GOVERNMENT AND POLITICS
OF ONTARIO

Government and Politics of Ontario

EDITED BY
Donald C. MacDonald

MACMILLAN OF CANADA
MACLEAN-HUNTER PRESS

ISBN 0-7705-1280-1 Cloth
0-7705-1281-X Paper

Printed in Canada

Contents

Preface

THE GOVERNMENT and politics of Ontario is a field of study which has been sadly neglected by scholars. Why this should be is almost worthy of a study in itself. There are many isolated topics falling within this field which have been covered in articles and theses. But most of them are unpublished, or in limited circulation, and therefore not readily accessible to the student.

There is, of course, *Responsible Government in Ontario*, the trail-blazing work of Fred Schindeler, the only systematic attempt to deal with the province's government and politics; but it is now out of date, particularly on the structure of the cabinet and ministries, legislative procedures and resources available to the parties.

The publication in 1974 of H. V. Nelles' *The Politics of Development* was a curtain-raiser to many major works now in preparation. The Ontario Historical Studies Series has initiated works in the social, political, cultural and intellectual history of Ontario, including biographies of all the premiers. By the end of the decade the traditional neglect of Ontario's past will, hopefully, have ended.

But no one has attempted an overview of the field of government and politics—a text which might be useful for the growing number of students in our universities and community colleges. This volume seeks to be that text.

Its genesis is significant in itself. The editor is something of a neophyte among political scientists. Some years ago I was engaged in the formal study of political science. But in the intervening years I have been involved in the practice of politics: in education and information work, in organizational work, and for twenty years a member of the Ontario Legislature, most of them as a party leader. In 1971 I was invited by Atkinson College, at York University, to become course director when Pol. Sci. 410, The Government and Politics of Ontario, was added to their calendar. Presumably it was felt that the experience of those years would be useful, as an interpreter of Ontario politics and of the veritable Niagara of material turned out at Queen's Park.

It has been a most rewarding experience, particularly when it could be conducted within such easy access of the Legislature and all the ministries. But even with all the advantages flowing to both the course director and the students from such close proximity to the seat of government, the absence of a basic study was felt. It is much more difficult for teachers and students operating at a distance from Toronto—an important consideration now that almost every university in Ontario has a course in the province's government and politics.

The solution seemed too obvious to be neglected any longer. Some fifteen to twenty university teachers active in the field were invited to share in producing such a text. Within little more than a year the team effort was completed, and in to the publisher.

From the outset, the contributors were firmly resolved on one point: to avoid, if at all possible, producing another volume modelled on the standard civic text which runs, seriatim, through the various components of government. The alternative model which has been attempted may not be immediately discernible, but if it is borne in mind, the whole volume should be more meaningful. So let me dwell for a moment on what has been attempted.

Basically the new approach is to introduce the reader to the government and politics of Ontario through five case studies. They illustrate how things work, rather than how the constitution says they should work; and they cover the spectrum from politics to government in many of its manifestations.

Thus, on the political side, the separate school question is reviewed as an illustration of how the political process responds to the conflicting pressure groups; or the Davis leadership convention for its operation at the party level. On the government side, there is an illustration of the legislative and political process in relation to how health insurance came to Ontario; or the development of regional government in the Hamilton-Wentworth area. Finally, the Workmen's Compensation Board is examined as an example of the hundreds of agencies, boards and commissions to which power has been delegated by the Legislature.

The first draft of these case studies was circulated among the authors of subsequent chapters who all came together for a one-day seminar when the manuscripts were discussed, both for a collective reaction to their content, and for suggestions as to how subsequent chapters might be related to them. The overall objective was to produce a volume which would have some degree of cohesion rather than eighteen unrelated essays which took no account of what preceded or followed.

Apart from this attempt at a new approach, the general format of the text is self-evident: following an introductory chapter, Part One presents the case studies; Part Two covers the government of Ontario, from the Legislature, through the cabinet and ministries, thence to the agencies, boards and commissions, with separate consideration of provincial-municipal relations, regional government and development, and federal-provincial relations. Finally, Part Three contains seven chapters isolating specific aspects of the politics of Ontario.

Obviously, many other topics might have been included. Both teachers and students may be led to them by the individual bibliographies at the conclusion of each chapter. Old government publications, as well as the regular flow of new material on current topics, are readily available from the Government of Ontario Bookstore, 880 Bay Street, Toronto—usually for a price, but sometimes free.

Special thanks must go to Diane Mew of Macmillan of Canada for her counsel in the preparation and revision of manuscripts. Mrs. Mew modestly contends that she is not an expert in any of the fields covered by a growing number of books which she has shepherded into existence; but she is a master in spotting points which are not clear to the general reader and in noting imbalances in the handling of a subject. Her suggestions, I know, have proven invaluable to all the contributors.

Finally, a personal word of appreciation to all my colleagues who have made this volume possible. I was told that the task of getting nearly twenty academics to operate as a team was a formidable one, but I have not found it so. Despite all the claims on their time, and the interruption of a federal election which inevitably involved political scientists in one way or another, deadlines were usually met. It was a rewarding cooperative effort.

DONALD C. MACDONALD
Toronto,
November 1974

GOVERNMENT AND POLITICS
OF ONTARIO

I
DESMOND MORTON

Introduction:
People and Politics
of Ontario

I N 1885 the Ontario government finally tore down the old lunatic asylum in Queen's Park and resolutely set out to erect Canada's ugliest legislative building. It stands there still, looking a little like a huge red toad, squinting through the trees and a couple of flagpoles at the traffic on Toronto's University Avenue.

Like the province's motto, *Ut incepit sic permanet fidelis*, the legislative building symbolizes Ontario's official allegiance to tradition. The ponderous sandstone monument that most Ontarians call Queen's Park is a museum for a theory of responsible parliamentary government which, if it ever had validity, has long since been eroded by generations of one-party dominance and public apathy. Students by the thousand are annually bussed to the Legislature to surge up the stairways and through the corridors and to listen dutifully to lectures on constitutional history. They are almost as close to reality at Old Fort Henry or Upper Canada Village.

When Queen's Park was completed in 1893, its legislative function mattered rather more than at present. After all, there were less than seven provincial employees for each elected member and most of them owed their jobs to party patronage or a politician's influence. The building itself was praised as a monument to the prudent management of the people's money. Sir Oliver Mowat, the provincial premier, boasted that construction had cost less than the estimated million and a quarter dollars. Mowat's boast was, as usual, a little deceptive. After all, the Christian Statesman (as he loved to be known) had promised in 1880 that his government's new home would cost only half a million dollars. However, well aware that similar projects in the United States had inspired prodigies of graft and extravagance, Ontarians could rejoice in fresh evidence that God had made them better than their neighbours.

In Canadian constitutional history, Mowat has earned most of the credit for expanding the trivial status envisaged for the provinces under the British North America Act. Within his own province, he bore faithful allegiance to the liberal doctrine that who governs best governs least. His constitutional struggles with Ottawa were, in fact, as strongly motivated by a healthy, partisan Liberalism as by any constitutional strategy. Control of liquor licensing, the core issue of several battles, mattered because liquor was the best known lubricant for switching a vote. Mowat's victory in the courts meant that the taps would henceforth be firmly in Liberal hands. If Mowat wanted additional powers for his government, it was to demonstrate in still more areas that he could offer cheap, efficient administration. The province's entire executive machinery, as well as its legislature, could be comfortably housed under a single roof; indeed, Mowat was reported as wondering how they would ever fill all the rooms. In 1893, a million dollars in statutory grants from the federal government and two millions more in revenue from the province's forests met almost all the cost of Mowat's government. The most significant form of provincial taxation, licence fees, netted only $294,757. The corporation of the City of Toronto spent almost as much as the provincial government to meet the demands of its 120,000 citizens.

Eighty years later the government of Ontario confesses to employing more than ninety thousand people. A far larger army, from child care workers to university professors, depends for the bulk of its income on the provincial treasury. Hardly a soul in Ontario can contrive to escape entirely from contributing some share of the $3.6 billion raised through provincial income, corporation or retail sales taxes, to say nothing of even more sophisticated and unperceived revenue sources. A toddler, shoving a sticky coin across the counter to buy a sucker, is in danger of becoming a taxpayer.

There are many explanations for the transformation of the provincial government in scope and cost. One is the distinct failure in prophecy by the Fathers of Confederation. If any of them could have imagined that education, roads and "hospitals, asylums, charities and eleemosynary institutions" would ever matter as much as railways, canals and promissory notes, they might well have added them to the responsibilities of the central government. However, in 1867 highways, hospitals, schools and poorhouses were, at best, marginal and largely self-financing concerns of government. The failure of prophecy was even more about people than about institutions. As Fred Schindeler has explained in *Responsible Government in Ontario*:

> The factor that has most profoundly influenced this change in the scope of government operations has been the gradual

change in the social attitudes of the people. Increased specialization in agriculture and industry, improved means of transportation and communication, and massive rural to urban population shift have made men less self-sufficient than they were in 1867. Economic and social interdependence have been an impetus to government intervention and gradually the people have come to expect the government to take a creative part in establishing a viable economy and the "good society." They have demanded that their government take steps to mitigate the more pernicious by-products of the free market; they have insisted that education should be made universally available, free of charge; and they have insisted that public funds be used to sustain them and assist them when they fall prey to the inescapable hardships of life.

A change in people's expectations is, in fact, only a symptom of other transformations in Ontario, particularly since Confederation. In 1867 the province was overwhelmingly agricultural. Toronto, the provincial metropolis, had only 59,000 people. As late as 1941, the census found that almost precisely as many people were gainfully employed in agriculture as in manufacturing—23.2 per cent of the work force. By 1971 agriculture had dropped to eighth place in the census categories of employment—a mere 3.8 per cent. An ancient populist nightmare had come true: the 129,910 farmers and farm labourers of Ontario were at last out-numbered by the 155,505 men and women sustained by the parasitic industries of finance, insurance and real estate. While 1,383,845 Ontarians were classified as living in a rural setting, 4,126,680 were not merely urban but lived in cities of 100,000 or more. In 1871 only Montreal had even approached that size.

Ontario has experienced other demographic changes which, in political terms, should have had just as traumatic consequences as the movement from farm to city. In 1871 the quarrelsome races from the British Isles, the Irish, English and Scots, virtually had Ontario to themselves with 82 per cent of the population. A century later their dominance had dwindled to a mere 59 per cent, while the Italians (whom census-takers had not even bothered to count in 1871) were ready to surpass the Germans as Ontario's fourth-largest ethnic group. A century ago Ontario's Catholics had formed a small and sometimes nervous minority of 17 per cent. Even in 1941 they mustered only 22.5 per cent, easily out-matched by the United Church and only a shade ahead of the Anglicans. As of 1971, the Catholics form Ontario's largest denomination, a clear third of the population. Unbelievers (coldly dismissed as "pagans") in 1871 included only a couple of thousand wayward souls, most of them Indians. In 1971, at a strength of 343,690, they were the fifth-largest denominational category, far out-numbering the Baptists.

Since Ontario politics frequently revolved around issues of religion, language and urban-rural friction, it might have been predicted that the political landscape would have been as unstable as the demography. In a localized framework this has sometimes seemed true. A visitor to the Ontario legislative chamber can still see a cruciform device in the plaster ceiling over the Speaker's chair. Spied by a vigilant Protestant in 1894, it was offered as evidence in that year's election that Oliver Mowat had sold out the province to the Pope. Such allegations helped to win six seats for the Protestant Protective Association. In 1919 the United Farmers and an equally astonished clutch of labour members swept from virtually nowhere to capture 34 per cent of the votes and fifty-five seats in the Legislature. In 1943, on equally short notice, the Co-operative Commonwealth Federation swept up 32 per cent of the popular support and thirty-four seats, nearly enough to form a minority government.

However, as observers of Ontario know, such episodes are exceptional. Despite radical alterations in the province's economy, the religious and ethnic composition of its people and the role and size of its government, Ontarians have safeguarded a reputation for political immobility. At most, they have appeared content to nibble at innovation. In only six of the twenty-nine provincial general elections between Confederation and 1971 did Ontario voters produce a transfer of power. From 1872 to 1905, the Liberals were in office. Thereafter, with interruptions only for the United Farmers from 1919 to 1923 and for Mitchell Hepburn's Liberals from 1934 to 1943, the Conservatives have been firmly in charge. The non-stop hegemony of the Progressive Conservatives after 1943 would be the envy even of totalitarian regimes both in its duration and in its lopsided legislative majorities.

The explanations for the durability of Ontario governments must be cautious, subjective and, frequently, flattering to the regime in power. The most significant reason may well be, quite simply, that Ontario is relatively easy to govern. As the chief beneficiary of the Confederation arrangement, her industrial and financial growth has been systematically secured by tariff protection and low-cost energy. Since 1867 Ontario has shared all of the booms and only some of the busts of the Canadian economy. When Ontario cabinets have contemplated expensive reforms, they have more often been restricted by their own ideology than by a barren treasury. By 1959, before the latest major instalment of welfare legislation across Canada, even the arch-conservative Duplessis government was spending 9.5 per cent of Quebec's personal income. Ontario, already more accomplished, was taking only 7.4 per cent. If, in the ensuing decade, Ontario voters demanded new hospitals, a network of community colleges, instant universities, multilane highways and medicare, the province could afford them. When an articulate and highly organized pressure group persuaded both citizens and newspapers that urban expressways had become an almost unspeakable evil, the premier of the day could actually win votes by writing off the billions of dollars spent on an unused ditch. Few other governments in Canada or elsewhere would have been rewarded for such prodigality by an enhanced legislative majority.

Prosperity, of course, is not quite enough to guarantee re-election, although it would have been a comfort to Sir William Hearst in 1919 or to the colourless George S. Henry in 1934. Paradoxically for a province of such apparent electoral stability, a factor in government longevity may be the surprising and largely overlooked degree of competitiveness in the Ontario political system. Despite their frustrations, Ontario's opposition parties maintain an impressive vitality. In five of the eight general elections in which Oliver Mowat and his Liberal successors held power, a bare percentage point separated winner and loser in the popular vote. Conservative victories since 1905 have usually been more clear cut but, since 1929, not even the popular Leslie Frost could draw more than half the province's popular vote for his party. Since 1943 the Tories have retained power largely because the discontented voters have divided themselves between the Liberals and the CCF or, since 1961, the New Democratic Party. In 1967 John Robarts could win 69 of the 117 seats with only 42 per cent of the vote; four years later, William Davis could boast of a landslide with only 44 per cent. Conservative party strategists are never allowed to forget that only a modest shift in voting support could deliver the same kind of one-sided majority to a rival party.

Lively competition means that few Ontario governments have been left to the quiet enjoyment of their power. At the same time, a fat majority in the Legislature fosters a kind of Pavlovian politics—making the voters miserable in the session immediately after an election the better to bribe them with favours as the next contest approaches. However, no government can afford comfortable inertia. Most successful Ontario premiers have imitated Oliver Mowat's style of bustling half-measures, to say nothing of his habit of scapegoating the federal government. The adoption of medicare, described below, is almost a paradigm of how other major reforms, including workmen's compensation and Ontario Hydro, have been achieved. Change comes most easily to Ontario if it is imperceptible, urged on by nudges and prods. Leading innovators perform best as reluctant dragons. If the sum total of reform in Ontario turns out to be unexpectedly large, it is possibly because the process has rarely halted. When it has (notably in the latter years of Hepburn's Liberal administration)° the failure has been noticed and fiercely avenged.

Another explanation for survival, particularly among the Conservatives, is that their party has never really depended upon a single strong man for its electoral appeal. While Sir Oliver Mowat bestrode his party and his province for so long that his departure left the Liberals seriously weakened, the Conservatives have been more fortunate. Death, transfer to the federal arena or ill-health ended the careers of James Whitney, Howard Ferguson, George Drew, Leslie Frost and John Robarts at junctures when their political stars were beginning to wane. By changing faces, the Ontario Tories have been able to combine the excitement of novelty with the reassurance of stability.

Prosperity, the pressure of competition and a collegiate rather than an individual sense of survival may help to explain why governments, specifically the Progressive Conservative administration of Ontario after 1943, could last for a third of a century. They explain very little about the consequences.

One outcome, described by Schindeler and increasingly apparent since his book first appeared in 1969, is an identification between the party in power and the provincial administration. "Members of the civil service," he observed, "are found equating the Government with the majority party and seeing themselves as the servants of the party instead of as servants of the administration. Publications concerned with various aspects of Ontario government seem as a matter of course to become vehicles for expounding the virtues of the Government of the day. In a thousand little ways it becomes evident that civil servants see their prime loyalty to be to a particular party instead of to the general public they are meant to serve." A thousand and first little way was illustrated in 1971 when the premier, William Davis, used the services of Treasury Board officials to assess the cost of the promises made by his Liberal and New Democratic Party opponents.

Any institution has its pride and its commitment to the status quo. Even a critical servant of that institution will understand its procedures and their justification better than the most informed outsider. Civil servants whose loyalties are stirred by an opposition party's philosophy or policies will still bridle at uninformed or captious criticism of their own government. The memory of Mitch Hepburn dismissing thousands of civil servants when he came to power at the depth of the depression, or auctioning government cars at Varsity Stadium, may delight resentful taxpayers, but it also brings a reminiscent chill to older government employees. Stability has its virtues, no less real than change. The long era of Conservative domination has helped improve the managerial efficiency of Ontario government, particularly on the approaches to cabinet level. The more capable ministers have learned the limitations of cabinet government and departmental structure from experience rather than theory and the resulting reforms may well have produced a more efficient executive than would have resulted from frequent alternations of power.

The price of such stable, invisible reform cannot be calculated. At a minimum, it is an absence of the occasional "new broom" politician, challenging departmental administrators on their most cherished beliefs. As the late R. MacGregor Dawson argued, such challenges can be among the most valuable contributions of the non-expert cabinet minister. For almost two generations Ontario government has rarely experienced either their creative stimulus or their potential for chaos.

Another feature of one-party government in Ontario is a relative absence of mass participation. The politics of prosperity normally become the preoccupation of an elite. Ontarians can certainly relish a well-fought election campaign. In contests at the federal level, they have acquired a reputation as discriminating and even fickle voters. However, few treat elections as more than a spectator sport. All three major parties in the province regularly sow the seeds for a mass base but the crop is never impressive. The New Democrats, who are most dependent on membership support and donations and who therefore cultivate them with special fervour, boast about 26,000 members—fewer than in the smaller province of Saskatchewan. The NDP also claims about 200,000 members affiliated en bloc through local trade unions, but they play only a slight role in the party's affairs. Both the Liberals and the Conservatives occasionally proclaim vast memberships but the figures, on closer examination, add up largely to those who have ever ventured to a party nomination meeting. William Davis' election as Progressive Conservative leader was accompanied by familiar promises of greater grassroots involvement: they did not survive the 1971 election.

For most Ontarians, provincial politics may flourish modestly during election campaigns—occurring, customarily, at four-year intervals—but the ritual of party competition in the Legislature draws little attention. Except when they can somehow engage the attention and sympathy of the press gallery, the two opposition parties at Queen's Park are effectively impotent. Apart from an occasional burst of publicity, engendered normally by sensationalism, opposition members enjoy an obscurity and a relative unimportance only exceeded by government backbenchers. At times, even Conservative premiers have felt embarrassed by the situation. Even before such a reform was conceived in Ottawa, John Robarts had extended modest research assistance to the opposition parties. The recommendations of the Camp Commission, discussed in chapter 7, may enhance the status of members on both sides of the Legislature.

They are unlikely to transform the weakness of the Legislature as a whole or to give it greater public prominence. Unless they have the power to defeat the government or at least to affect its intentions, the opposition parties possess little interest for the media or the public. Of course this is not uniquely true of Ontario. The overwhelming power of the executive in all parliamentary systems, even at Westminster, renders even the mythology of responsible government and popular sovereignty suspect. However, almost a third of a century of one-party rule has robbed even mythology of its power to charm. Even a change of party in power would probably not restore the authority legislatures once allegedly possessed. A new regime, armed with a full agenda of reforms, would be quixotic indeed if it deliberately strengthened the opposition.

Ontario experience suggests that the politics of a one-party government are extra-Legislative. From time to time during the political year, throngs of farmers, teachers, students or trade unionists gather on the parking lot in front of Queen's Park to demonstrate their grievances. Only the most naive imagine that they are close to the seats of the mighty. The Legislature is conveniently accessible by public transit and it is a recognized backdrop for the television cameras. The rugged façade gives a pleasant resonance to the amplifiers. However, the politically sophisticated normally shun vulgar or chilly displays and find their way through the maze of office buildings to the east of Queen's Park Crescent. It is there that truly influential people may be found.

If there is a power centre in the Ontario government, it must be the cabinet, the gathering of policy secretaries and ministers with or without departmental responsibilities (or "portfolios"), assembled under the benign guidance of the man who gave them their jobs, the provincial premier. Ontario cabinets have grown. When the province came into existence in 1867 only five cabinet offices were authorized. By the time J. P. Whitney took office in 1905 he could appoint seven departmental ministers and three more without portfolio. In 1974, in addition to the premier and three co-ordinating ministers (or "policy secretaries"), there were the heads of seventeen "ministries," as departments had come to be called, and three more ministers without portfolio either on their way up or down in the cabinet hierarchy.

The Ontario cabinet, like its counterparts in Ottawa and the other provinces, matters because it amalgamates political and policy influences at the highest level. Admittedly, its decisions normally arrive after lengthy processing through committees and ministries, through public hearings and private consultations with affected organizations and after cautious surveillance by legislative draughtsmen. Otherwise, cabinet business would be hopelessly bogged down. However, for most decisions, the cabinet is the court of last appeal. Like its federal counterpart, it also has an informal but vital representative function. Almost regardless of talent, ministers may be included because they can speak for regions, religious and ethnic groups and for industrial and economic interests. Roman Catholics, Franco-Ontarians and the North can be expected to scrutinize the balance of cabinet membership and to protest any fancied slight. So, in more recent years, have New Canadians, women and the young.

The cabinet is normally very much the expression of its first minister. It did not require television to emphasize the importance of leadership in Canadian politics. Lacking more than a surrogate monarchy, Canadians moved to the presidential version of prime minister earlier and faster than their Westminster model. For all her Loyalist trappings, Ontario was no exception. If few Ontario premiers have imitated the dictatorial pretensions of a Mitch Hepburn or his taste in wine and women, all of them, from the time of John Sandfield Macdonald, have acted firmly as the leader and spokesman of the provincial government.

Ontario premiers have been appropriately identified as the symbols of their periods of government, lightning rods for public praise or condemnation. They have also normally functioned as their party's chief political manager. As in so much else, Oliver Mowat set the pattern. In addition to his constitutional battles to keep the saloons safe for Liberal licence-holders, Mowat took a well-informed interest in the adjustment of constituency boundaries, keeping his party in office long after its agrarian base had begun to melt. Once the farmers had begun to turn Conservative, rural over-representation and oleaginous flattery of farmers became a bipartisan Ontario tradition.

Mowat's Grit farmers professed to be sturdy yeomen, uninterested in pelf and plunder from the public treasury; in fact, the crude and brutal politics of party patronage operated in Ontario at least until 1943, when the newly elected Drew government held back from wholesale dismissal of provincial employees. Minority standing in the Legislature and a wartime shortage of manpower undoubtedly contributed to Drew's moderation: he had been a victim of an earlier slaughter in 1934. In time, Drew and his successors found a satisfying and generally acceptable way of rewarding the network of local notables on which Progressive Conservative power rests. The expansion of the Ontario government has largely taken the form of a proliferation of agencies, boards, commissions and crown corporations. A current government pamphlet claims that there are more than two hundred and fifty of them; most casual observers have long since lost count. They range from relics like the Soldiers' Aid Commission to the currently fashionable Ontario Council on the Status of Women. Some, like the Hydro-Electric Power Commission of Ontario or the Liquor Control Board, are household words; others, like the Athletics Commissioner or the Ontario Heritage Foundation, are known, if at all, to specialists. Virtually all of them provide opportunities for government jobs—as directors, counsel or advisors. Outside the sprawling realm of government, there is a host of other positions to fill—as government-nominated directors of marketing boards, as governors of universities and regents of community colleges. Since the nominations purport to give the people of Ontario a voice in controlling some of their vital institutions, party allegiance is far from being the only or even the primary factor in filling vacancies. Most of the familiar categories have to be kept in mind. If business is represented, there must be at least a token trade unionist. Religion, ethnicity and youth must normally be served and someone will almost certainly remind the government that 50 per cent of the population is female. Somehow, though, the ranks of the Progressive Conservative party seem better stocked with the appropriate worthies than either the plebeian New Democrats or the upwardly mobile Liberals.

The innumerable government appointments are more than comfortable and respectable sinecures for deserving supporters; they also provide a pervasive infusion of values, ideas and directions through most of the governmental and quasi-governmental agencies of Ontario. Their presence is a guarantee that the divine right of private property will be defended against too obtrusive claims of public interest or that the blessings of the profit motive will be brought home to socialistic bureaucrats. Because the Tory philosophy can be ambivalent on the rival claims of public and private interest, community concerns may occasionally carry the day, as they sometimes did before the Ontario Municipal Board under the chairmanship of J. A. Kennedy.

The ambivalence of Toryism in government is also apparent in the transformation of the Queen's Park bureaucracy during the sixties into an impressively modern and highly talented machine. Largely unknown to the electorate, the top echelons of the Ontario civil service experienced the same kind of quiet revolution in competence and expectations that the Quebec government underwent in the early years of Jean Lesage. New blood was introduced, salaries were improved and modern administrative procedures were adopted, all with uncharacteristic haste. Ontario did not, of course, lead the way. The smaller and relatively impoverished province of Saskatchewan had been developing a modern, innovative public service since the CCF victory in 1944. However, the new sophistication and competence of Ontario civil servants help to explain the province's positive role during the complex federal-provincial constitutional and fiscal negotiations of the sixties. It also underlies the provincial government's positive role in restructuring municipal government, land-use planning, public housing and a variety of other activities which might have seemed inappropriate for an administration espousing conservative, free enterprise principles.

With its impressive bureaucracy, its elaborate patronage network and capacity for self-renewal, Ontario's long-lived Conservative regime might seem destined to last forever. Undoubtedly, in the view of its supporters, it should. However, the apparent stability is really the result of an impressive balancing act in which clever political management, an acute sense of the public mood and a partially fortuitous continuation of prosperity all play a part. It would take less than a 10 per cent shift to one or other of the opposition parties to topple the Ontario Conservatives, and the volatility of the province's voters, particularly in the cities, could be transferred from the federal to the provincial arena.

Even without serious and explicit sins of commission or omission, the Tories could find themselves with an unpopular leader and no means of either replacing or redeeming him. The affluence of Ontario's industrial heartland has long depended on the grudging acceptance by other provinces and of Ontario's own hinterland of roles as suppliers of cheap energy, raw materials and labour. By the mid-seventies few would predict that this relationship could endure forever. The Conservatives would be logical scapegoats for a reversal in the economic fortunes of Canada's most favoured region. In such circumstances, the incredible demographic changes which the Conservatives have so far weathered could have a delayed reaction. The heart of Tory voting strength—middle class, middle-aged and Protestant —is dwindling in relative importance. Like the Mowat Liberals, the Conservatives may preserve the power of a shrinking constituency by careful adjustment of constituency boundaries, opportune alliances with the young or with Eastern Europeans or even by eye-catching policies. Sooner or later, other groups in the Ontario mosaic will demand a more authentic access to power as they did in Manitoba by supporting a predominantly ethnic New Democratic Party.

The Conservatives could even be the victims of their most impressive achievement, the development of a government capable of extensive planning and innovation. Much of the most vociferous criticism of the current provincial administration is not directed at its conservatism but at its reforms—in education, municipal government, urban transit and land-use planning. Among the moods which were sweeping the province's opinion-leaders in the mid-seventies was a nostalgia for small-town Ontario, even in the midst of an intensely urbanized and industrialized society. The preservation of neighbourhoods, farmers' markets, bric-à-brac and clean air all reflected a kind of conservatism which ran headlong into the achievements of a Progressive Conservative government. It presented that government with the most serious challenge to its survival.

14 / Desmond Morton

NOTES FOR FURTHER READING

The absence of secondary material on Ontario history and politics both available in print and fit to read is one of the grievances that teachers and students meet and regularly deplore. Among the more successful attempts to fill the enormous gaps are Neil McKenty's brilliant biography of Mitchell Hepburn (Toronto, 1967), E. C. Drury's memoirs, *Farmer Premier* (Toronto, 1965), and Fred Schindeler's *Responsible Government in Ontario* (Toronto, 1969), already transformed into history by changes in the government structure. H. V. Nelles, *The Politics of Development: Forests, Mines and Hydro-Electric Development in Ontario* (Toronto, 1974), explores the fascinating relationship of business and provincial government at the turn of the century. Jonathan Manthorpe's *The Power and the Tories* (Toronto, 1974) is a long-awaited study of the remarkably durable regime that governed Ontario for a third of a century after the Second World War.

These are only examples of some of the important and valuable books on Ontario published in recent years. Others are expected and their quality may be anticipated by articles collected by the Ontario Historical Society in *Profiles of a Province* (Toronto, 1967) or Donald Swainson's edited collection of papers, *Oliver Mowat's Ontario* (Toronto, 1972). Among the articles in *Ontario History*, a number deal with more recent provincial political history. The Ontario government itself is endeavouring to fill the shelves with a massive series under the general editorship of Goldwin French.

PART ONE

CASE STUDIES

2
WALTER G. PITMAN

The Limits to Diversity:
The Separate School Issue
in the Politics
of Ontario

ON AUGUST 31, just a few days before he was to announce an autumn election for late October 1971, Premier William Davis issued a statement "re the Question of Extended Public Assistance to the Separate School System." He indicated that he and his colleagues had "considered this matter exhaustively" (it was well over two years since the Trustees' brief "Equal Opportunity for Continuous Education in Separate Schools in Ontario," requesting further aid had been presented), but the Premier stated that the government had "concluded that it cannot support the proposals of the Ontario School Trustees' Association."

The Conservative victory on October 21, 1971, thereby confirming William Davis' leadership and his position on separate school extension, settled the question for the moment. But the campaign of separate school supporters and their failure to move the Ontario government raises many problems for the political observer. How do minority groups, and in this case a substantial minority, effectively approach the government? Did separate school supporters engage in legitimate lobbying, or was it too intense and pervasive, arousing partisan opposition which otherwise might have remained dormant? Were the supporting methods impressive and, if so, what methods were most impressive—briefs, letters to and interviews with politicians, student picketing at Queen's Park, a mass demonstration at Maple Leaf Gardens? Whose activities were the most helpful—trustees, teachers, students, their parents, the Roman Catholic community, the bishops? Was the timing of the approach faulty, being some two years before an election, thereby allowing a period during which the force of the campaign could be dissipated? Should opposition parties have waited for a government reaction before moving so positively in support of the separate school case for extension? Could, in fact, anything have moved the Conservative government towards an acceptance of the separate school claim for additional assistance, or was it a lost cause from the outset?

The issue can be simply stated: the Roman Catholic separate school supporters wished to have the Government of Ontario fund grades 11, 12 and, until it ultimately disappeared, grade 13, in the same way that these grades were funded in the public school system. There was no question of the continued public support of the elementary grades, one to eight, and historical precedent had extended that assistance to grades 9 and 10. The issue was whether the province should allow the Roman Catholic community the right to educate its young in its own schools to the end of the secondary system at public expense.

However, it must be recognized that no issue has had a more pervasive influence on the politics of Ontario than the controversy over the role of the separate school system. Ever since the concession granted in the old Province of Canada (before the creation of Ontario at Confederation) that there could be, in effect, a second public system, the question of its continued existence, the extent of its support, and the possibility of its extension in size and function, has been debated at elections in every single decade, has resulted in major court battles and has influenced the future of each political party and its leaders.

Although the issue has deep and abiding roots in the history of the province, the decade of the 1960s brought with it a number of serious problems for the separate school system, especially in terms of its capacity to provide secondary education.

The Robarts Plan, or the Reorganized Program, introduced in 1962, increased dramatically the cost of secondary education. It envisioned the development of three streams: arts and science, business and commerce, and science, trade and technology. Each stream was to be offered at the four- and five-year level. The capital cost of this remarkable expansion of secondary schooling was to come largely from the grants emanating as a result of the federal government's recently acquired commitment to vocational training and a generous allowance of 80 cents on the dollar to boards of education who would provide these facilities. However, the continuing cost of providing for these expensive programs had to be borne by the local jurisdiction, with grants, of course, from the provincial level. With much less support at its disposal, it meant that separate secondary schools were restrained to providing programs in the regular arts and science branch, and, to a lesser extent, in the business and commerce stream.

As well as coping with the problem of more expensive offerings, the numbers of students who had expectations of remaining to the end of the secondary system increased substantially. This had been one of the main hopes of the Robarts plan, but for the separate schools it meant a significant pressure of expectation on the part of students, many of whom would have normally left the schooling system after grade 10, and now began crowding into grades 11 and 12 in Catholic high schools where no provincial grants were available. This pressure had to be passed on to the parents of these students in the form of higher fees, and ultimately on to the Roman Catholic community. Many of the parents were in a desperate situation, having to cope with the increasing municipal tax burden for education and, as well, having to pay, over and above, the fees of their offspring who had succeeded in reaching the grade 11, 12 or 13 level—an average amount of $412 per pupil in 1969.

In many cases, Roman Catholic students transferred to the public school system when they reached the high school level. Some transferred for the financial reasons already explained, others for valid academic reasons. The Roman Catholic separate high schools could not offer the vocational programs which were more appropriate to the interests and capacities of many Roman Catholic young people. Occasionally, these transfers from one system to another resulted in a traumatic experience for individual students, damaging irreparably their educational careers. It was the knowledge of the effect which the truncated system had had on a number of young people that gave an element of poignancy to the struggles of the "complete the system" campaign in the late sixties.

As early as 1962, the Bishop's Brief to the Ontario Government had expressed the need for further assistance, particularly at the secondary level, but in 1964 the Robarts government had made a generous response—at least in so far as the support of separate elementary schools were concerned. Though there had been no argument that public assistance to separate elementary schools was threatened, the level of funding had been far from sufficient and only the dedication of teachers and parents had allowed the schools to survive. The Foundation Plan, introduced in 1964, compensated through provincial funding those school boards which because of inadequate local assessment revenue did not receive sufficient support. This gave all the elementary schools, both public and separate, in areas of low assessment, a "shot in the arm." Yet, even with this assistance, the reality was that a pupil in the separate elementary school in 1969 was supported by $577 in grants and taxes, compared to $641 for a student in the public elementary system.

It is strange that the Foundation Plan which strengthened the financial base of the separate schools was passed with virtually no opposition from even the most virulent anti-religious school critics. The Foundation Plan did not, however, solve the problem of inadequate support for the secondary school program, because the right to support grants beyond grade 10 had not been conceded, and the grants for pupils in grades 9 and 10 of the separate secondary schools were at the elementary level. By 1969 a pupil in the separate secondary school was being supported by $577, compared to over $1,000 for a pupil in the public secondary school.

There was a further pressure within the Catholic educational system which had come to a head by the mid-sixties. The French-Canadian Roman Catholic was in an even more difficult position than the English Roman Catholic. The disruption in the life of an English Catholic youngster who had to transfer mid-stream in his secondary career to another public school was minimal compared to the French-speaking student who had to transfer to an English-speaking high school. The 1960s was the decade when the bilingual rights of French-speaking people were finally recognized in this country, and the trustees of the French-speaking Catholic schools came to the conclusion it was time to push for a full secondary system which would be both Catholic and French.

The English-speaking trustees were reluctant to push such a proposal only a year after the Foundation Plan had been achieved, but the impatience of their French-speaking colleagues carried the day. The only course was to transfer the jurisdiction and capital assets of the Catholic private high schools over to the public separate school system and ask for grants which would support the extension of its activity and responsibility to the end of grade 13. This intense concern of the French-speaking Catholic community had the effect of pushing the entire Catholic separate school system towards a confrontation with the government on this matter before it would otherwise have transpired.

Largely as a result of these internal events, the Association of Catholic High School Boards of Ontario was formed in January 1966. It was to include two lay representatives from each diocese and its purpose was "to study the Catholic secondary school needs in Ontario." This new organization was to be a member of the English Catholic Educational Association of Ontario, which included all the trustee, teacher and parent organizations associated with the separate school system. The association carried out its study and produced a formidable submission to the Separate School Teachers' Association's Special Working Committee on Upward Extension, entitled "Completing their Schooling." However, while this work was going on, two events took place which gave separate school supporters great confidence that their expectations would bear fruit.

The first was the tabling in the Legislature on June 12, 1968, of the Hall-Dennis Report. This document received a warm response, not only from government sources, but from the NDP and, after a short flurry of criticism, from the Liberal party as well. It stressed the importance of equality of opportunity for every child and saw this equality in the context of a continuous progression from kindergarten to grade 13. On the basis of this concept of increased integration, the division between grades 10 and 11, the point of demarcation for grant purposes, would disappear altogether. Although the report did not specifically call for immediate extension of support to grades 11 to 13 in the separate schools, everything in the report seemed to point in that direction. Indeed, both of the men whose names came to be identified with the report, did subsequently articulate this as a solution to the problem of a truncated system which, they believed, worked such a hardship on so many young people who had to transfer at a difficult point in their educational careers.

The other event which gave a spurt of encouragement to separate school supporters was the introduction on March 15, 1969, of Bill 44, a piece of legislation designed to completely overhaul the educational system, creating county boards across southern Ontario to replace the hundreds of small boards which had previously fragmented the education process for every young person. These larger boards would have a stronger local tax base and would, as well, provide more sophisticated special and administrative services. All of this was related to the pervasive slogan of this decade in Ontario: equality of educational opportunity. Some weeks later an amendment to the Separate Schools Act was introduced into the Ontario Legislature, reducing the number of boards to thirty-one (excepting northern Ontario).

The climax in the Roman Catholic separate school supporters' approach to government came with the presentation in 1969, of the brief, "Equal Opportunity for Continuous Education in Separate Schools of Ontario." This document stressed the restrictions which restrained the separate school system from "offering a complete education from the Kindergarten to Grade 12 (13) at the present time." These restrictions included "(a) a limitation of jurisdiction to a K to 10 program; (b) unavoidable retention of grade distinctions in spite of the development of ungrading elsewhere; (c) classification of grades 9 and 10 as elementary grades for grant purposes; lack of adequate voice at Department of Education levels." If equality meant anything, it meant an individual educational experience appropriate to every child. The document pointed out a tangible link between the reorganization of larger units of jurisdiction, and the concept of continuous education, making use of the words of the minister himself at the time of the introduction of the bill creating county boards for the public school system, that "the first principle related to our major and ultimate goal, is that all children . . . have equality of educational opportunity . . . the second is that this program of public education be a continuous and integrated process from Kindergarten to Grade 13."

The brief argued with some cogency that the basic claim on which public assistance for secondary education had been denied in 1915—that there was clear separation between elementary and secondary learning—had been destroyed if the K to 13 continuous ungraded educational system was to be established. Recognizing the general concern for the cost of duplication of facilities which might be assumed if a separate school system received sufficient public funding to strengthen its secondary school system, the brief concluded with assurances that cooperation in the use of public resources, rather than competition for funds, would be encouraged by the extension of aid to the end of grade 13.

The brief had been presented on May 26, but by mid-June it had provoked no response. It was at that point that a very marked change in strategy took place. The Trustees' Association had assumed that this issue, like the movement towards the Foundation Plan, could be carried out in a spirit of quiet negotiation with the Department of Education, its minister and officials. But the involvement of nine organized affiliates of the English Catholic Educational Association of Ontario, representing the beleaguered private separate high schools, and the increased participation by more militant teachers, students and parents, forced the campaign to an intensity not originally conceived to be appropriate by the Trustees. It is not unfair to say that the leadership of the Ontario Separate School Trustees' Association was more politically sophisticated than that found in other Catholic organizations. The executive secretary was Chris Asseff, a man who had been a Conservative candidate in Fort William in the 1963 provincial election and the president of the association was Dr. N. A. Mancine, an active Liberal from Hamilton. Behind them were hundreds of trustees whose experience in election campaigns had produced a practical judgment about strategy and who saw real dangers in a heightened confrontation between the government and the Catholic community.

In response to evidence of impatience, the president of the Ontario Separate School Trustees' Association reconstituted the working committee which had prepared the brief; it met on June 25 "for the purpose of formulating future plans in regard to the follow-up program." At that meeting, activities for the coming months were discussed, and it was decided that county committees should be formed, made up of the Catholic Parent-Teacher Association, Ontario English Catholic Teachers' Association, Association of Catholic High School Boards of Ontario, and the Students' Federation.

That meeting determined the basic strategy, which was outlined in an urgent and confidential memorandum dated June 30, 1969. "It was decided (1) that the campaign should be a 'quiet campaign'; (2) that it should continue for three months; (3) that it should involve every major Catholic organization in the Province." It was assumed that the government would make a decision in the fall of 1969, an expectation that was to be disappointed. Nonetheless, the purpose of the campaign was "to create a political climate that will facilitate a favourable decision by the Government." There were two immediate tasks, to "drive home to the public the basic still-not-well-understood facts and contentions set forth in the 'Equality in Education' brief," and, secondly, "to bring every appropriate influence to bear on members of the Ontario Legislature, the political parties and their riding organizations, to win support for the brief." Emphasis was placed on the fact that "the campaign will *not* be characterized by dramatic statements or militant demonstrations. This is a time for real restraint."

The first task, that of reaching out to the wider public was to be accomplished by a number of publications, including a periodical entitled "The Spotlight, News and Views on Catholic Education," published by the English Catholic Education Association of Ontario. The purpose of these pamphlets, information sheets, copies of articles and speeches, which issued forth in some profusion, was obviously that of arousing a deeper commitment on the part of the wider Roman Catholic community, many of whom had children in the public schools or had no children at all. As well, there was the hope that this information would reach beyond the Roman Catholic community to the Ontario citizenry at large, in part at least through an active campaign of letters to the editors of Ontario newspapers.

The second step, that of contacting every MPP in Ontario within the months of July, August and September, was carried out with considerable dispatch and the issue was brought to the attention of provincial legislators in no uncertain terms. The brief had already been presented to both the Liberal and New Democratic parties in June, and this initial approach, strengthened by the interview with each individual MPP, had an immediate effect on both opposition parties. In the expectation that a solution would be forthcoming from the government in the early fall of 1969, the NDP caucus formed a sub-committee and worked throughout the summer, attempting to understand the problems of the separate schools and searching for solutions. A committee of the Liberal party had already been

formed and had been at work on the problem. This flurry
of intellectual effort on the part of the opposition parties
produced similar results, with both Liberal and the NDP
caucuses supporting the main contentions of the Separate
School Trustees' Association brief. In late October, the
NDP issued its discussion paper, entitled "The Financial
Crises in the Separate Schools," in which all the historical,
constitutional, financial and philosophic arguments for
extension were stated. Although the paper endorsed the
extension, and this endorsation was supported by the
provincial convention a year later, there were strong statements supporting mechanisms to ensure that no duplication of facilities resulted from such a policy.

However, it was the decision of the Liberal caucus to
support extension of aid which created the greatest amount
of attention in the fall of 1969. An endorsement by Robert
Nixon and his caucus virtually assured the acceptance of
this policy position by the Ontario Liberal party. Front-
page headlines followed by observations of newspaper
editors appeared across the province.

For example, the Toronto *Globe and Mail* of November 5,
in an editorial entitled "The argument is flawed," struck
out at the Liberal and NDP positions. It admitted that
Roman Catholic students might be disadvantaged, but concluded that the Hall-Dennis ideal of educational equality
for every child could best be achieved by a single system.
It rejected the argument for diversity by taking it to *ad
absurdum* lengths suggesting that this meant every group
could demand its own system. "In education (in the past
five years, the Ontario bill rose by $1 billion) the costs of
true pluralism are on the edge of infinity."

The Toronto *Telegram*, in an editorial on November 6,
rejected the brief and the views of its supporters: "We do
not believe it is in the best interests of all Ontario children,
of whatever faith, to extend the present Separate School
system."

The only political trial of the separate school issue in
1969 took place in the by-election held in the constituency
of Middlesex South. It was an important riding, including
within its boundaries part of the city of London and surrounded moreover by a number of constituencies held by
Ontario cabinet ministers, including the Premier, John
Robarts. The battle was watched with great interest. The

victor was the NDP candidate, Archdeacon Kenneth Bolton, who, in a prepared statement for the local press, had been most generous in his reaction to the separate school cause. The Conservative candidate, in the collective press statement, had confused the extension issue with support for private schools and had stated that persons wishing to send their children to them must be prepared to assume the added expense. The Liberal candidate, unaware of the direction in which the caucus of the party was moving, was most negative to separate school hopes, commenting, "I do not favour the further extension of this inadequate project into further grades." In reality, the issue played little part in the election and its results, though it may have given false hopes to those who saw in Bolton's victory a vindication of the view that support for the separate school position was politically viable.

In the fall of 1969 and early months of 1970, the opposition to the separate school cause began to organize. Two inter-church groups produced totally opposite reactions to the brief. A group called the Inter-Church Committee on Protestant–Roman Catholic Relations, representing the Anglican Church of Canada, the Baptist Federation of Canada, Churches of Christ (disciples), the Presbyterian Church of Canada, the Salvation Army of Canada, the United Church of Canada (but significantly lacking any representation from the Roman Catholic Church) issued a pamphlet entitled "A New Separatism in Ontario?" and claimed that both Catholic and non-Catholic would be hurt by the proposed full separate school system. This intense, emotional response assumed that the granting of support to grades 11, 12 and 13 "may well lead to a demand for Separate Teachers' Colleges, a Separate Department of Education and a separate curriculum," even though at that point Teachers' Colleges were being transformed into faculties of education associated with provincial universities, and the Catholic position had been for a clearer voice within the existing department, and not a single word had been written to suggest any future appeal for a separate curriculum. This committee saw a "serious threat to Canadian unity," and was convinced in its own mind that "a large percentage of Roman Catholics evidently do not want it." As evidence for the last statement, the fact that 40 per cent of the Metro Toronto Roman Catholics directed their school taxes to the public school system was cited, even though in many cases these Roman Catholics had no choice, there being no separate school available to them.

On the other hand, the Ecumenical Study Commission on Religion in Education, representing almost the identical major Protestant denominations as the Inter-Church Committee, but including the Roman Catholic community as well, came out strongly in favour of the brief and its basic arguments. It recognized the existence of a separate school system by right under law and pointed out with some clarity that whether they regarded "this situation with favour or not, this is NOT the issue under discussion in 'Equality of Education' nor, therefore, in this memorandum." The brief recognized that there might be a slightly higher cost but that this should be borne "as an act of justice towards those Roman Catholic citizens of the province who have so far carried on their shoulders the cost of educating 16,000 pupils who might have all this while been a charge on public funds." The Ecumenical Study Commission recognized that the decision to complete the separate school system would arouse demands "for similar privileges to private schools." The commission argued that only the Roman Catholics were recognized "by the Constitution as having specific educational rights," that the Roman Catholics would "bring with them a dowry of many of their buildings" and that the commission would find it "doubtful if private schools would wish to surrender their sovereignty and become part of the public educational system." This brief stressed the importance of "shared facilities and services," and concluded with a statement of commitment to "unity in diversity" as "a viable possibility—both church and society are not necessarily weakened by plurality."

Perhaps more important than these denominationally oriented briefs, was the one submitted on behalf of the Ontario Public School Trustees' Association. In this document, there was a strong appeal for a "unified Secondary School educational system"—an indication that not only was this organization prepared to fight the extension of support to grades 11, 12 and 13, but was calling into question the very existence of a separate school system. "We take a positive approach that any step which would tend to segregate any part of the school population by reason of race, colour, language or creed, is an invidious one and should be foreign to Canadian concepts." Harold Greer, the *London Free Press* special correspondent at Queen's Park, in an article on January 28, 1970, criticized in harsh terms that particular statement, "which is about as close as one can come to saying that separate schools are un-Canadian and that to extend public support for them through the high school level is high treason." The brief concentrated its attention on the financial situation and concluded that not only should no further grants to separate secondary schools be contemplated, but that the existing grants to separate elementary schools should be reduced.

The "quiet campaign" of the OSSTA had been organized for the three-month period leading up to the expected decision in the late fall of 1969. When no decision was forthcoming, the campaign, which in itself had become more noisy than its originators had intended, lost its purpose and came to an end. From that point, the initiative increasingly fell into the hands of the more militant leadership of the separate high schools.

Not only did this transfer of real leadership escalate the nature of the rhetoric, it also focused attention on the least appealing aspect of the problem. The students and parents in the separate high schools were, to some extent, an elite and could be linked, to the disadvantage of the cause, to the other private schools of the province. The initial focus had been on the extension of the public separate school system; now it was on justice to the existing private separate high schools and gave some credence to the government argument that helping the Catholics would bring appeals from every private school interest in Ontario.

Throughout 1970 there was a lively debate in the letters-to-the-editor columns of newspapers and at meetings organized by numerous committees. Letter-writing campaigns overflowed the mail-boxes of MPP's. Even municipal councils debated and in many cases passed resolutions supporting the Separate School Trustees' brief. Before the year was out, a huge rally was held in Maple Leaf Gardens, and although Catholic high school students were responsible for organizing the program, the entire Roman Catholic community was involved. The event was a success as an estimated fifteen thousand people filled the largest building in the province and speaker after speaker appealed for justice and equality of treatment for separate school students and their parents.

In the fall of 1970, John Roberts announced his decision to step down as premier of Ontario and leader of the Conservative party and for the next few months attention was centred on the choosing of a leader and new premier. The question of aid to separate schools came up on many occasions, but the candidates for leadership were obviously unwilling to see this issue become a major area of contention in the Conservative party. With only the slightest variation in emphasis, each of the candidates made very cautious statements which gave little hope to Catholic separate school supporters and no commitment to a change of policy.

During this period, while pedestrian day-to-day politics came to a halt at the provincial level until the Conservatives had picked a leader, the OSSTA had commissioned Elliott Research to do a survey of public opinion on separate education in Ontario. The survey was conducted in ten Ontario cities and involved two thousand respondents, 60 per cent of whom were non-Catholic, and was completed in January 1971. The Trustees were able to conclude that there was not very strong opposition on the part of non-Catholics to the extension of aid to grades 11, 12 and 13 in the separate school system. This survey was confirmed in a way by surveys taken by both the Liberal and Conservative parties in the winter and spring of 1971, but not revealed until after the election. It indicated that the Ontario electorate was not particularly incensed or excited by the proposal to give aid to enable the separate schools to complete their system. In fact, Ontario's citizens were much more concerned about pollution and the cost of living; the separate school issue was well down on their list of political priorities.

One might ask why Premier Davis decided to arouse interest in this issue just a few days before the announcement of an election. Certain observers have suggested that William Davis, who had barely won the leadership race and in doing so had alienated many individuals whose support was imperative, saw this historic issue as one which would,

above all others, unite the Conservative party behind him
before the election was called. Was this the reason for his
dramatic announcement on August 31?

The results of the election of October 1971, ended all
further discussion on extension of support for separate
secondary education in the province. Both the NDP and the
Liberal party were committed to the separate school supporters' position. The Conservatives were aligned against
that position. The Conservatives won a decisive victory,
increasing their strength in the Legislature, reducing substantially the number of seats held by the official opposition, and eroding marginally the complement of the NDP.

In certain areas, the separate school issue played a major
role; in Windsor, Welland, Ottawa and parts of northern
Ontario rallies were sponsored by separate school supporters which were well attended and aroused much
enthusiasm. But there were several other issues which took
precedence. Certainly President Nixon's announcement on
trade and tariff, which appeared to threaten the well-being
of Ontario's industrial system, was paramount in the mind
of the electorate.

Yet the extension question had wider ramifactions. The
Premier's statement, coming as it did only a few days
before the election announcement, became another element
in the formation of an image, an image of a tough, decisive
leader. The separate school issue, along with the celebrated
cancellation of the Spadina Expressway, provided a specific
example of decisiveness in the face of strong opposition.

As well, this issue contributed to the Conservative cause
in another way. It deflected attention away from what
might have been the Achilles' heel of the new premier.
William Davis had built a costly educational system and
the unpopularity of high local taxes to support this system,
accompanied by a lack of confidence in that system's
capacity to live up to the unrealistic expectations, could
have created serious embarrassment on the hustings. But,
ironically, education was scarcely discussed at all. The
entire focus was on the separate school issue during the
weeks which followed the announcement, while the election campaign was being fought.

Perhaps there was no hope from the outset. A letter from
Premier John Robarts to the North Bay Council, who had
given its endorsement to the separate school cause (as did

many other municipal bodies) and printed in the *North Bay Nugget* of July 23, 1969, was "interpreted by several North Bay officials as a clear statement of policy that spells out the government's intention not to bend to a current province-wide campaign." The reasons for Premier Robarts' rejection of the brief centred on the identical areas emphasized by Premier Davis' statement of August 31, 1971: the fragmentation of the existing system, the costliness, and the implications for the support of other denominations.

Yet Catholic supporters believed that the burgeoning strength of the separate school system, with some four hundred thousand students and growing faster than the public school system, seemed to have a logic of its own. As well, the example of other provinces (five had given government support, another province seemed moving in that direction and a seventh provided tax concessions in lieu of direct financial aid), seemed to support the extension position.

Any assessment of voting strength of those who might support extension would inevitably be inexact. Yet the reality was that if this became a major issue, the majority of the province was non-Roman Catholic, and the Liberals and NDP had placed themselves in the position of dividing between them the Roman Catholic minority who would most likely provide the votes in favour of extension. The sophisticated polling techniques used by the Conservative party which had been used to gauge the political atmosphere indicated a further reality—that many Roman Catholics did not, in fact, agree with the position of the separate school trustees. At this time of the loosening of the power of the church over personal affairs characterized by a variety of approaches to such matters as birth control, the dissident Roman Catholic was likely to use his vote to express his individual preference rather than line up slavishly behind a particular program.

For those outside the Roman Catholic community, the issue was complex. The arguments raged on whether separate schools and their public support was appropriate in a secular or ecumenical decade. The fact that the continued existence of the separate school system was not in question rarely had much impact in the confusion which invariably accompanied a public discussion of the matter.

Further, the question of the cost continued to arise and the wildest predictions were put forward as accurate estimates. During 1970 and 1971, the opposition parties called on the Minister of Education and then the Premier to give some cost analysis of the separate school trustees' demands. No figures were forthcoming and the resultant void was filled with unsupported cost predictions which undoubtedly struck fear into the hearts of many taxpayers and placed the philosophic arguments well to the rear.

However, all these observations pale in significance compared with the reality of October 21, 1973—a clear mandate for the Conservative party. The Conservative victory made it clear that Premier Davis and his colleagues had assessed the mind of the electorate more perceptively than either the Liberals or the NDP. The government had remembered the history of the province, had understood the nature of Ontario society and were aware of the vote-getting capacity of the separate school extension issue. Yet bitterness has not departed and, although aid to separate schools is unlikely to remain an issue in the public domain, or become a source of contention in the next provincial election, there is every reason to believe that the events of 1969 to 1971 have forged new political alliances and broken old partisan links. It is significant, for example, that when the first strike of teachers took place in the last days of 1973, it was the Catholic teachers who were the most difficult to assuage; it was the Catholic affiliate of OTF who reached the highest level of militancy against a Conservative government. The scars have not healed.

Although a more secular society will not give prominence to church-state relations with quite the intensity of the first hundred years of Ontario's existence as a province, the continuing reality of a separate school system in parallel relationship to the public school system will continue to make the extent of its function and support a factor in the political life of Ontario.

3
KENNETH BRYDEN

How Public Medicare
Came to Ontario

ONTARIO medicare assumed its present form in 1972,[1] nine years after the first government medicare bill was introduced in the provincial Legislature. Those years witnessed recurring and often acrimonious disputes involving political parties, pressure groups, the news media and other attentive segments of the public. The federal government also got into the act and relations between it and Ontario were embittered as a result. At stake were conflicting interests and ideologies. A reluctant Ontario government was driven relentlessly to adopt a plan which the Premier at one stage described as a "Machiavellian scheme." Events in other parts of Canada had a decisive influence on policy-making in Ontario in the medicare case, and it is necessary to describe those events in some detail in order to understand how public medicare ultimately came to Ontario.

In urbanized, industrialized societies like Canada, there are many risks—unemployment, ill health, penury in old age, etcetera—for which most individuals and families cannot make adequate provision on their own. As a result, there has been continuous pressure over the last one hundred years for governments to step in with public social security plans. Medical, hospital and related expenses are among the significant risks of a modern society. In past years such expenses have placed many families and individuals in serious financial straits and in some cases have even reduced them to poverty. Thus, public health insurance in a variety of forms now constitutes part of the battery of social security measures in most modern societies.

In Canada, health insurance was a subject of intermittent public discussion from World War I on, but it was not until World War II that it became a significant public issue. During that war, the great depression of the 1930s was fresh in memory and there was a determination to avoid such a disaster in the future. More and more people came

1 "Medicare" has become the popular designation of insurance covering doctors' bills. The term was invented in the United States in relation to a plan applying only to the aged. It was quickly adopted in Canada with the broader meaning of all medical insurance without age restriction. "Health insurance" has a still broader meaning, embracing both hospital and medical care and often other health services as well.

to see governments as having a positive role to play in maintaining employment and in providing social security. In Canada, the federal government established a cabinet committee to study postwar problems early in the war; it also referred such matters to committees of the House of Commons for study. Health insurance emerged as an important issue in those investigations, with labour, farm, church and other groups urging federal government action. So great indeed was the emotional impact of the war that the Canadian Medical Association (CMA), later an implacable foe of public medicare, stated that the medical profession was willing and anxious to cooperate in a national health insurance plan. Not even the private insurance industry was opposed: it had not at that time developed a significant amount of business in this field.

The only apparent obstacle to immediate federal action was constitutional: court decisions over the years had left little doubt that health insurance was under the jurisdiction of the provinces. The federal government decided that it could overcome the constitutional problem by sponsoring a joint federal-provincial plan. Accordingly, one of its proposals to the federal-provincial conference on postwar reconstruction held in 1945–46 was for federal payment of 60 per cent of the estimated costs of health insurance plans established and operated by the provinces.[2] This proposal was part of a larger package of proposals which the provinces had to accept or reject in toto and which included provincial agreement to exclusive federal ocupancy of important tax fields. The wealthier provinces balked and the federal package went down the drain.

In the meantime, some initiatives were coming from the provinces. In 1944 the democratic socialist Co-operative Commonwealth Federation (CCF) was elected to power in Saskatchewan. The new government placed high priority on health insurance. It did not believe that a relatively poor province like Saskatchewan could establish complete health insurance without federal assistance, but to demonstrate the seriousness of its intentions, it launched a hospital insurance plan of its own which came into effect

2 Dominion-Provincial Conference on Reconstruction, *Proposals of the Government of Canada* (Ottawa: King's Printer, 1945), pp. 28–36.

in 1947. British Columbia and Alberta followed the Saskatchewan example in 1949 and in the same year Newfoundland, which already had a government-operated cottage hospital system, entered Confederation as a Canadian province. Thus, hospital insurance was in effect in four of the ten provinces by 1949.

In Ontario the CCF, which formed the official opposition from 1948 to 1951, pressed hard for adoption of a hospital insurance plan on the Saskatchewan model. So did trade unions and other groups. For a time the Progressive Conservative government of the province resisted these pressures, claiming that public health insurance of any kind represented unwarranted government interference with private initiative. With the cost of hospital treatment increasing rapidly, however, such a position was hard to maintain in Canada's most highly urbanized province. In 1955, shortly before a provincial election, Premier Leslie Frost reversed the field on his critics by demanding at a federal-provincial conference that Ottawa provide financial assistance to the provinces for hospital insurance plans. In later years, Frost recalled with relish the consternation which spread over the face of National Health and Welfare Minister Paul Martin as the Ontario demand was enunciated. The federal government had got into the comfortable habit of proclaiming its intention to do something about health insurance later. Action could no longer be postponed, at least on hospital insurance, now that Canada's most populous province was demanding it and four other provinces already had it. Legislation was passed authorizing the federal government to pay half the cost on average of provincial hospital insurance plans, and by 1961 all provinces had adopted such plans.

In Ontario a new government agency, the Ontario Hospital Services Commission (OHSC), was set up to operate the plan, and private agencies such as Blue Cross and insurance companies had to withdraw from standard ward coverage and concentrate on supplementary benefits. The government claimed that its new plan was voluntary, but in fact coverage was compulsory for all workers in employment units of fifteen or more employees—that is, more than 60 per cent of the population. Intensive promotional campaigns by cooperatives among the farm population and growing awareness of the benefits of hospital insurance among the public generally combined to induce most people not in the compulsory groups to come in, so that there was nearly universal coverage in a few years.

With the federal government now subsidizing hospital insurance, the CCF government of Saskatchewan decided to take the next step of covering doctors' bills in a medicare plan. The CCF made such a plan the main plank in its 1960 provincial election platform, and after winning the election, the government launched a full-scale study preparatory to introducing a plan. A rocky road lay ahead; gone were the halcyon days of the early 1940s when almost everyone was in favour of public health insurance including medicare. Two powerful interests opposed to medicare had grown up in the interval. Insurance companies had built up a profitable business in the health insurance field and had set up a special organization, the Canadian Health Insurance Association, to protect their interests. Even more important, organized medicine over the years had reversed its position completely from that of the early 1940s. The medical associations of most provinces had established medicare plans of their own. Being strong supporters of private enterprise, they were ready to accept the competition of insurance companies, but they were bitterly opposed to any kind of public plan which would supersede both their own and the insurance industry's plans. That industry for its part was unhappy at having been pushed to the fringes of hospital insurance. With organized medicine on its side, it could hope for a more favourable outcome of a battle against medicare.

Most doctors, and especially the leaders of the CMA and the provincial medical associations, were convinced that public medicare would lead to crude government interference in the practice of medicine and in the doctor-patient relationship. The intensity with which this view was held bordered almost on fanaticism. As a result, when the Saskatchewan government proceeded with its new medicare plan in 1962, most of the doctors of the province engaged in a concerted withdrawal of medical services. For a short time the province teetered almost on the brink of anarchy, until a face-saving formula worked out by a mediator brought in from Great Britain enabled the doctors to resume their duties under the new government plan.[3]

The events in Saskatchewan focused public attention on medicare in the late 1950s and early 1960s and revived demands for federal action of the kind proposed in the mid-1940s. The federal government, now in Progressive Conservative hands under Prime Minister John Diefenbaker, temporized by appointing a royal commission (the Hall Commission) in 1961. A perusal of the personal backgrounds of the commissioners suggests that the government had in mind a report that would be unfavourable to extension of public health insurance beyond the provincial hospital insurance plans already in operation. If so, the result was different than anticipated. The exhaustive studies produced by the commission's research staff convinced the commissioners, and especially the chairman, Justice Emmett Hall, that only a public health plan would adequately meet the needs of all residents of a modern society. The commission's report, issued in 1964,[4] recommended introduction by stages of comprehensive health insurance financed jointly by the federal and provincial governments and administered by the provinces. The first stage of hospital insurance having already been achieved, the next logical stage in the commission's view was medicare, to be followed in due course by coverage of other personal health services. Organized medicine and the insurance industry subjected the report to a withering attack, but Justice Hall counter-attacked. He proved to be a formidable platform speaker who defended the report vigorously in a number of public appearances. The Hall Report and the chairman's defence of it placed powerful weapons in the hands of the proponents of public medicare.

Organized medicine and the insurance industry had not, however, been letting the grass grow under their feet. Conscious of the growing pressure for public medicare, the CMA had worked out its own alternative long before the

3 For further information on the Saskatchewan medicare controversy, see Robin F. Badgley and Samuel Wolfe, *Doctors' Strike: Medical Care and Conflict in Saskatchewan* (Toronto: Macmillan, 1967); Edwin A. Tollefson, *Bitter Medicine: The Saskatchewan Medicare Feud* (Saskatoon: Modern Press, 1964).

4 Royal Commission on Health Services, *Report*, 2 vols. (Ottawa: Queen's Printer, 1964, 1965).

Hall Commission appeared on the scene. The CMA argument was that, with the growth of private medicare sponsored by the medical associations and other non-profit organizations and by the profit-making insurance companies, the great majority of Canadians already had medicare coverage. Therefore, the only proper role left for governments was to subsidize the minority of people who were not covered by group plans in their places of employment and who could not afford to buy individual coverage. The Hall Commission rejected this line of argument. Its investigations showed that, though a majority of people had private medical coverage of some kind, most of them had inadequate, in some cases grossly inadequate, coverage. The commission was satisfied that universal coverage at reasonable cost could be achieved only through a public plan.

Organized medicine and the insurance industry stressed the voluntary nature of the CMA proposal and compared this feature favourably with the compulsion inherent in a public plan applying by law to the entire population. Freedom of choice, they argued, is the hallmark of a free society, and under their plan consumers would be free to decide the kind and degree of coverage they wanted and to make their own choice of carriers from among the many insurance companies and smaller number of non-profit organizations offering coverage. Moreover, making coverage depend on choice in the market place would help to keep costs under control. Under a public plan, everyone would be covered willy-nilly for a full range of medical services, but under the CMA proposal every consumer would decide whether he wanted to pay the cost of full coverage or accept partial coverage and use the money saved for something else. At the same time, government subsidization of the poor would ensure that no one would be deprived of coverage because of inability to pay.

Supporters of public medicare countered these arguments with the claim that in actual fact the free operation of the market was resulting mainly in duplication and waste in the case of medicare. A multiplicity of carriers, offering a bewildering variety of coverages and devoting large sums to promotional and selling expenses, inevitably led to cost inflation. The CMA proposal would perpetuate this state of affairs. The only change it would effect would be to make public funds available to increase the business of private carriers through subsidization of the poor. The large number of people whose incomes were no more than enough to get by on but not small enough to qualify for subsidization (probably a majority of the population) would be faced with the Hobson's choice of paying larger premiums than they could afford or of settling for less than adequate coverage. At the same time, the tax money of these people and others would be used under the CMA proposal for paying private carriers to provide coverage for the poor. Medical services were like education, it was argued, in that they represented a universal need. The only way of ensuring that they would be universally available was through a single universal plan in which everyone would be covered automatically and from which therefore promotional and selling expenses, as well as duplication of services, would be eliminated.

Though organized medicine and the insurance industry did not manage to sell the CMA proposal to the Hall Commission, they were successful with some provincial governments. In 1963 the Social Credit government of Alberta, strongly oriented to private enterprise, implemented a plan based on the CMA proposal. The Progressive Conservative government of Ontario was also sympathetic. This was especially true of John Robarts who became leader of the party and premier of the province late in 1961. Robarts had a strong philosophical commitment to the proposition that the role of government in social security was to supplement, reinforce and regulate rather than to supplant the insurance industry. This came out clearly in his attitude to contributory pensions, the other major social security issue in Canada in the 1960s. Robarts and his government battled stubbornly, though unsuccessfully in the end, to establish a plan in which insurance companies would be used to provide contributory pensions, as an alternative to the Canada Pension Plan under which such pensions came to be provided through a government-administered fund.[5] The same attitude was evident in the Robarts government's response to medicare.

5 For an account of the Ontario plan and its relationship to the Canada Pension Plan, see Kenneth Bryden, *Old Age Pensions and Policy-Making in Canada* (Montreal: McGill-Queen's University Press, 1974), pp. 165–69, 173–75.

During the 1950s the opposition parties in the Ontario Legislature had been reduced to numerically minute groups. The 1959 provincial election increased opposition strength substantially with a consequent increase in pressure on the government. On the medicare issue, the official (Liberal) opposition was ambivalent for some years, wavering between the CMA type of proposal and public medicare; but eventually it came down solidly in favour of a public plan. As for the smaller CCF group (NDP after the formation of the New Democratic Party in 1961), medicare was an issue for which this group had a natural affinity, and it pushed ceaselessly for a public plan. Under persistent pressure in the Legislature and with public debate mounting outside, the government eventually found it necessary to declare its position on medicare. In 1962, Health and Welfare Minister Matthew Dymond, a medical doctor, appointed a small private committee to advise him confidentially on medicare.[6] The committee consisted entirely of representatives of the medical profession and of the insurance companies and non-profit carriers in the health insurance field. Obviously, Dymond had made up his mind in advance about the kind of advice he wanted to get. That advice was incorporated in a bill introduced in the Legislature but not enacted in the spring of 1963, in the dying days of the 1962–63 session, the last session before an anticipated provincial election. The bill was based in principle on the CMA proposal but with some refinement of detail to eliminate the more objectionable features of some of the medical insurance contracts then being sold by private companies (for example, the practice of many companies of cancelling a contract as soon as the subscriber reached sixty-five). The bill set forth a standard contract which all carriers in the province were to be required to provide on demand, and the government was to have authority to set a maximum premium for this standard coverage. The public was to be free to buy this or any other coverage or to refrain from buying. The government itself was to offer the standard contract to the very poor on a subsidized basis.

During the provincial election in the fall of 1963, the government used the bill as evidence that medicare was for

6 Legislature of Ontario, *Debates*, 1965, pp. 1163–65.

all practical purposes an accomplished fact in Ontario. In actuality, the bill had been introduced for discussion only. It was referred in August to a committee chaired by J. Gerald Hagey, president of Waterloo University, for further consideration and refinement. With the exception of a labour representative, all members of the committee, including the chairman, were already committed to the CMA approach to medicare. The committee heard briefs advocating public medicare from organizations with large memberships such as the Ontario Federation of Labour and the United Church of Canada, but it had no ears for such views. It recommended that the government should proceed with the 1963 bill with only technical changes.[7]

In the spring of 1965 the government brought in a new medicare bill, which filled in details not adequately provided for in the 1963 bill but which contained no changes of principle. The new bill was the subject of a prolonged and bitter debate in the Legislature and of much criticism from labour, farm, church and welfare groups, but the government mustered its majority to push the bill through. After doing so, it had second thoughts and it refrained from proclaiming the bill in force. The reason was that it had run into difficulties with supporters of the bill. In particular, the insurance companies objected to being required to offer the standard contract provided for in the bill. The government decided to relieve them of this obligation, and in 1966 it brought in an amending bill under which it undertook exclusive responsibility itself for providing insurance under the standard contract. The private carriers were free to offer whatever coverages they wished. Moreover, they were given all the group contract business, the lucrative part of medical insurance, while the government took responsibility for the costly part, including the subsidized groups.

A special medical services insurance division was established in the Health Department to provide the coverages for which the government was now responsible. The OHSC already had a fully developed structure for administering hospital insurance, and the logical administrative procedure would have been to extend OHSC responsibilities to

7 Medical Services Insurance Committee, *Report* (Toronto: Queen's Printer, 1964).

include medical coverage as well. Organized medicine was, however, opposed to administration of medical insurance by a commission on which doctors were not in the majority. Thus the provincial government had to establish separate structures or risk a fight. In an attempt to rationalize at least premium collection, the government set up the Health Insurance Registration Board in 1967 to collect both the hospital and medical premiums. If anything, this complicated rather than simplified the existing administrative complexity because three agencies were now involved —HIRB, OHSC and the Medical Services Insurance Division.

Meanwhile, developments were occurring at the national level which in time were to render obsolete Ontario's hybrid policies and confused administrative structures. The national Liberal party, after its crushing defeat in the federal election of 1958, went through a period of intense self-examination. New figures came to the fore with the aim of restoring to the party the reform image they conceived it had once had but had lost in the later St. Laurent years. As a result, the party's platforms in the 1962 and 1963 federal elections were oriented to substantial extension of social security, including a firm commitment to joint federal-provincial public medicare. Returned as a minority government in 1963, the Liberals were under strong pressure both from within their ranks and from outside to act on the medicare pledge. The pressure became irresistible when the Hall Commission presented its report in 1964. In 1965 Prime Minister Lester Pearson proposed that the federal government would pay 50 per cent on average of the cost of provincial medicare plans. To qualify for federal subsidization, the provinces would have to meet four conditions: universality of coverage, comprehensiveness of benefits, portability of coverage from province to province, and non-profit administration by an agency of the provincial government. In other words, the federal government committed itself to a universal public medicare plan similar to that introduced in Saskatchewan in 1962 and recommended by the Hall Commission in 1964. After extensive discussions with the provinces, the offer of subsidization and the qualifying conditions were incorporated in a statute that came into effect on July 1, 1968.

It was abundantly clear that Ontario's hybrid policy did not qualify for federal subsidization. Premier Robarts complained bitterly that the federal government was trying to determine provincial priorities. Noting that health insurance was a provincial responsibility under the constitution, Robarts argued that Ontario was in the process of developing a policy that suited its needs. The federal government was now threatening to penalize the province financially for refusing a quite different kind of plan. The proposed federal plan would cost governments more than Ontario's and Ontario's priorities dictated that any available additional money should be devoted to matters that the provincial government considered more urgent than full public medicare. If Ottawa wanted to assist in financing medicare, it should make its subsidies available for plans which the provinces rather than Ottawa devised. Robarts' plea was to no avail. July 1, 1968, arrived with no relaxation of the federal conditions. This fact added financial pressure to the growing political pressures on the provincial government to go the whole way to universal public medicare. It was estimated at the time that, by failing to qualify for federal subsidization, Ontario was sacrificing approximately $175 million a year.

The provincial government reacted by intensifying its pressure on Ottawa to relax the conditions, and finally, in 1969, Ottawa gave some ground. It was agreed that Ontario could meet the federal requirement of non-profit provincial administration by designating private carriers or consortiums of them as provincial agents. These carriers would be required to provide the basic coverages required under the federal conditions on a non-profit basis, but they would be free to provide additional coverages on their own terms. It was also agreed that the province would be permitted to achieve the federal condition of universal coverage in stages, covering 90 per cent of the population at first and gradually working up to 95 per cent. Provincial legislation to authorize the new arrangements was passed in June 1969. To achieve the immediate objective of 90 per cent coverage, the government resorted to the device it had used for hospital insurance of making coverage compulsory for everyone in employment units of fifteen or more employees. It was estimated that these people, together with those being subsidized by the province and those who sought coverage voluntarily, would produce the required 90 per cent.

Premier Robarts and Health Minister Dymond announced the new arrangements with satisfaction, but they
had won a Pyrrhic victory. The overly complex structure
for administering hospital and medical insurance in the
province was reduced to an absurdity by the addition of
designated agents. Herculean efforts by provincial administrators to make the new setup work ended in failure for
the simple reason that it was unworkable. The provincial
government finally accommodated itself to this hard fact.
After passage of preparatory legislation in December 1971,
a new Health Insurance Act was adopted in June 1972. That
act established a full-fledged public medicare plan and
integrated its administration with hospital insurance into
a single health insurance plan operated by the province.
Public medicare had finally arrived in Ontario.

SELECTED BIBLIOGRAPHY

A good brief description of Canada's public medicare plan
in its historical setting is contained in Malcolm G. Taylor,
"The Canadian Health Insurance Program," *Public Administration Review*, vol. 33, no. 1 (Jan.–Feb., 1973), pp.
31–39.

Just about the only convenient source of information on
the political controversies surrounding the evolution of
public medicare in Ontario is Legislature of Ontario, *Debates*, especially, 1965, pp. 2755–60, 3209–93 and 1969, pp.
5724–30, 5965–6040.

For a discussion of the pros and cons of public and
private medicare, see W. P. Thompson, *Medical Care: Programs and Issues* (Toronto: Clarke, Irwin & Company,
1964).

An excellent analysis of the medicare issue in the light of
the perceptions of the medical profession is found in
Bernard R. Blishen, *Doctors and Doctrines: The Ideology
of Medical Care in Canada* (Toronto: University of Toronto
Press, 1969). Another valuable study of the profession is
J. W. Grove, *Organized Medicine in Ontario*, a study for the
Committee on the Healing Arts (Toronto: Queen's Printer,
1969).

The problems involved in the administration of health
programs generally and of public medicare in particular
are analysed in Peter Aucoin, "Federal Health Care Policy"

and G. R. Weller, "Health Care and Medicare Policy in Ontario," in G. Bruce Doern and V. Seymour Wilson, eds., *Issues in Canadian Public Policy* (Toronto: Macmillan of Canada, 1974).

The legislative bases of the current federal and Ontario medicare programs are *Medical Care Act*, Revised Statutes of Canada, 1970, chap. M–8, and *Health Insurance Act, 1972*, Statutes of Ontario, 1972, chap. 91.

4
HENRY J. JACEK

Central Governmental Planning *versus* Conflicting Local Elites: Regional Government in Hamilton-Wentworth

AN IMPORTANT problem facing all governments is how to develop and implement policies which make efficient use of public resources while at the same time do not upset the values and traditions of local political leaders who are in much closer personal contact with the mass of voters. This problem is especially important for the central political leadership of Ontario because this province is vast in size and heterogeneous in population. Perhaps no recent issue is more indicative of this problem than local government reorganization. And in the Hamilton-Wentworth-Burlington area the clash between the Ontario government and local elites was especially severe.

In the 1960s two complementary trends were occurring in the Ontario government. First, the Ontario government was concerned about the efficient use of tax revenue. This concern resulted in the Ontario Committee on Taxation and its findings, the Smith Report. The basic conclusion of this report was that a general reorganization of the structure of local government was needed in order to create a fair and efficient use of governmental tax resources. At the same time, the Ontario Department of Municipal Affairs, in cooperation with various municipalities, was continuing a study of municipal government through local government review commissions.

These two trends were more than complimentary. The review of local governments was a direct result of the Ontario government's concern over increasing provincial expenditures to an out-of-date inefficient municipal system. As these expenditures increased, the costs associated with such a policy rose quickly while the benefits increased at a much slower rate. Thus, the Ontario government could foresee the day when provincial voters would react negatively at the polls to the ever-widening gap between heavy taxes and correspondingly insufficient governmental services. To prevent this expected negative voter reaction, the provincial government was forced into a positive policy initiative, an action also supported by some important provincial civil servants. This policy initiative, fraught with a different set of political risks, was the consolidation and reorganization of local governments.

In the mid-1960s a review was made of the local government structure in the counties of Halton and Peel. The town of Burlington was in the southwestern part of Halton

County and was a rapidly developing bedroom suburb of Hamilton. Burlington officials at this time were wary of municipal reorganization and preferred to be left alone. Nonetheless, the Peel-Halton Local Government Review recommended that Burlington be included in a revised Peel-Halton region. However, this report specifically stated that the case for Burlington's inclusion in such a region was not conclusive. While this report was not what Burlington wanted, it did raise the hopes of the Burlington officials that they could avoid being tied to a metropolitan Hamilton government.

About a year later, on August 29, 1967, the Hamilton-Burlington-Wentworth Local Government Review Commission was created by the Department of Municipal Affairs with the approval of the city of Hamilton, the town of Burlington and the county of Wentworth. Later the town of Grimsby and the township of North Grimsby were included in the study at their request. First, a large mass of data was collected and published in the Hamilton-Burlington-Wentworth Local Government Review, *Data Book of Basic Information*, in June 1968.

Although all the municipalities studied have strong ties to the city of Hamilton, the communities are very different in character. As the map indicates, Hamilton is at the centre of a crescent. In this centre exists a dense mass of population and most of the industry of the region. Almost all of the population is tied occupationally to the city's industry, giving the city an overwhelmingly urban, industrial outlook. The population of Hamilton is also distinctively working class in nature with large concentrations of Catholics and first- and second-generation Canadians of southern and eastern European origins. Hamilton's suburbs are quite different. Some, like East Flamborough, West Flamborough, Beverly, Glanford and Binbrook, are rural communities based on an agricultural economy and outlook. Others, like Ancaster, Saltfleet and the Grimsby and North Grimsby area, adjacent to Saltfleet, are a mixture of small built-up areas surrounded by agricultural lands. Three communities—Dundas, Waterdown and Stoney Creek—are small towns whose communities have a strong pride in their extensive historical heritage. Finally, there is Burlington, northeast of Hamilton and east of East Flamborough, with a large land area strongly populated with middle-class

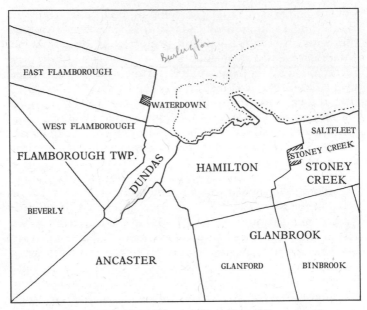

Regional Municipality of Hamilton-Wentworth

Hamilton suburbanites. This town of approximately ninety thousand is heavily populated by people who are upwardly mobile socially and who have left behind their working-class roots in Hamilton. All of these suburbs, in sum, have a population which is middle class or agricultural, Protestant and British in background and which fear being dominated by the large industrial centre of Hamilton and its working-class population.

In the second phase of the Hamilton-Burlington-Wentworth Local Government Review, written and oral submissions, based partially on the information in the Data Book, were made to the commission. The city of Hamilton and the county of Wentworth emphasized to the commission the importance of having Burlington in a new metropolitan Hamilton regional government. As the appendix on page 61 indicates, there was an impressive amount of data to show that there was substantial interaction between the residents of Burlington and the people of Hamilton-Wentworth. At the same time, there was substantial pressure from the residents of Burlington to the commission to leave Burlington as it was and certainly not to bring Burlington into a metropolitan Hamilton regional government. Thus, it was clear to the commission as it ended the submission stage of the review that the recommendation on Burlington's future was to be its most controversial proposal.

Even before the commission members were selected the prospects for regional government became controversial, beginning in Burlington. In that community, a few present and future leaders decided to mobilize the townspeople against the possibility of regional government with Hamilton. In early 1967, some members of the community, including five members of the town council, were even opposed to a joint study with Hamilton and Wentworth. The reason for the opposition was that it was believed that the study would lead to proposals for Burlington's amalgamation with Hamilton. A telephone survey of one thousand homes in Burlington was organized and it was found that 73 per cent opposed being absorbed by Hamilton and 52 per cent were even opposed to Burlington's participation in the commission. The results were quickly released to the media. Soon after, the appointment of a well-known Hamilton politician to the commission caused even more concern. In addition, an attempt to have a plebiscite on the question of regional government in the 1967 Burlington election was frustrated. At the same time, a formal interest group was organized called the Citizens' Association for an Independent Burlington.

In December 1968 a brief from this interest group was submitted to the commission. During January, February and March of 1969 a petition was brought around the community opposing Burlington's inclusion in a regional government with Hamilton. This petition with over fifteen thousand signatures was presented to the Minister of Municipal Affairs. Finally in the December 1969 Burlington election a plebiscite was held. Only 12 per cent of those voting on the question favoured Burlington's inclusion in a regional government with Hamilton. On March 10, 1969, the town council voted for a resolution which emphatically opposed regional government with Hamilton-Wentworth. Early in 1970, the Citizens' Association once again presented a brief to the minister opposing a Hamilton-Burlington region.

The Burlington leaders of the opposition to regional government with Hamilton were not ordinary citizens. Rather they were drawn from the political and economic elite of the community. The Citizens' Association was run mainly by two women. The head of the group, a well-known Liberal, was a close friend of numerous local politicians including the town mayor in 1967. Her husband ran successfully in 1967 for town councillor and helped draw up the materials for the 1969 petition. The second-in-command was even more politically prominent as the vice-president of the Halton West (provincial) Progressive Conservative Association and as an unsuccessful candidate for councillor in the 1970 town election. Her husband was also an unsuccessful town council candidate in 1967, losing to the then most outstanding opponent of the anti-Hamilton group.

Other local elites were also important. The town council, at a crucial point in March 1969, voted against Burlington's participation in a Hamilton region. The Junior Chamber of Commerce provided many volunteers for the 1969 petition drive and the Burlington Chamber of Commerce spent approximately $6,000 prior to the 1969 plebiscite on a campaign to reject a Hamilton-Burlington region. The media also played their part, especially a Burlington weekly newspaper, the *Burlington Gazette*. Typical of this newspaper's support was the free printing of the 1969 petition materials. Leaders of other important groups supporting the anti-Hamilton movement were the Upper Burlington Citizens' Forum and the local leaders of the three major political parties. Thus, by 1970 the community was fully mobilized against a Hamilton-Burlington region. This fact, plus the presence of an important provincial cabinet minister, George Kerr, from Burlington while there were no ministers from Hamilton or Wentworth prior to 1972 made it increasingly clear that a Burlington-Hamilton region was politically improbable.

Finally, in November 1969, the commission prepared a report for the Minister of Municipal Affairs. The basic recommendation of this report was that Hamilton, Wentworth County, and the southern suburban part of Burlington be united in a regional government with a two-tier system. The two-tier organization would contain a regional tier responsible among other things for overall regional planning and transportation, while the lower tier would consist of regional municipalities handling other more local functions.

Besides recommending South Burlington's inclusion in a Hamilton area regional government, the commission also recommended the inclusion of Grimsby. Although the town councils from the latter area had asked to be included in the commission study, the local elites opposed the report's recommendation. Between these two points in time, the Grimsby area had been incorporated into the new regional government of Niagara and the local elites felt another rapid change was unwise. Since there was no intense opposition from the Hamilton area municipalities to the exclusion of the Grimsby area from the Hamilton region, the idea of Grimsby remaining in the Niagara region was quietly accepted.

By 1972 an uneasy feeling developed among Hamilton leaders, although they were still prepared to accept and argue for the basic commission proposals on the geographical boundaries for the proposed new region. Among the elites of Wentworth County, feelings were more than uneasy; rather, panic set in. These leaders were convinced that Burlington and Grimsby were lost to the expected Hamilton-Wentworth region. In such a region over three-quarters of the population would be in Hamilton. They also knew that such an unbalanced situation could easily lead the provincial government to opt for a single-tier region. In effect, Wentworth County would be annexed to Hamilton and the power and status of the rural officials would be vastly reduced and many, if not most, would lose public office.

Faced with this dismal prospect the county officials searched desperately for an alternative plan which would ensure a better rural-urban balance. They tried, as a result, to construct the case for a Brant-Wentworth region. So in November 1972, Wentworth County presented a brief to the provincial government entitled "An Alternate Proposal for a Regional Municipality of Brant-Wentworth." The brief proposed a very large region, which was to contain Hamilton, Wentworth County, part of Burlington, Brantford, Brant County, Caledonia, and the northerly parts of Oneida and Seneca townships. As expected, this brief proposed a two-tier region and gave as a major argument the need for a balance between Hamilton and the rest of the region. Because the proposal covered a large area without a coherent, natural community of interest and because two different watersheds were contained in the area, this alternate proposal was not seriously considered by either the city of Hamilton or, more importantly, the provincial government.

The confrontation came to a climax when the provincial government in January 1973 released their tentative plans, "Proposal for Local Government Reform in the Area West of Metropolitan Toronto." The proposal was, in effect, a reform of three county governments, Peel, Halton and Wentworth. Although these three counties seemed to have two natural communities of interest, Peel-Oakville and Burlington-Wentworth, a major stumbling block was the opposition of Peel officials to joining with Oakville. Since the provincial premier's home constituency was in Peel County, it was most unlikely the Peel County officials' wishes would be overridden. As Burlington officials wanted regional government with Oakville while Peel officials didn't, the joining of Burlington and Oakville was an easy decision. What was left over was regional government for Hamilton-Wentworth. The provincial government was well aware of the intense criticism that would come from this latter area. The government needed a tactic to soften the expected criticism, so it did something highly unusual. It gave Hamilon-Wentworth two choices, alternatives that were sure to divert some criticism from the government by having Hamilton and Wentworth officials quarrelling among themselves. The provincial government advanced two proposals: one single-tier, the other two-tier. The one-tier proposal, which the province seemed to favour, would join Hamilton, Dundas, Ancaster, Stoney Creek, Saltfleet, Binbrook, Glanford and small parts of Beverly and West Flamborough. Parts of Wentworth County would go to the Waterloo-Kitchener area, Brant, and the proposed Halton region, leaving the remaining suburban and rural parts of Wentworth greatly unbalanced against the Hamilton population. The two-tier proposal was to include a larger part of Wentworth although Waterdown and East Flamborough would still go to Halton. It is important to note that both alternatives would abolish the Hamilton Board of Control, in effect the city council's executive committee.

At this point, city and county officials began intense lobbying activity with the provincial government and these officials, especially in Hamilton, put great efforts into mobilizing public opinion against the proposals specifically and against the provincial government in general. The county officials quickly prepared a response to the government's proposals. They argued, quite correctly, that the province ignored all the briefs, studies and proposals for the area and, in fact, disregarded the province's own criteria for regional governments. The county officials especially dreaded one-tier government and they argued that one-tier municipalities had been established only in Northern Ontario and such a system was inappropriate for an area with long-established local communities. The county officials declared themselves in favour of two-tier government but not the kind outlined in the government's proposals. These officials correctly pointed out that the proposed two-tier region was far too small to adequately cover the natural community of interest in the metropolitan Hamilton area. Officials from Wentworth, agreeing with Hamilton leaders and the earlier Hamilton-Burlington-Wentworth Commission report, said that it was in keeping with the province's guidelines on regional government to include Burlington in the area's local government. The Wentworth officials said that if the government went ahead with either of its proposals, the city of Hamilton would so dominate the region that the county residents would be left virtually without any control over their local government. In sum, the county officials rejected both government proposals and in turn offered the provincial government two two-tier proposals of its own, the report recommendations or the alternative Brant-Wentworth region.

Don Ewen, the Conservative member for Wentworth North in the provincial legislative assembly, quickly became a strong opponent of the government's proposals. Although his area had been consistently Conservative in provincial elections over the past thirty years, he thought that if either government proposals went through, his seat was lost. He especially feared the fact that under the one-tier proposal his constituency would be cut up into several pieces in four separate regions, Hamilton-Wentworth, Halton, Waterloo and Brant.

Perhaps even more intense efforts against the government's plans occurred in Hamilton. Here the mobilization of public opinion by the local political elite was a key factor. The mayor and the other four members of the Board of Control took the lead in rallying negative public opinion. All five members of the Board had a great deal to lose even beyond the fact that the Board of Control was slated to be abolished. The mayor, Vic Copps, could see his power and status diminished. As a well-known Liberal who had previously sought the provincial Liberal leadership and as an outspoken critic of the provincial government, he could not expect to be appointed to the regional chairmanship. Additionally, he was feared by the county officials as an outspoken champion of the city's interests.

Since the majority of the Board of Control including the mayor were Liberals, it seemed clear that local Conservatives were needed to give visible leadership to the negative reaction against the government's proposals. The first person to come to mind was Hamilton's only provincial cabinet minister, Jack McNie. But arrayed against him in the cabinet was a formidable trio—Premier William Davis from Peel County, Secretary for Justice and Government George Kerr from Halton West (Burlington), and Services Minister James Snow, MPP for Halton East (Oakville). Thus, if the battle was to be decided only by those in the cabinet room, then the recently appointed junior minister from Hamilton was heavily outweighed.

Thus, it appeared to be a good tactic to bring Hamilton Conservative party workers into the visible leadership. At the same time, Hamilton Conservatives were only too willing to become active leaders. The Conservative members of the city council were quick to respond. Pat Ford, a well-known Conservative party activist and alderman, publicly warned provincial Conservatives that the party could be politically destroyed in the area as a result of the regional government proposals for Hamilton-Wentworth. The Conservative alderman warned that the Conservative seats of Hamilton West, Hamilton-Mountain and Wentworth North were in great danger. This alderman also pointed out that the adverse reaction to the Tories could carry over into federal elections as well. In a rare show of Conservative partisanship on the city council, all the Conservative councillors sent a letter to the provincial government urging a change in the government stance while pointing out the precarious position of the city and county Conservatives.

At the same time, the mayor decided to launch a citizens' group opposing the province's proposals. This group was to utilize well-known city Conservative party workers who were not on city council. This group was called VOTER, the first letters of the words, Volunteers Opposing a Toronto Enforced Region. The main positive purpose of this group was to encourage the province to include Burlington in the metropolitan region. The general chairman and co-ordinator of the campaign picked by the mayor was an important Hamilton Tory, Rodger Inglis, who supported Premier William Davis in the 1971 leadership contest and a past president of the Hamilton West Provincial Progressive Conservative Association. Named as honorary chairmen were two additional prominent Tories.

The major tactic of VOTER was to circulate a ballot-like petition against the government's proposals. Currently with the petition drive media advertisements were used to encourage people to mark the petition so as to protest the province's proposals. The cost of the advertising and the petition totalled over $9,000 and the expenditure was approved by the Board of Control. The day-to-day handling of the petition was run by another Hamilton West Conservative who had been active in past provincial campaigns. But support for the unofficial plebiscite was not limited to the Conservatives alone. The provincial New Democratic Party candidate in the Hamilton Centre riding, Michael Davison, canvassed door-to-door to collect signatures. In this activity he was joined by his campaign workers in his riding.

Still further support for the petition drive came from federal Labour Minister John Munro, Liberal from Hamilton East, and the Hamilton East Liberal riding association. Using the free mailing privilege accorded members of Parliament, Munro sent out in his riding 23,000 copies of a letter accusing the provincial Conservative government of ignoring public opinion in Hamilton and urging residents to express their views in the ballot-type plebiscite. In addition, the Hamilton East Liberal riding association (federal) paid for mailings to approximately five thousand households outside the riding of Hamilton East.

Complementing the activities of the city and county officials and other local politicians were the efforts of citizen groups. An example of this type of activity was a seven-page booklet entitled "Towards Regional Government" submitted by the Dundas Heritage Association in February 1973 to the provincial Minister of Treasury, Economics and Intergovernmental Affairs. This booklet argued that the natural region at the head of Lake Ontario comprises Halton and Wentworth counties including the city of Hamilton. Since it appeared that the provincial government was not prepared to introduce true regional government in the area, it was better that the municipal structure of the area be left unchanged while at the same time encouraging Hamilton, Halton and Wentworth to cooperate on planning for regional development and services.

After receiving many briefs and taking note of the various activities to mobilize public opinion, the province on June 13, 1973, submitted to the Legislature Bill 155, an Act To Establish the Regional Municipality of Hamilton-Wentworth. As expected, Burlington was excluded from this region but major concessions were given to both the county and city. In general, Wentworth received the major concessions. The municipality was to be two-tier, not the one-tier the city wanted if Burlington was to be excluded and, just as important, the county was not to lose major areas to Brant, Waterloo and Halton. Representation on regional council was not to be on the basis of population alone, since the city with 77 per cent of the population would have only 61 per cent of the regional seats. The expected amalgamation of some of the lower-tier municipalities was not as drastic as earlier proposed. For example, Dundas and Ancaster would still be separate as they wanted. Also, although the number of elected officials was reduced, the reduction was not as radical as expected. Both Dundas and Ancaster kept the same number although there were minor changes in some titles.

Why were these concessions made to the county officials? A primary reason was the government's fear of losing Wentworth North. A great many of the county officials were actively committed Conservatives who formed the backbone of Tory organizational strength in the riding. In addition, the depth of negative feeling against the previous regional government proposals by the rank and file voters in this area was far more intense than in Hamilton. Opposition to the basic concept of regional government, even after the province's concessions, was still far greater in the Wentworth North communities of Beverly, Dundas and Ancaster than in Hamilton.[1]

At the same time, some concessions were also made to the Hamilton elite. The Conservative government, recognizing the very strong opposition from the mayor and the Board of Control, reversed its previous stand and left the internal structure of Hamilton city government relatively unchanged. This probably reflected the government's fear that some of the displaced Liberals, who were popular with Hamilton voters, would run in the Tory seats of Hamilton West and Hamilton-Mountain in the next provincial election. The former constituency was especially vulnerable. Most of the city Conservatives who were active in fighting regional government were from Hamilton West. Their continued active campaign support seemed crucial since that riding's elections usually resulted in close Conservative victories over strong New Democrat and Liberal opponents. The provincial Conservatives did not want to lose this seat, especially since it was held by a cabinet minister who was a close personal friend of the Premier.

The last important regional government decision to be made by the province was the choice of regional chairman. The act instituting regional government for Hamilton-Wentworth provided initially for a provincial appointment. The province let it be known that the two-tier form was the major concession to the county officials. So the next major decision, that of the chairmanship appointment, would be a concession to the city. At the same time, the province was prepared to give an informal veto to the county officials. It was also generally known that the regional chairman would have to be a person acceptable to the Conservative activists in Hamilton. Initially the leading candidate for the chair-

1 This generalization is based on a comprehensive survey of the attitudes towards regional government and its various aspects among residents in the city of Hamilton and the county of Wentworth. See Manisha Bhargava, Maxine Carmichael, Ida Deutsch, Steve Gibbs, Don Kersey, John Neale, and Ian Newcombe, *Survey Dundas Report: Regional Government, An Attitudinal Survey of the Hamilton-Wentworth Region* (Dundas, Ontario), Summer, 1973, p. 71. The map of the communities of Hamilton-Wentworth was also taken from this report, p. 19.

manship was a former Hamilton controller, Jack Mc-
Donald, who probably was the most important city Tory
not currently holding public office. But the county officials
would be unhappy with such a choice. McDonald, like
Mayor Copps, was identified as an overly strong booster of
city interests and, in addition, it was felt that his personality was too abrasive. The next leading candidate was
Hamilton's deputy mayor, Anne Jones, a current controller.
She seemed to have all the necessary qualifications. Besides
being an important city official, she was also known to be
a diplomat who took a moderate stance in most issues in
which she became involved. Finally, she was quite acceptable to area Conservatives, especially those in Hamilton
West. Indeed, many city Conservatives had previously
hoped that she would run provincially for the Conservative
party. Thus, the provincial government chose her to be the
first regional chairman of Hamilton-Wentworth.

In the local debate over regional government, it was
clear that public opinion was being led, formed and sometimes distorted by the established local elites, whether
municipal or political party officials or both. In rural and
suburban Burlington and Wentworth County the latent
dispositions of the population were one-sided and strong
although they still needed mobilization by local elites. In
Hamilton, popular opinion was clear but not nearly so
one-sided as elsewhere. Because of the shape of elite
attitudes and public opinion in the various areas, the
government needed to make its major compromises with
Burlington and non-urban Wentworth. It was clear that the
vast majority in Hamilton-Wentworth wanted a plebiscite
on regional government.[2] But if the government allowed
that, a serious defeat was highly predictable although not
completely certain. Although over three-quarters of the
Hamilton-Wentworth population wanted the plebiscite,
including both those for and against regional government,
the negative group did not quite have a majority with the
balance of power held by those with no formed opinion,
about one-fifth of the voters.[3] On the whole, those who

2 Seventy-seven per cent wanted a plebiscite, 17 per cent were opposed and 6 per cent had no opinion. Ibid., p. 38.
3 Forty-seven per cent would have voted against regional government, 33 per cent for it and 20 per cent did not have a formed
   opinion. Ibid., p. 71.

opposed regional government were more politically involved compared to those who were favourable.[4] Since politically involved people by definition are more likely to vote versus uninvolved people, the plebiscite would most probably result in a defeat for any provincial plan.

The informal plebiscite carried out in Hamilton in 1973 was really more like a petition drive. The city voters in this informal plebiscite were shown to be 14 to 1 against regional government. But this was a distortion of public opinion in that 42 per cent of Hamiltonians were in favour of regional government, excluding the undecided.[5] Thus, in the city there was not overwhelming opposition. Although the opposition was widespread, it was not nearly as one-sided as the local elites and their informal plebiscite indicated. The reason for the variance between the expressed opinion of the plebiscite and actual public opinion lies with the bias of the elite organizers. Participation in the informal plebiscite was characterized as a vote against regional government. The consensus was among the city elite not the city voters because it was the interests of the elite which was most directly and immediately affected. Thus, in a conscious decision only one sector of public opinion was being mobilized while the somewhat smaller but substantial opposite sector was being ignored.

The process by which regional government came to Hamilton-Wentworth indicates the way in which a central government must modify its goal of efficiency in the face of widespread opposition from local elites. Not only must compromises be made to all the local elites in general but the pattern of adjustments must take into account the severe differences in opinions among the local elites themselves. The need for compromise becomes more intensely acute when the local party organizers of the governing party are especially upset.

APPENDIX

Patterns of Social Interaction by Burlington Residents with the City of Hamilton and the County of Wentworth.
1. Percentage of Burlington homes subscribing to *The Spec-*

4 Ibid., p. 72.   5 Ibid, p. 71.

tator (Hamilton's daily newspaper), 96 per cent.[a]

2. Percentage of leaders (n = more than 60) of the City of Hamilton, both public and private sectors, who are residents of Burlington, roughly 90 per cent.[b]

3. Percentage of Real Estate firms in Burlington who are members of the Hamilton Real Estate Board, about 90 per cent.[c]

4. Percentage of telephone calls between Burlington and other communities in the surrounding area that were between Burlington and Hamilton, 81 per cent.[d]

5. Percentage of active members of the Junior League of Hamilton who resided in Burlington, 59 per cent.[c]

6. Percentage of Burlington lawyers who belonged to the Hamilton Law Association, the majority, 20 lawyers.[c]

7. Percentage of Burlington residents who worked in Hamilton, 48 per cent.[e]

8. Percentage of the directors of the Greater Hamilton YMCA who lived in Burlington, 40 per cent.[c]

9. Percentage of all vehicle trips originating or with final destination in Burlington that were to or from Hamilton, 39 per cent.[f]

10. Percentage of the membership in the Hamilton Rotary, Kinsmen and Kiwanis Clubs who resided in Burlington, about 33 per cent.[c]

11. Percentage of Burlington employees who resided in either the City of Hamilton or County of Wentworth, 32 per cent.[g]

12. Number of Burlington residents who used the services of Hamilton social agencies in 1968, 11,000 (incomplete).[c]

13. Number of Burlington doctors belonging to the Hamilton Medical Association, 41.[c]

NOTES

a Dominion Bureau of Statistics domicile survey, 1966.

b *Commercial Development in Hamilton*, A Report to the Hamilton Economic Development Commission, Arthur B. Little, Inc., October 1968.

c Hamilton-Burlington-Wentworth Local Government Review, *Report and Recommendations* (November 1969), pages 36–37.

d Hamilton-Burlington-Wentworth Local Government Review, *Data Book* (June 1968), Table C-6.

e Burlington Traffic Planning Study, 1964.

f Metropolitan Toronto and Region Transportation Study, 1964.

g Burlington Chamber of Commerce, 1967.

SELECTED BIBLIOGRAPHY

Peel-Halton Local Government Review, *Report of the Commissioner*, September 1966.

Ontario Committee on Taxation, *Report* (Toronto: Queen's Printer, 1967).

For a comprehensive set of data and maps on the Burlington, Grimsby, Hamilton and Wentworth area see *Hamilton Burlington Wentworth Local Government Review: Data Book of Basic Information*, June 1968.

The commission recommendations are contained in Donald R. Steele, E. A. Jarrett, and Brian W. B. Morison, *Report and Recommendations: Hamilton Burlington Wentworth Local Government Review*, November 1969.

An excellent study on the basis of the anti-Hamilton movement in Burlington is contained in Barbara Epstein, "Community Resistance to Regional Government: An Exploration Study of Status Politics," a research report submitted to the Department of Political Science, McMaster University, Hamilton, Ontario, no date.

The provincial government's initial proposals, sometimes called "the blue book," for regional governments in Hamilton-Wentworth, Halton and Peel are found in *Proposal for Local Government Reform in the Area West of Metropolitan Toronto*.

An example of the type of brief put forward in response to the provincial government's initial proposals is the Dundas Heritage Association's seven-page booklet, "Towards Regional Government," February 1973.

The final legislation instituting regional government for Hamilton-Wentworth is Bill 155, An Act to Establish the Regional Municipality of Hamilton-Wentworth, submitted for first reading on June 13, 1973.

For a comprehensive survey of the attitudes towards regional government and its various aspects among residents in the city of Hamilton and the county of Wentworth, see Manisha Bhargava, Maxine Carmichael, Ida Deutsch, Steve Gibbs, Don Kersey, John Neale, and Ian Newcombe, *Survey Dundas Report: Regional Government, An Attitudinal Survey of the Hamilton-Wentworth Region* (Dundas, Ontario), Summer, 1973.

5
DAVID SURPLIS

The
Progressive Conservative
Leadership Convention
of 1971

THE APPARENTLY unshakeable hold that the Progressive Conservative party has had on the government of Ontario since 1943 is often the subject of discussion and debate. While explanations of the regime's longevity may include considerations of the opposition parties' inability to mount effective campaigns, the Conservative party's ability to create and to maximize its own opportunities must not be overlooked. The leadership convention of 1971 is a case in point.

When John P. Robarts indicated his intention to retire from the office of premier in December of 1970, he provided his party with an excellent chance to continue its hold on the reins of power. His resignation from office and from the party leadership would be expertly executed to allow the Conservatives to choose a new premier; the timing of each step was nearly perfect. In the first place, all the attention which is naturally focused on a leadership convention in any party would be heightened in the case of the Conservatives because they would be choosing not only a new leader but a new premier. This would give the party an advantage in exposure and publicity which its opponents could not buy. Secondly, by selecting a new leader so close to the date of an expected general election, Robarts' successor would have just enough time to demonstrate some capacity to govern before dissolving the House. It seems, therefore, that the vehicle of leadership selection—the largest, most widely covered, most expensive convention in Ontario's political history—was of immeasurable assistance in lengthening the Conservative party's tenure in office.

Once Robarts' intentions were formalized, it was a relatively simple task for the party to arrange for a convention to choose his successor. Easy, that is, in the sense that the procedures for such an event are fully covered by the party's constitution and by the experience of many party organizers who had staged two similar conventions in the previous twenty-three years. The logistics of a leadership convention are complicated but the procedures are straightforward. By virtue of the constitution, direction of such a convention is assumed by the executive council of the extra-parliamentary party, the Ontario Progressive Conservative Association. In this task the council is assisted by the staff of party headquarters, by the party's organizers and by its nominees.

The council decided to hold the leadership convention in Toronto on February 10, 11, and 12, 1971. Special events were to be held at the Royal York Hotel with plenary sessions and voting to take place at Maple Leaf Gardens. Once these decisions were arrived at, notice was sent to each of the 117 riding associations throughout the province to select delegates. The constitution provides for ten voting delegates and ten alternate delegates who must be elected at a special meeting called for that purpose. "Wherever possible," the constitution reads, "the delegates should be composed of four men, four women and two members of a recognized Young Progressive Conservative Association for the Riding, one of whom should be a woman or if there is no recognized Young Progressive Conservative Association in the Riding, two persons under the age of 30 years."

In addition to the delegates from the ridings, the party makes provision for voting privileges for delegates "ex-officio" (MP's, MPP's, senators, party executives), delegates from recognized district associations, and the delegates of student and businessmen's clubs. There is also a special category of delegates "at large" nominated by the party president (not numbering more than half the ridings in the province) who are given voting rights by virtue of their contributions to the party as a whole. The total number of delegates eligible to attend the convention in 1971 was thus 1,748 comprising 1,170 from the ridings, 255 ex officio, 265 from the districts, and 58 at large.

The selection of delegates went relatively smoothly, except for a charge by the provincial YPC executive (led by Sean O'Sullivan, now a member of Parliament) that certain ridings had not included the two young persons required by the constitution, and by the charge by a few disgruntled Conservatives that some riding delegates had been chosen by executive fiat rather than at open meetings. The YPC charge was rectified by prompt executive action and the others were largely ignored because in a cadre party such as the Conservative they are not of such moment as they are to mass parties. (Joseph Wearing discusses the subject of mass parties in more detail in chapter 18.) By and large, the delegates chosen were happy in the anticipation of an exciting time in Toronto.

Even easier than the selection of delegates, of course, was the finding of candidates who aspired to succeed Robarts. Five members of the provincial cabinet had officially entered the race by January: William Davis (Education), Allan Lawrence (Mines and Northern Affairs), A. B. R. Lawrence (Financial and Commercial Affairs), Darcy McKeough (Municipal Affairs), and Robert Welch (Provincial Secretary). Each had been chosen by Robarts for cabinet responsibilities and each came from a different area of the province. It was generally conceded that Davis was in the advantaged position going into the contest because he had been a highly visible Minister of Education. The Education portfolio gives a minister a great deal of publicity (not all of it good) and Davis had been very active in his duties. (Robarts himself, it must be remembered, went from Education Minister to Premier in 1961.) But each of the other candidates was serious in his belief that the elevation of Davis to the leadership was not a foregone conclusion and began building a campaign organization.

Davis at first appeared to have the easiest time of organizing because a majority of both the cabinet and caucus supported his candidacy; he had ample talent from which to draw. But Allan Lawrence soon had to be acknowledged as a serious contender because he was able to attract into the management of his campaign the nucleus of the organization which had worked successfully to establish Robert Stanfield as national leader of the party in 1967. Despite the seeming advantages of the two leading figures, the others were able to mount serious campaigns largely staffed by organizers from their home ridings and by the personal assistants in their offices. They were aided as well by friends they had made throughout the province both from their official and party connections.

Each candidate rented office space in Toronto which became the headquarters, or nerve centres, of the campaigns. It was here that the lists of delegates were analysed, speeches were written, brochures planned—in general, where the overall plans of attack were formulated. The main concern of the candidates was contact with delegates. To aid in this task, the party played its part by staging six large meetings at various locations throughout the province where all the candidates could be seen and heard at once

(Seven were scheduled but one had to be cancelled because of a violent snowstorm.) As well, convention organizers made lists of delegates and alternates available to each candidate as they were received from the ridings. But apart from these services, it was largely up to the candidate to curry favour with potential supporters. And in this age, the process is extremely sophisticated, demanding and expensive.

Each of the leadership campaigns had two main thrusts: activity prior to the convention and activity in Toronto. The first of these is hard to evaluate in terms of effectiveness, especially since the excitement and intensity of activity at the convention itself can obliterate the memory of earlier, quieter, meetings. But no candidate dared overlook it. Each candidate did his best to get in touch with each delegate before the others, usually by letter or by telephone. In this way the candidate's name and one or six of his attributes could be impressed on the voter. But hearing a man make a brief speech or chatting privately for a few moments is surely no measure of a man's ability. Unless a firm commitment to active support can be wrung from a delegate, the best one can hope for is that he at least has not alienated anyone. But all the candidates believed in "getting around" —so much so that they all either rented or borrowed private airplanes to aid in the task. Tours were arranged by headquarters staffs, set up by "advance men" and dutifully, if often tardily, followed by the candidates. Sometimes adjacent ridings would get together to allow the contenders to make their appeals more conveniently. None of these meetings was particularly lavish, with the speech of the candidate usually being supplemented by the offer of a drink or some light sandwiches and coffee.

In a province with 117 ridings, the schedules of preconvention activity were very demanding on the candidates. Darcy McKeough estimated, for instance, that he had travelled over four thousand miles a week for the five weeks prior to the convention. And besides the grind of visiting sometimes four or five communities in one day, it must be remembered that each of the candidates was a cabinet member responsible for the affairs of his ministry. The campaigns were often hindered as well by inclement weather. In this regard, Robert Welch often made friends by promising that if he were elected leader, he would not resign in any season other than summer. The rigours of campaigning did not seriously affect any of the candidates, however, and all of them seemed genuinely to enjoy it. A leadership campaign, after all, affords to candidates, their spouses and close staff members an opportunity to meet thousands of people and to see far-flung parts of the province which is a felicity not available to many others.

The hectic weeks preceding a leadership convention may have many of the appearances of a general election campaign but there are some specific differences. Generally, candidates do not have to convert voters to a particular philosophy; they have only to convince people that their own abilities to carry out a program of action are greater than those of their opponents. From a purely pragmatic point of view, it is not to be expected of leadership candidates that they will attack each other, for the main beneficiaries of such action would only be the opposition parties. The situation is even more acute when it is cabinet ministers who oppose each other; each of them, through the vehicle of collective cabinet responsibility, is equally responsible for the legislation of the others. They must keep their criticism to a minimum and say, in effect, "We're all wonderful but I'm more wonderful than they."

Within these limits then, it should not have been expected by the general electorate that many far-reaching discussions or debates on government policy would take place. Of course each contender had views on how things could be done better but he had to be mindful at the same time of not giving his leader, Robarts, a rebuke. These considerations had the effect of turning the leadership campaign very much into a popularity contest. All the candidates had strong support from their local areas which was supplemented by that of friends from other parts of the province. The true support of each candidate can only be estimated because none of them knew exactly who supported them at voting time, but it can be assumed that the candidates picked up support from clients of their ministries as well as from friends that they made at previous party gatherings. For instance, quite a few northern delegates supported Allan Lawrence and several municipal councillors supported Darcy McKeough. So once the basic patterns of support were roughly gauged, the real business of conventioneering began. "Who will you support after your favourite candidate is knocked out?" became the operative question. It was this jockeying for support that assumed the greatest importance as the campaign wore on.

These observations are not intended to portray the candidates as a bland group. Each had strong opinions on where the province should be headed and each had demonstrated leadership abilities in the cabinet. In particular, Allan Lawrence and Bert Lawrence gave very definite outlines of the changes they would like to see. But most Conservatives seemed to sense that what was really important was the continuation of the image of "good government" which would be instrumental in the upcoming general election. Most elections are fought in terms of generalities in any event and it was this which appeared to deal a severe blow to the campaign of Allan Lawrence. Through the years Lawrence had developed a reputation for candour and criticism of his own party; he was known as a disturber of the status quo. If Davis and the others portrayed an image of "more of the same," it was Lawrence who offered the possibility of a clear break with the traditions of Drew, Frost and Robarts. When the convention came, it was to be found that the Conservative delegates were not quite willing to gamble on this "newness." The wisdom of this action cannot be denied since the new leader was able to increase the party's standings in the Legislature, but it is interesting to speculate what changes Allan Lawrence might have brought to politics in Ontario.

The second phase of the leadership campaign, the activity in Toronto, was particularly important and interesting. Once the delegates had been contacted personally and had had their preferences roughly catalogued, it was up to the candidates' organizations to convince further by extravaganza. What a treat it was to be a registered delegate in 1971!

Most delegates chose to stay either at the Royal York in downtown Toronto or at the Westbury Hotel which is closer to Maple Leaf Gardens. Wherever they were lodged, however, it was certain that they would not be alone for long. The various campaign organizations tried to ensure that every whim of the delegates was looked after. Their planes were met, transportation was provided, hunger and thirst were unknown, and there was plenty of reading material for the studious. Except for a few brief hours through the night there was something for every delegate to do, and many willing lobbyists to help him do it. Not that activity stopped through the night. Many delegates were amazed to find special newspapers at their hotel-room doors in the mornings which summarized the previous day's activity, suggested a program for the present day and, of course, extolled the virtues of the candidate whose team had produced the paper.

Each candidate had hospitality suites in the larger hotels which served food and liquor (always known to conventioneers as "beverages") and which, nominally at any rate, gave the delegate a chance to talk to the candidate "quietly." Robert Welch's group even provided a "beauty spot" for female delegates where they could set their hair, freshen their makeup, or just relax. The candidates held parties, receptions, lunches and dances throughout the time in Toronto which, taken together, produced a scene of frenzied activity for observers and a bonanza for free-loaders. All the while campaign workers were meeting to assess protestations of support and to plan further action for the true test: voting.

The convention organizers arranged for plenary sessions at which the candidates would speak on two areas of policy concern rather than having the delegates consider policy resolutions. But these speeches did not particularly enhance any one candidate's image; they were of much more value in that they provided information to the general public who were being kept aware of the convention events by the media. It is fair to state that the concern of the delegates was not policy anyway; it was on the central question of who would win the voting. Bill Davis had entered the convention as the front-runner but as the convention progressed, Allan Lawrence made considerable gains with the aid of his well-coordinated team. The possibilities of stopping Davis or Lawrence, or the chances of one of the other candidates becoming a compromise selection were increasingly the topic of conversation.

The candidates were officially nominated on the afternoon of Thursday, February 11, at Maple Leaf Gardens and they gave their final speeches that evening to the accompaniment of "spontaneous" demonstrations so familiar now in Canadian politics. The demonstrations were in fact carefully orchestrated well in advance because there was a strict time limit on them (eight minutes); if a demonstrating group went on too long, it would cut into the fifteen minutes allowed their candidate for his speech. Officially nominated along with the five cabinet ministers was a student from the University of Ottawa, Robert Pharand. (To this point Pharand has not been considered because, although his candidacy was serious insofar as he had a point to make—more opportunities for French-speaking students in Ontario—he had no real backing and could not possibly have been considered a threat to any other candidate.) The candidates' speeches were uniformly well delivered but no one speech in particular appeared to win over more supporters. The candidate who did gain from the speeches was Darcy McKeough who made a hard-hitting attack on socialism. His remarks may not have won him many extra votes at the convention but McKeough gained notice from many outside the convention. He became someone to watch in the future—which just might have been his intention all along. When the speeches were over, the candidates and their advisers retired to prepare themselves for the crucial voting on the Friday.

The convention organizers believed that they had done everything possible to ensure a well-publicized, smooth-running selection of a new premier for Ontario. They had rented fifteen voting machines from a corporation in the United States which they felt would maximize efficiency and speed at voting time. They had arranged for tight security for the Gardens and delegates had ample briefing on how the election was to be held. Press, radio and television reporters were assigned choice locations from which to send messages to the general public not able to be present in the arena (seats had been allocated to the public free of charge but there simply wasn't room for more than four to five thousand). The first ballot was to begin at 3 p.m. with subsequent ballots planned for one and a half hour intervals, with the low man dropping out each time until one man had an overall majority. Everything, the party officials believed, had been arranged so that the new leader could be presented to Ontario on prime-time television. But their best laid schemes went agley.

Immediately after the completion of the first vote, scrutineers for the various candidates checked the tallies of the machines against their own counting of the people who had voted and found discrepancies. Some machines had recorded a total vote higher than the number of people entitled to vote, some lower. Party president Alan Eagleson called an immediate conference of the candidates, convention officials, and the man who had rented them the voting machines. The result of the conference was that it was decided to disregard the results of the first vote and to proceed with paper ballots and ballot boxes. Howls of dismay greeted Eagleson's announcement and the provincial NDP sent a telegram to Eagleson offering to show the party how to hold a vote.

More than four hours from the time the first machine voting had started, delegates voted once again on hastily-printed paper ballots. The results of the vote were announced as:

William Davis	548
Allan Lawrence	431
Darcy McKeough	273
Robert Welch	270
Bert Lawrence	128
Robert Pharand	7
	1,657

Pharand was dropped for the next ballot and Bert Lawrence withdrew. Each of the four remaining candidates and their supporters raced over to the Lawrence delegation to try to get them to make some public show of transfer of allegiance. But Lawrence stated flatly that he could not and would not direct his supporters and refrained from accepting anyone's insignia or badges.

The second ballot results were as follows: Davis 595, Lawrence 498, McKeough 288, Welch 271. It was apparent that Allan Lawrence was the major recipient of the votes cast by Bert Lawrence's followers. When Welch was dropped for the third ballot, he too refused to show support for anyone else. But the floor managers for the remaining three candidates were undaunted; they raced about proferring hats, buttons, stickers and signs to those who had been wearing Welch colours. In this process the Davis team had an edge because their communications system was a little faster than that of the other organizations. This enabled Davis' managers to get the word out to their operatives in the audience by walkie-talkie, telephone and signal.

Following the lobbying after the second ballot, the third was taken in an air of great anticipation. If Lawrence were to gain the same percentage of Welch's votes as he appeared to have gained Bert Lawrence's, it would be an extremely tight contest. The results of the third ballot were: Davis 669 (a gain of 74), Lawrence 606 (a gain of 108), and Mc-Keough 346 (a gain of 58). The Lawrence team and supporters were tremendously enthusiastic about the result; they had gained the most and it appeared that they would have a very good chance of upsetting Davis on the fourth and final ballot. Lawrence tried to get over to see McKeough to gain his support but he was rebuffed. Instead, at precisely 12:45 a.m., McKeough went over to Davis' box and embraced him in the grand style of kingmakers. The Davis supporters were exultant but the Lawrence team were only momentarily dejected. Lobbying and chanting continued right through the next ballot. In fact, just before the final result was announced, a great cheer went up from the Lawrence delegation. Their operatives had reported a win for their man but they were in error. The official final count was Davis 812, Lawrence 768. A mere forty-four votes separated the final contenders for Robarts' mantle.

All the contestants were called to the centre stage by party president Eagleson, Lawrence made the customary motion that the results be declared unanimous, Davis made his acceptance speech, and the delegates went out into the winter morning air to party or to sleep. The Gardens cleanup crew then went about clearing the twenty-five hundred pounds of garbage, dismantling TV towers and so on in readiness for the morrow's hockey action.

So despite the fact that he had not been able to do so on prime-time television, Bill Davis became leader of the Progressive Conservative party. Although it had been his goal for a long time (one Conservative noted that "being premier of Ontario has been on Bill Davis' schedule ever since he was a youngster") and although he had been campaigning unofficially for the post for over two years, his victory was not won easily. And this was good for the party. Because Allan Lawrence's campaign was so well organized and because the other candidates kept fighting to the very end, an extremely interesting political spectacle was presented to the voters of Ontario. Davis and at least four cabinet ministers had been shown off to the public at, or near, their best. Those Conservatives who attended the convention went home with a heightened sense of accomplishment and camaraderie. It would be a relatively simple job for Bill Davis to call them all back together within a year to fight an election. And he did. He gave each of his opponents a prominent cabinet position in the new government and he gave the organizers of Allan Lawrence's campaign influential positions within the party hierarchy. Premier Davis produced some interesting legislative programs, called an election for October and, with an election organization combining the best talents from the leadership convention, went on to score an easy triumph over the Liberals and NDP.

Although the Davis election effort in the fall of 1971 was superbly executed, the leadership convention which preceded it contributed greatly to his success. The leadership campaign was in all senses well-planned. The convention was called at a very convenient time; the candidates were able to muster extremely capable assistants and supporters; the participants were able to generate a tremendous amount of enthusiasm because the race was so close; and the public could see and hear most of the activity because, after all, the Conservatives were not only choosing a leader for themselves but a premier for the province. For the Conservative party, the convention was a huge success.

All the activity before and during the convention was not without cost, of course, and this is where the opposition parties raised the loudest wails. It was estimated that the party itself spent over $150,000 on the convention and that each of the major candidates spent between $40,000 and $100,000 on his campaign. The party recovered a large part of its outlay from registration fees but each candidate had to rely on fund-raisers of his own. Each had an agent who supervised the collection of money and these men were often able to get support in the form of loans of equipment as well as in cash. The candidates relied on personal solicitation for their fund-raising and a few small dinners were thrown for potential supporters with the intention of getting financial donations as well as ballot strength. None of the contestants complained about a lack of funds and it is certain that the delegates did not complain about the manner in which the money was spent. It may be regretted by some that free bars, parties, dinners and the like can generate political enthusiasm but it is nonetheless a reality.

Electoral advantage always seems to lie initially with the governing party. In a sense, the Conservative leadership convention of 1971 and the calling of the election were almost copied from the federal Liberals' agenda in 1968: Trudeau was elected leader in an exciting convention and shortly thereafter went to the people. The fact of the matter is that the Conservative party in Ontario took advantage of its opportunities to maximize the exposure of its leaders and platforms. It is precisely this ability which has kept the party in the forefront of Ontario politics for over a generation.

But lest we get the impression that the planning by the party was totally successful, it should be noted that a hockey executive walked into Maple Leaf Gardens on voting day, saw all the activity, and demanded, "What the hell is going on here anyway?"

6
JONATHAN MANTHORPE

One of Our Agencies Is Missing: The Crisis of Change at the Workmen's Compensation Board

WHEN the act establishing the Ontario Workmen's Compensation Board was passed by the provincial Legislature in 1915 it was one of the most advanced, humanitarian pieces of legislation relating to employment in any industrialized society. Indeed, it was so advanced that it became a model to be copied by much of the rest of the world for the next fifty years. Like all good ideas it was simple. In setting up the Compensation Board the Ontario government was in fact establishing an insurance operation which compensated workmen or their dependants for injuries or death resulting from the negligence of employers. To pay the compensation, the board made annual levies of all Ontario employers in amounts based on the number of people employed. The board's officials judged claims for compensation and built into the system was an appeal structure which could be used by both workers and employers against decisions held to be unfair. To avoid criticism that decisions were politically motivated, and to give the board some stature as a quasi-judicial body, it was largely independent of the Ontario government. It didn't rely on government funds for any of its operations, subsisting on the levies it collected from industry and the interest gained from the investment of that money. The board made annual reports of its dealings to the Legislature through the Minister of Labour; but although the three government-appointed members of the board which governed the organization met now and then with the minister, successive men in that post have held it to be unnecessary and wrong to meddle in the board's affairs.

This system was immeasurably superior to that which had existed before. Previously there had only been the principle of common law which held that a master or employer was responsible for injury to or death of employees resulting from a negligent act by the employer. Thus injured workmen had to sue their employers and prove in a court of law that their injuries were the result of negligence. It was a long, expensive and uncertain process which left the workman without money at a time when he could not earn anything for himself and his family. The Workmen's Compensation Board (WCB) could react swiftly to a claim (often beginning compensation payments within a few days of being consulted), helping rehabilitate those

permanently injured, and setting pensions for those who
could not work again.

It worked well for fifty years, but in the late 1960s the
first indications began to appear that the structure of the
WCB had not adapted to the tremendous industrialization
of the province in the 1950s and early 1960s. By 1973 the
board had become a mammoth operation. It had an annual
income from levies of nearly $170 million which was raised
from about 140,000 employers. It processed about 400,000
claims each year and itself employed 1,400 people. The WCB
had become a cumbersome bureaucracy, highly structured
to maintain efficiency under the pressure of the great work-
load it had to carry, and in doing so it had become in-
sensitive to the feelings and needs of the injured people it
was there to serve.

In the late 1960s the WCB became the target of demonstrations and campaigns by labour unions and other groups
representing injured workmen. All the complaints were
similar. Compensation payments, particularly for those
permanently disabled, were low, claimants were treated
abominably by WCB officials, and the appeal system brought
only a tangle of red tape and little justice. The WCB reacted
violently to the criticism, an uncharacteristic response
from a government agency. A dramatic high point of the
confrontation came at the opening of the Legislature in
1970. A man somehow evaded the police guards on the door
of the Legislative chamber and began shouting his complaints against the WCB from the floor of the House. When
tackled by policemen he clung, still shouting, to the chair
of the wife of former Premier John Robarts, who was
among the guests invited to watch the opening ceremony.
But there was no significant reaction from the government.
It seemed as reluctant as ever to mix in the affairs of one
of its agencies, even though the strength and persistence of
the complaints and demonstrations gave a clear indication
that something was wrong.

The government's sensitivity in the area of its relationships with its agencies goes back many years. It is partly a
philosophical stance that holds that these agencies—there
are about three hundred in all—can operate more sensi-
tively, efficiently and swiftly if they have a high degree of
independence. The attitude has also grown as a result of

the government's experiences with the Ontario Hydro Electric Power Commission. Ontario Hydro has been since its inception the great source of government discomfort and scandal bar none. After the last wave of allegations in the 1930s, Hydro was placed firmly outside the mainstream of government and it stayed there until recently when concern about its isolation caused it to be placed under stricter control.

The government may have been unwilling to step into the internal problems of the WCB—and it may even have been unaware that serious problems existed, but the back-bench members of the Legislature certainly knew there were problems. In the last few years by far the largest single source of the problems that people bring to the doors of their members of the Legislature has concerned the WCB. This was to be of prime tactical importance later because it meant the WCB had few political friends at the Conservative court and retribution when it came was only marginally affected by the dictates of Tory party loyalty. For even the most loyal Conservative backbencher, the stinging rebuffs they had received from board officials, the hopeless quagmire of bureaucracy they encountered when seeking information or assistance, and the dissatisfaction among their constituents were of greater influence on their attitudes than the fear of the passing embarrassment the government might feel from a full disclosure of what had been going on at the WCB.

The beginning of a massive reassessment of the board, which lasted nearly two years, began in March of 1972 when the Toronto *Globe and Mail* published a series of articles about the WCB and its inner workings. The stories contained a series of sensational charges, including statements that an additional levy on a company with a poor safety record was dropped after an anti-WCB lobby in which it was represented was scuttled. Another charge was that a vice-chairman of the WCB, who was critical of some of the organizational changes that had been instituted, had been pressured into retiring early and "paid off" with about $60,000. Subsequent charges were made by the vice-chairman and others before a committee of members of the Legislature which investigated the allegations. Some of the charges were not proven, but the committee did find that the making of the

allegations was symptomatic of the situation within the
WCB. Morale, the committee said, was at a very low level,
the number of employees quitting the organization over the
previous few years had been incredibly high, the organization was badly structured and authoritarian in nature. The
committee encountered practices of which it heartily dis-
approved, such as the widespread tapping of telephone
calls.

The method by which the Ontario Legislature conducted
its investigation of the charges against the board became
central to the whole theme of reassessment of the WCB
because it was such a difficult and painful process. Had the
WCB been more closely tied to the Ministry of Labour or
had it been the practice of successive Ministers of Labour
to maintain regular and meaningful lines of communication with the board, the whole affair might never have
happened. Because no one in government appeared either
to know or to be sufficiently concerned about conditions at
the board, those conditions achieved crisis proportions
before being tackled.

Initially, the opposition Liberal and New Democratic
parties pressed the government to establish a royal commission to look into the charges that had been levelled at
the WCB. The Conservatives, on the other hand, leaned towards the matter being dealt with the standing committee
on resources development, a committee of the Legislature
made up of MPP's. The opposition parties wanted a royal
commission because these are judicial inquiries chaired by
a judge, and they felt this would give the Conservatives
less chance to bring political pressure to bear to cover up
what had happened than if the inquiry were handled by
the committee. But the government decided the committee
should conduct the inquiry. The committee was made up
of eighteen MPP's with the parties being represented in
roughly the same proportions as they were in the Legislature. Thus the Conservatives had twelve members on the
committee, the Liberals three and the NDP three. The
Liberals and NDP therefore felt that any moves they made
to extend the inquiry or to push it into areas that might
embarrass the government would be quickly squashed by
the Conservative majority.

But the opposition had not counted on two factors.
Firstly, the Conservative backbenchers' experiences with

the WCB were as bad as their own. The government members were used to receiving special treatment from departments and ministries when they called for information or assistance. The WCB had treated them much like anyone else and this rankled with the Conservatives. Secondly, a few weeks before, the government had begun to implement plans for a complete reorganization of all its operations in the name of efficiency. There was considerable concern among MPP's of all parties that in making the policy-formulating functions of the government highly efficient, the role of the individual member of the Legislature would be downgraded. The Conservative backbenchers wanted to demonstrate that they had a role to play in the government process and the committee investigation was a handy device with which to do it.

The Conservatives showed the way they intended to go from the first organizational meeting of the committee. They allowed a very loose framework for the governing of the inquiry to be established. It turned out to be too loose and the first two days of hearing evidence were chaotic. Witnesses made the most outrageous statements with impunity and the hearings became a shouting match that gave the committee members no hope of making any judgments on the truth or otherwise of what they heard. After a few days' recess Premier William Davis stepped in and introduced a motion into the Legislature to regulate the committee hearings. The motion said the committee would be provided with a counsel who would question the witnesses under oath and a transcript would be kept of the proceedings. The granting of legal counsel to the committee was an important precedent. Members of the opposition parties had been pressing for years for expert assistance to be provided to the committees. On one or two occasions Mr. Davis had refused these demands, but now, almost in self-defence, he had been pushed into doing so.

The committee sat for twenty-seven days, mostly from 10.00 A.M. to 8.00 P.M. The transcript of evidence covered 2,050 foolscap pages and in addition there were over five hundred pages of exhibits tabled. Within the bounds of what they were investigating—whether or not anyone in government or at the board had acted improperly—the members conducted an exceptionally thorough inquiry.

In the end, the committee concluded that the problem at the board was partly a result of the highly structured organization and partly a result of the divisive atmosphere and bad morale. The committee didn't feel competent to suggest how the organization might be improved and it laid the responsibility for the bad atmosphere largely at the door of one man, the board chairman, Bruce Legge, who had held that post since 1965 and who had implemented a number of efficiency-oriented procedural changes. The wording of the committee's comments on Mr. Legge was hard and uncompromising. It referred to repeated evidence that he was "arrogant, impatient, and condescending with lesser mortals," and tempered that statement by saying only, "In his favour it must be said that he was described as being compassionate and understanding" when dealing with appeals by injured workmen whose claims for compensation had been turned down or who felt they were not being given enough money.

Later in its report the committee attempted to make a general description of the conditions at the wcb as it saw them. It said:

> Although not amounting to fear, hatred or mistrust, there was an underlying uneasiness amongst personnel at the Board. The individual origins and resultant apportionment of fault thereof are shrouded in the mists of time, but the atmosphere was related in some way to the introduction of change, the insertion of and the manner of selection of personnel, the exodus of some senior officers, a lack of feeling of job security and generally the structure and tone of the administration.

That then was the problem, but what to do about it? The committee recommended only that a team of management consultants be hired to thoroughly investigate the board's operations and to suggest a new organizational structure. The Ministry of Labour would have liked some stronger recommendations so that it could have cleaned the wcb house rapidly, but it was not prepared itself to take the steps the committee had shied away from suggesting. So in January 1973, Fern Guindon, the Labour Minister, appointed a three-man task force to investigate the board's operations. The men on the task force were management consultant A. R. Aird, who was chairman of the task force; Deputy Labour Minister Robert Johnston; and former federal Labour Minister Michael Starr.

Their report, completed in August 1973, painted a picture of an organization that had completely lost track of its purpose, that had become an authoritarian bureaucracy which neither dealt with the problems of those it was there to help, nor gave its employees any satisfaction in their jobs.

While the legislative committee had imparted the perception that somehow beyond the clouds of conflicting and unresolved evidence Bruce Legge, the board's chairman, was personally a large part of the WCB's problem, the task force, with the aid of more time than the committee and a more intimate look at the operation, took a more subtle view of what had gone wrong.

Until recently the WCB operated in a stable social environment. The need for active policy planning was limited to recommendations for benefit increases to counter the effect of inflation.

Today, with the gradual encroachment of external influences caused by legislation covering health care, income maintenance, job placement and training services, and as a result of greater interest by the general population in the nature and administration of social programs, the WCB inevitably becomes a high profile organization.

These subtle but profound social policy shifts, taken together with general social trends, mean change for the WCB. The organization for the fifties and sixties is operationally inadequate, indeed obsolete, in the seventies.

The task force summed up its feelings by saying: "Currently the WCB is in the unenviable position of embodying most, if not all, the characteristics for which government is often criticized—the faceless bureaucracy, lack of service orientation to the public it serves, lack of vigour in promoting change, and time-serving staff."

The WCB was organized in what the task force called a "vertical hierarchy," with most of the work relationships being between superior and junior and very little lateral coordination. At the top of the structure was the chairman of the board. With him were his two fellow board members, who served with him in judging appeals and had some slight administrative functions, but who were com-

pletely overshadowed by his authority. The lines of authority ran from the chairman to the executive manager of
the WCB as well as to the directors of the eight separate
departments which made up the board's organization.
Four of these departments—adjudication, safety, rehabilitation and medical services—dealt with services to the
public, while the other four—finance, employee relations,
legal, and the office of the assistant to the executive manager—dealt with internal administration.

Most injured workmen, however, dealt only with one
branch, the adjudication section, and generally only with
one department of that section, the claims department. It
was to the claims department that an injured workman
went and it was here that his entitlement was determined
and the money paid. Should the workman be unhappy with
the amount of compensation offered, or should he be
turned down entirely, a three-level appeal structure was
open to him. The first level was the review committee of
officials. This group simply reviewed the evidence in the
current file on the claimant and then made a decision. The
review committee conducted no hearings.

If he was still dissatisfied, the workman could then appeal to the appeal tribunal which was made up of officials
more senior than those on the review committee. The
tribunal conducted hearings and the appellant could appear with a representative. Generally these representatives
have been union officials, members of the Legislature from
the claimants' home ridings, and sometimes lawyers. The
final level of appeal was to the three-man board itself,
which also conducted hearings in a semi-judicial atmosphere.

The report found that for both the employees of the
board and the injured workman the system was unsatis-
factory and often unpleasant. For the injured person, first
contact with the WCB was often by letter, but the board's
replies tended to be abrupt, couched in officialese and often
incomplete or unclear. Should a visit to the WCB head office
be necessary, the claimant was subjected to an unpleasant
and sometimes threatening experience, the task force
found. Uniformed security guards were placed throughout
the building and some at least of them regarded the injured
workmen as shirkers intent on dunning the WCB for as
much as possible. It could only be assumed that this outlook was learned from more senior WCB employees, the

task force commented. Waiting areas were inadequate, particularly as the average waiting time for someone visiting head office was four hours, a fact the task force felt to be intolerable. The whole business of visiting the head office should be as pleasant and easy as possible, the task force said. The uniformed guards should be replaced by properly trained receptionists, claims officers should wear name tags so the claimant knows with whom he is dealing on a more personal basis than previously, and there should be concessions to human comfort, such as providing free coffee for visitors.

Having gone through the initial harrowing experience of entering the building, the task force found that the speed with which the workman's claim was dealt with could well depend on whom he knew. Claimants who were being represented by "important" people had their files tagged with a distinctive marker and their claims were dealt with by a special group of senior officials. This discriminatory practice was part of the board's whole defence mechanism which had made it so resistant to outside pressure for change. Should a claimant be unsure, or unable to speak English, he would also have a slow and difficult time at the WCB as translation facilities were inadequate.

The fundamental aim of the task force was to personalize the service of the WCB. In this way not only would the injured person feel that his problems were being looked after sympathetically, but the board employee would feel some sense of pride and involvement in what he or she was doing. The task force also wanted to wipe from the minds of WCB employees the idea, which it found to be prevalent, that the board dispensed charity. In its place the true picture should be implanted that compensation for injuries received as the result of negligence by an employer is the right of every employee.

When it recommended a new organization for the WCB, the task force hoped to both streamline and homogenize the structure. At the top of the organizational chart would be, instead of the board chairman, the board itself, expanded from three to five members. To one side would be a joint consultative committee which would be made up of the board members, members of the public, government officials, employers, and union representatives. This group would hopefully stop the board again becoming an isolated bureaucracy. Beneath the chairman and general manager would be six departments instead of eight, combining the functions of the WCB in what the task force felt would be more manageable and harmonious groupings. Decision-making would be spread throughout the structure in order to make the process viable and to make working for the WCB a job with interest and challenge.

On the sensitive issue of appeals, the task force recommended that the review committee and appeals tribunal be scrapped and that instead a two-stage, fully automatic appeal process be created. If a claims administrator turned down a request, his decision would automatically have to be reviewed by the claims supervisor. If he also said no, that decision, again automatically, would go to a claims review group of senior officials. If they too rejected the claim, the injured person would be informed of the reasons for the rejection (the task force found too many situations where this had not been done) and would be told of his right to appeal to the board, which could be done on request. By making the appeal structure automatic, the task force hoped to get away from past practices where on many occasions road blocks had been placed in the way of claimants who wanted to institute an appeal. This structure was set up at the end of 1974.

There were in all close to a hundred recommendations in the task force report covering matters both large and small. Nothing much seemed to have escaped them and they even commented that they didn't like the name Workmen's Compensation Board because it had sexist overtones. Ontario Compensation Commission would be an improvement, they said.

The report was completed at the end of August 1973, and Labour Minister Guindon accepted it with enthusiasm, saying it heralded a new and brighter day for the WCB. He tabled the report in the Legislature on September 5 and announced that board chairman Bruce Legge had resigned four hours before. "In my opinion there was no way we could implement the recommendations of the report unless a change was made in the chairman," Mr. Guindon commented at the time. He had told Mr. Legge the same thing at a meeting at the Royal York Hotel in downtown Toronto shortly before.

Mr. Legge had hardly had time to place his letter of resignation on the desk before the cabinet appointed an acting chairman to replace him. In searching for a replacement the government looked no further than the members of the task force and picked out Michael Starr. Mr. Starr had much to commend him, both politically and personally. As a member of the task force he had an intimate knowledge of the existing situation at the wcb and the recommendations for change. He had been federal Minister of Labour from 1957 to 1963 in the Diefenbaker cabinet, was a loyal Conservative, but also had been a strongly union-oriented minister. His riding had been Oshawa just east of Toronto which, because of a large General Motors plant there, is politically dominated by the United Auto Workers union. Organized labour, which for years had seen the wcb as more a servant of the employers than the injured employees, could see in Mr. Starr one of their own. Although born a Canadian, Mr. Starr is of Ukrainian stock and for years in federal politics was seen by ethnic minority groups as their standard bearer. After leaving politics he was appointed a judge of the Citizenship Court. With an ever-increasing number of immigrants in Ontario's labour force it was obviously a bonus to the provincial government to have at the head of the wcb a man with an in-born sensitivity for the problems of racial, cultural and linguistic minority groups.

In addition, Mr. Starr had a number of personal attributes that encouraged his appointment. He is loyal and has a sense of frankness tempered with considerable humility. He thrives on work, and set the federal Labour Ministry on its ear in his first few days there. The choice of Mr. Starr was an obvious one and it was received with enthusiasm all round. The only cautionary notes to be sounded were not about Mr. Starr, but about the powers he would wield under the reformed wcb. When the amending legislation was introduced in December 1973, Frank Drea, Conservative backbencher from Scarborough Centre riding, pointed to the chairman's power over job classifications, salary ranges and hiring and firing, and commented that this "scared the hell" out of him.

"If you can guarantee Mr. Starr will be chairman for as long as the act applies, okay," Mr. Drea said. "I have confidence in him, but you're making it a one-man show." The opposition parties were also concerned and the NDP pushed through an amendment that would require the board to submit proposed changes in its regulations to the joint consultative committee for comment before the changes could come into effect. Mr. Guindon commented that this would take too much power away from the chairman.

The whole WCB episode points to the government's tendency when dealing with its agencies to appoint a person or group in whom it has confidence to run the organization and then leave it to them. There is little consultation, little accountability. Perhaps the most astounding thing about the whole situation was that it took the government some seven years to become aware that there were problems at the WCB. It was apparent at the first committee investigation of the WCB that successive Ministers of Labour over that period had paid little or no attention to what was going on at the board.

In suggesting how this gulf in communication might be bridged the task force drew on its own experience and also that of the Committee on Government Productivity, a group which had dealt with the reorganization of the entire government structure. There should, the task force said, be monthly meetings between the Minister of Labour and the chairmen of the WCB, and the entire board should meet with the minister at least twice a year. There should also be a day-to-day working relationship between the chairman and his officials, and the Deputy Minister of Labour and his staff. In the future there should be informal ties with other ministries, such as Health and Social and Family Services, which deal with problems closely aligned to those of the WCB. Finally, to keep the reviving breath of fresh thoughts and attitudes gusting down the WCB's hallways, board members would only be appointed for five years, though this would be renewable.

Shortly after Mike Starr took over the chairman's office in the forbidding building down by Toronto Harbour, an injured workman, a frequent visitor in the past, went down to get a problem with his compensation sorted out. After he left, he said with a smile, and with a note of astonishment in his voice: "You know what, they gave me free coffee."

PART TWO

GOVERNMENT

7
DONALD C. MACDONALD

Modernizing
the Legislature

THE PUBLIC image of the Ontario Legislature is often negative—at best mixed—because there is such a gap between the historical ideal and the reality. Actually, the Legislature is deeply involved in a modernization process of which the public has little knowledge or appreciation. Constitutionally, so the British North America Act tells us, the province has the responsibility (often exclusive, sometimes shared with the federal government) for education, welfare, labour and agriculture, resources, property and civil rights, consumer and corporate affairs, administration of justice—matters which touch the daily lives of all who live within its borders. In addition, municipalities are the creatures of the province, and may at any time have their powers, boundaries or resources altered, or even their very existence terminated.

Surely the men and women, elected members of the provincial Parliament, who wield such far-reaching powers must be the most important assembly of individuals in the province. But are they? The reality falls far short of the constitutional theory. In fact, the public doesn't perceive the Legislature to be the centre of power. As Fred Fletcher points out in his chapter on news coverage in Ontario, provincial affairs runs a poor third to federal and local politics in the media.

Most of these conditions are not unique; they are to be found in varying degrees in every democratic society. But if they are to be corrected in Ontario, improvements must come from within the province. And the Legislature itself is a major point of initiative.

In his *Responsible Government in Ontario*, Fred Schindeler has documented the basic reason for the eclipse of the Legislature. During the past hundred years, the scope and complexity of government has greatly increased. The executive branch has developed to cope with this growing burden, but until very recent years the operation and procedures of the legislative branch continued much as they were in the years following Confederation.

The average length of a session between 1867 and 1964 was 44.5 days, just under nine weeks. As late as the premiership of Leslie Frost (1949–61), sessions were almost invariably tucked into the eight to ten weeks before Easter. Though Ontario has moved in this century from a predominantly agricultural economy to become the industrial heartland of Canada, the activities of the Legislature remained geared to farming: it met between ploughing in the fall and seeding in the spring. This part-time effort left the responsibilities of government even more to the executive branch and the growing bureaucracy at Queen's Park.

It was John Robarts who brought the Ontario Legislature into the twentieth century. During his years as premier (1961–70) legislative sessions ran as long as 173 days in 1968–69, and averaged close to one hundred days. It was in keeping with Robarts' no-nonsense, chairman-of-the-board approach to the business of government, that not only did the Legislature meet for a longer period, but the first steps were taken to acknowledge the special needs of opposition parties, and to provide MPP's with the necessary resources to do their work on a full-time basis.

Though the modernization of the legislative branch of government was begun during the 1960s, it tended to lag behind even more intensive efforts to improve the efficiency of the executive. In his closing years in office, Robarts appointed the Committee on Government Productivity (COGP) to recommend changes in government administration, particularly at the policy-making level. George Szablowski will examine the nature and effectiveness of these changes in the next chapter. But to the extent that the recommendations of the COGP have increased the efficiency of the executive branch, they have resulted in a further diminution of the power of the Legislature.

Significantly, consideration of the Legislature was specifically excluded from the terms of reference of the COGP. Only after the first six of its ten reports had been released, almost as an afterthought the government appointed the Ontario Commission on the Legislature, popularly known as the Camp Commission.

Time alone will tell whether the recommendations of the Camp Commission can arrest the eclipse of the Legislature, or point to ways and means by which the role of the MPP can be made more meaningful. But the commission's appointment came at a time when the growing dominance of the executive and administrative branches over the Legislature had reached a point where the Legislature is little more than a rubber-stamp, approving (on rare occasions, disapproving) decisions which have already been made by the cabinet or the bureaucracy.

What, then, is the historic function of the Legislature? That private members should play a more active and positive role in the legislative process. That, collectively, members of the Legislature should keep under critical review the government's actions (or failure to act), particularly when they involve expenditure of public monies. That as the key link with the electorate, private members should have more effective opportunities to reflect day-to-day needs, and to initiate corrective action, instead of the government having to rely so completely on outside experts or inside bureaucrats.

The Ontario Commission on the Legislature was established in June 1972, to examine how the Legislature might more effectively fulfil these historic functions. Specifically, its terms of reference were "to study the function of the Legislative Assembly . . . with particular reference to the role of the Private Members, and how their participation in the process of government may be enlarged, including the services, facilities and benefits to the Members of the Assembly."

The personnel of the commission raised high hopes. Farquhar Oliver had been a member of the Ontario Legislature for forty-one years, some twelve of them as leader of the Liberal party. Chairman Dalton Camp and Douglas Fisher had had extensive experience with the Progressive Conservative and New Democratic parties, respectively, and had established reputations for an imaginative and innovative approach to politics. Together the commissioners represented an almost unparalleled wealth of political experience from which to chart the first major effort at reform of the Ontario Legislature.

The commission's major concern was for "the decline of the Legislature as an institution of unchallenged strength and independence." Historians might well ask when the Ontario Legislature was an institution "of unchallenged strength and independence," but no one will dispute the decline. The commission pinpointed the cause as being in the general erosion of the Speaker's powers and the placing of the Legislature in an administratively subservient role to the executive. It pursued these issues with singular purpose and determination. In the process it had to tackle head-on the government's reluctance, if not opposition, to the reforms it proposed.

In the preface to its second report, for example, the commission pointed out that there had been four special papers dealing with the Office of the Speaker at various intervals during the previous five years. These interviews and studies had enabled the commission to reach two conclusions: first, that "the Office of the Speaker, and consequently the administration of the Legislature itself, has not grown and developed along lines consistent with modern parliamentary democracy"; and second, that "although virtually all the Ontario government reports dealing with the matter recognize this fact, and made worthwhile recommendations, none of these were adopted. . . ." The commission commented acidly: "We can only assume that the government, for its own reasons, declined to act upon the recommendations of these reports, or, perhaps more likely, there was a failure to attach sufficient priority to implementing them."

After reviewing the situation at Westminster and Ottawa, the report concluded: "The Commission is intent on a similar independence for the Speaker and the Clerk in Ontario, and on emphasizing the privacy of their function as officials of the Assembly. . . . Respect for the offices, and a deep belief in the good will and high purpose of the Speaker and the Clerk, are slow to develop when these officers are dependent on the Ministry for the fulfillment of their smallest personnel or financial needs."

Not only did the commission spell out the administrative staff which the Office of the Speaker should have, but it drove the point home with the recommendation that in the Table of Precedence for Ontario, the Speaker should rank next to the Lieutenant-Governor, the First Minister and the Chief Justice of the Supreme Court of Ontario.

After another six months of contemplating the issue, the government responded on June 25, 1974, in a statement to the Legislature by the Honourable Eric Winkler, Chairman of the Management Board of Cabinet. He announced acceptance of most of the commission's second report, and in particular welcomed those recommendations relating to the status of the high office of the Speaker and of the Clerk.

The administrative subservience of the Legislature is being removed, but experience suggests that the basic problem remains because the government has really not accepted the idea of an independent legislature. Too often, it reverts to playing the game according to the old rules. Moreover, too often the Speaker and the Clerk are willing to go along; they are captives of the traditionally subservient role.

In fact, there is another fundamental problem which the Camp Commission apparently never considered. Is it possible to develop an independent legislature without an independent Speaker? And is it possible for a Speaker to be genuinely independent as long as he is chosen from among the ranks of the government members, usually for only one parliament, and therefore is always aware that he will ultimately have to return to the partisan ranks? In short, the long-debated question of a permanent Speaker cannot be evaded; but on this, the Camp Commission had nothing to say or recommend.

The task faced by the Speaker in the Ontario Legislature is virtually impossible. The government, and all its members, know that he is one of them, and the pressures are always there in a subtle way. On occasion they are open, blatantly so, as a couple of incidents in recent history will illustrate.

During his term as premier, Leslie Frost operated on the assumption that there were two sets of rules in the House —one for himself, and one for all other members. Thus he intervened in debates whenever he chose, and nobody, including the Speaker, could do much about it. No one present will ever forget the look of stunned surprise on Mr. Frost's face on the one occasion when the Speaker, Rev. A. W. Downer, asked him to take his seat because he was out of order!

Or that more spectacular occasion when George Drew publicly challenged the Speaker on the petty issue of where seats had been assigned for his visitors in the gallery. To his credit, the Speaker of the day, W. J. Stewart, removed his tricorn hat, placed it on the Speaker's chair, and vacated the office, never to return.

In the mother of Parliaments at Westminster, the Speaker was long ago given the "permanent" status which makes an independent role possible. It is at least highly debatable whether the kind of independence envisaged by the Camp Commission for the legislative branch can ever be achieved until the Speaker is freed from former, and the likelihood of future, partisan association with the government.

But quite apart from the question of whether any Speaker can be the first officer of an independent legislature unless he himself is independent, it cannot be assured that the government's acceptance of the Camp Commission recommendations means the battle for a genuinely independent legislature is won. In fact, it has only begun. The way may now be cleared for the Office of the Speaker, and consequently the administration of the Legislature itself, "to grow and develop along lines consistent with modern parliamentary democracy," but it is an evolutionary process. It cannot be decreed, or legislated.

In fact, the Camp Commission's recommendations were predicated on the recognition that members of the Legislature are masters in their own House, and that, in a very real way, the independence of the Legislature depends on them. Repeatedly, the commissioners pointed out that the erosion of legislative powers was not so much a calculated usurpation by the executive as it was the filling of a vacuum left by members who had not exercised their responsibilities. Once the Legislature has clearly been given the responsibility to run its own affairs, there will be no excuse for failing to accept the obligation.

For example, the commission felt that it was of paramount importance that the members "regulate their own affairs, apply their own standards, and assert their authority" in matters which clearly fall within their jurisdiction. That will involve a degree of self-discipline hitherto not exercised. Having escaped from the paternalism of executive control and regulation, the Legislature will now have the obligation of regulating itself on such things as select committee expenditures, which are frequently being questioned publicly.

This is true not only in dealing with essentially administrative matters, but also with devising ways and means of redressing the imbalance arising from the growing dominance of the executive and administrative branches over the Legislature in all modern government. The Camp Commission contented itself with seeking restoration of the traditional rights of the Legislature which had wasted away over the years. It left to the MPP's themselves the responsibility for devising new techniques for keeping the ever-more powerful executive in check by an independent legislature. It will be the obligation of members to guard their rights more jealously, and in the evolutionary process by which these parliamentary changes are normally achieved, to seek constantly for ways and means by which the role of the Legislature vis-à-vis the executive can be strengthened.

Within the context of this broad overview, it is now appropriate to examine particulars of the role of the private members and consider how their participation in the process of government can be enlarged. Within the past generation the work of MPP's has become much heavier. This is the case, in part, because their responsibilities, along with government, have grown in size and complexity, and, in part, because the average citizen has become more aware of his rights under the growing body of legislation which now touches every facet of life. Thus, the MPP's "case-load" (responding to problems and requests raised by constituents) has become the heaviest part of his work. Moreover, the work-load has not been lightened by the appointment of an ombudsman, as is the case in many other provinces. Often it threatens to overwhelm the member, or at least to occupy him so completely that his role as a legislator is neglected. In other words, the job of an MPP is now full-time. If it isn't, it should be; and the public is entitled to demand as much of its elected representatives.

The length of the sessions is growing. In fact, the Camp Commission proposed a scheduling for the legislative year which would begin with the second Tuesday in February, run until the last Friday in June, with one week's break for the mid-March school holiday and the 24th of May; resume after the summer recess on the second Tuesday in September till the second week of December, with one week's break at Thanksgiving.

When the House is not actually in session, there is often select committee work or an extensive range of constituency obligations. In addition, every politician has party activities, certainly within his riding, often at the provincial, and sometimes even at the federal level. Such duties are still all part of a democratic political system to which an elected representative has a special obligation.

That being the case, the job of an MPP can no longer be regarded as part-time, for which he is paid an "indemnity" to compensate for time off from his regular employment. Consequently, the commission argued strongly for improvement in both the income and working conditions of the member and virtually all of its recommendations concerning "the emoluments of office" have been implemented. An MPP's basic income is $15,000 (still anachronistically called an indemnity), plus a tax-free expense allowance of $7,500. The indemnity paid to members of Ontario's first parliament after Confederation was $450, and as late as 1955, it was only $2,600, plus $1,300 tax-free allowance.

For members living outside Metropolitan Toronto, a travel allowance is paid for fifty-two round-trip economy flights a year, or an accommodation allowance of up to $3,000 a year, provided reasonable proof of the expenditure is made. In addition, all members are entitled to a 15-cent-per-mile allowance for travel within their constituency, or to and from their home and Queen's Park by car. Maintaining personal contact with constituents is always a problem. MPP's have access to government lines to most key centres in the province, and the use of a telephone credit card when those lines are not available. In addition, there may be two mailings per year to each household within the constituency. As a safeguard against abuses, all accountable expenditures by each member are to be reported annually in Hansard.

Because of the insecurity of politics, pensions have become widely acknowledged as a necessary attraction to bring capable men and women into public life. The average tenure of office by an MPP was reported by the Camp Commission to be nine years. MPP's contribute 7 per cent of their salary to the pension fund, which is matched by the government; and they become eligible when their years of service (which must be a minimum of five), together with their years of age, total sixty or more. The maximum pension can be 75 per cent of the salary, but that is attainable only after some twenty-two years of service. Finally, each member is now provided with an office at Queen's Park, and a secretary or personal assistant.

This updating of conditions is important for reasons far beyond the well-being and greater efficiency of the members themselves. In the words of the commission report:

"Constituency demands are such that substantial resources and services must be provided to Members, if they are to hold, let alone increase, their capacity to take part in the work of the Legislature." In short, the revitalization of the Legislature is possible only if something is done about what the Camp Commission describes as "the constituency syndrome—the belief that the priority role of the Member is to look after his 'case load,' rather than to be, in terms of priorities, a legislator and a scrutinizer of government spending."

But in addition to their individual work loads, members operate as a team through their party caucus. Here, too, the Ontario Legislature began to move into a new era during the Robarts regime.

Traditionally, new governments treated the opposition with the vengeful attitude reserved for civil servants known to have partisan associations with the old government. They couldn't fire the opposition, but they were damned if they'd do anything to help them! Premiers like George Drew and Leslie Frost, who became active in politics during the thirties, were understandably captives of this traditional attitude. They had vivid memories of Hepburn's wholesale firing of civil servants in 1934 and the scornful way in which he treated the opposition. But John Robarts entered politics in the fifties, and was free of these past attitudes. Moreover, during his years as premier, the executive branch first became conscious of the overwhelming burden of policy-making and administration in modern government, and therefore responsive to the plight of opposition parties which had traditionally operated without any resources to fulfil their role as critic of the government.

Throughout the sixties, a combination of pressure from the opposition parties, particularly the NDP, and Robarts' appreciation of the problem, resulted in the gradual increase in resources for research, public relations and other staffing of opposition caucuses. That process received a strong boost from the Camp Commission.

The formula for assistance to opposition caucuses is subject to change almost yearly, but as of 1974, each caucus was given an annual and unconditional grant of $5,000 per member. To provide additional staff support for opposition leaders, and therefore a more adequate balance with the

Premier's Office, which has a staff of seventy or more, there is a further grant of 30 per cent of the unconditional allowance, plus a research grant of $137,500 for the official opposition, and of $99,000 for the third party.

Thus, the Liberal opposition of twenty-three members is now financed to the extent of $301,950 per year, while the NDP, with twenty members, receives $242,000—in both instances including research staff.

The government caucus deserves special mention. Some forty of its seventy-three members (the Speaker is the seventy-fourth Progressive Conservative member) are in the cabinet, or parliamentary assistants to ministers, or one of the government appointees to various boards and commissions, for which there is extra emolument, often including office facilities and staff. The role of these forty government members is presumably a meaningful and satisfying one. But for the government backbencher, political life can be doubly frustrating. If perchance he cannot get what he feels to be an adequate response to the needs of his constituents, his only recourse is to raise the matter privately with the minister, or in government caucus. Beyond that he is hesitant to play the maverick, and publicly berate the government—a course which is fully open to an opposition member.

But collectively, the government caucus has some compensation for the greater frustration of some of its members. There are only just over thirty so-called backbenchers without appointment to the cabinet, as parliamentary assistants or to some agency, but the caucus is in receipt of a per capita allowance of $5,500 for its total membership of seventy-four. That represents a budget of $387,000. In addition, government members have, for obvious reasons, readier access to the administrative bureaucracy. The relations between the opposition members and the civil service are not, as the Camp Commission notes, as paranoid at Queen's Park as in Ottawa, but there are limitations to the extent to which ministries can provide information to an opposition member when that information might turn up as ammunition against the government the next day in the Legislature.

Thus, while opposition parties have been more adequately provided for in Ontario than in any other provincial parliament (with the possible exception of the Quebec National Assembly), the imbalance between the resources available to the government caucus and to the opposition caucuses still remains—perhaps inevitably so.

Another major area for enlarging the participation of private members in the process of government lies in reform of the procedures and practices of the Legislature itself.

This topic is worthy of a book, let alone part of a chapter in an overview of the government and politics of Ontario. Schindeler's *Responsible Government in Ontario* is the only major study, and still provides much of the historical background and basic procedures. But unfortunately Schindeler's study is out of date; it was completed at the end of our first one hundred years, precisely when government and legislative procedures were being subjected to a much-needed overhaul. The second and fourth reports of the Camp Commission provide an up-to-date picture of legislative procedures, along with recommendations for further changes. Our focus here will be to pick and choose among those legislative procedures which have reduced the opportunities for fuller participation of the private member, and especially to suggest how that participation can be enlarged.

Where does the primary responsibility for reform of the Legislature rest: with the government or with the opposition? Obviously, the answer is with all members, on whatever side of the House they sit. As indicated earlier, members are masters of the House, and can reshape its procedures as they wish, assuming there is a consensus and the government is willing to permit it.

But the reports of the Camp Commission laid special blame on the opposition. "Members in Opposition to the Government, individually and in their parties," the second report states, "have not been persistent or zealous in taking advantage of the rights they have under the rules of the Legislature and the British parliamentary traditions in order to defend or even assert their responsibilities."

While there is a measure of truth in that assertion, those involved would counter, by way of explanation, that there are limits to the amount of time and energy which can

profitably be spent in seeking procedural changes when the whole mood and attitude toward changes is resistant beyond the point of reason.

However, for the future, the commission's point may be well taken. Now that there is a general desire to improve procedures, hopefully there will be a more sympathetic attitude toward efforts for achieving it, and inevitably the thrust is likely to come from the opposition more than from the government side of the House.

The one area of virtual unanimity is in the criticism of how the business of the House is managed. The commission's conclusion is unequivocal: "The business of the House is arranged and carried out in an inefficient or haphazard manner. The scheduling of what the Legislature will be doing, or actually does, is arranged without enough prior notice, without enough consultation between parties, and results in flat days and weeks without much pressure and then speed-ups and near-bedlam just before recess."

While this criticism was expressed "with more irritation and occasionally with outrage by Members of the Opposition," the commission reported that "a surprisingly large minority of the supporters of the government agreed that the management of the business of the Legislature was unpredictable. . . ." The reason for this disturbing feature of the Legislature's activities remains a matter of conjecture. The commission noted that early in its studies the Premier indicated that he was most willing to look favourably on suggestions for better planning of the legislative business, "even to attempting the establishment of a routine parliamentary year which would spread out the sittings and recesses more evenly over the twelve months."

In addition, the commission's proposals for strengthening the role of the party whips may encourage greater inter-party consultation. But in the final analysis the solution to this problem, which bedevils the operations of the House more than any other single thing, rests with the Government House Leader, backed by the Premier, through an orderly scheduling of government bills and ministerial estimates of expenditure.

Assuming a more efficient handling of the business of the House, the work of committees is the next most important aspect of the legislative process. They have become a vexing problem. The Ontario Legislature has been attempting to develop a more effective committee system for many years, without much success, particularly with standing committees.

Select committees are another matter. They meet only when the Legislature is not sitting, and over the past twenty years have evolved significantly. The ostensible purpose for appointing a select committee is to provide an opportunity for a group of members, not more than fifteen in number, drawn from all parties, to investigate a topic of public concern. There is no doubt, however, that their appointment has often been as much to keep backbenchers occupied in a Legislature with top-heavy majorities.

Select committees have been appointed to recommend overhauling of major statutes, such as the Labour Relations Act or the Companies Act; to investigate problems arising from consumer credit, tile drainage or snowmobiles; or to explore general policy areas such as the more effective use of our school facilities or economic and cultural nationalism.

Usually select committees are provided with the necessary expert staff. They enable members to become more thoroughly conversant with the topic under study and also provide for public involvement from all across the province —and sometimes from other provinces or countries. They have proven to be useful devices in exploring old or emerging problems.

One reason why select committees have been so successful is that members' attendance has been good, no doubt in part because an honorarium of $50 a day, plus expenses, has been paid. The Camp Commission has recommended that membership on select committees should be considered an integral part of an MPP's work, for which a reasonable income is now provided, and therefore the honorarium should be stopped. The government has hesitated to implement this recommendation (just as it delayed on the recommendation of the Camp Commission that government members should no longer be appointed to agencies, boards and commissions), and the future of select committees is somewhat in question.

Standing committees are more closely related to the day-to-day work of the Legislature. Normally, they can meet only on days when the House is in session, but in the free mornings when it is not actually sitting. Until 1970 they were identified, more or less, with the interests of the various ministries. But they tended to become so numerous that it was physically impossible to schedule them in the limited morning time available.

As a result, Ontario moved in 1970 to a variant of the British system, with five omnibus committees: one to deal with Procedural Affairs; three tied to the policy fields of Administration of Justice, Social Development and Resources Development; and a Miscellaneous Estimates Committee. In addition, there are two committees dealing with the specialized fields of Public Accounts and Regulations.

In theory this is a much more viable set-up; but in practice it hasn't worked out. The Estimates Committee, of course, is very busy. It has taken a sizable proportion of the load which hitherto was carried by the Committee of Supply, involving the whole House. In the parlance of Queen's Park, there is now a "two-ring" rather than a "one-ring" circus, but the time schedule for consideration of estimates is squeezed into the seventy-five sessional days after the budget is brought down.

Unfortunately, the other committees have tended to be neglected. In order that the government can keep a tight rein on their activities, the Standing Orders do not permit a committee to deal with any matter that has not been specifically referred to it by the House. In addition, whereas it used to be a relatively common practice for every new bill of any substantive nature to be referred to the appropriate committee in order that representatives of the public might testify as to its impact on them, this is being done much less frequently. The result has been graphically underlined by an analysis made by the Liberal Caucus Research staff which revealed that in 1966 some 44 per cent of bills introduced to the House were referred to a standing committee, whereas since 1972 that percentage had dropped below 10 per cent. Thus, a major means of involving the public has been neglected.

Committees represent a mini-meeting of the Legislature; they are in fact an extension of it. Members are often freer to follow their own judgment rather than the party line. Thus, there tends to be a less partisan, more objective consideration of issues. For all these reasons the failure to develop a more effective committee system has greatly inhibited a more effective operation of the Legislature.

There are a number of procedures, deeply embedded in the traditions of the British parliamentary system, which have weakened, or even withered away, in the Ontario Legislature. Their recent restoration offers some opportunity for the private member, individually on either side of the House, or collectively through opposition parties, to have a greater influence over the legislative process. Three of these traditional procedures merit brief reference.

First is the right of any private member to introduce a bill or resolution. This right was never denied, but for some years it was treated with such disdain by the executive branch that private members' bills and resolutions were invariably called in the late hours of the final days of the session. For a time, two one-hour periods a week were set aside for their debate; that has now been reduced to one period. But most damaging of all has been the government refusal to permit such bills or resolutions to come to a vote, as is the case in most other provincial legislatures.

The result is that, while the debate might receive some publicity, it is often conducted before a near-empty House, with virtually all of the cabinet members absent. In contrast, in the Nova Scotia Legislature, for example, private members' bills introduced by the opposition command a full attendance, frequently witness divisions within the parties and even the cabinet, and conclude with a free vote. Hopefully, the recommendation of the Camp Commission for providing more time, and the holding of votes, will prove acceptable to the government, and thereby permit of the more meaningful involvement of private members which these traditional rights envisaged.

Second is the right of an opposition party to introduce want-of-confidence motions on any public issue which might emerge. For some years this right completely disappeared in Ontario. From the origins of parliament, the legislative branch has cherished the privilege of seeking redress of grievances before voting money for the upkeep of the sovereign's household. Down through the centuries this right remained as a check of the legislative branch over the executive. It is symbolic of the general problem in the Ontario Legislature that it should have fallen completely into disuse for many years. With the updating of the Standing Orders of the Ontario Legislature in 1970, three such opportunities for want-of-confidence motions were granted in each session, as amendments to supply motions, two of which may be used by the official opposition and one by the third party.

Third is the right of a private member to seek adjournment of the regular business of the House for consideration of a matter of urgent public importance. Once again, for practical purposes this right withered into virtual disuse. The Speaker must be notified by the member of his desire to move a motion, and throughout most of the postwar years it was the Speaker's right to accept or deny it privately, so that the member's intention would never become publicly known. The Speaker usually refused, arguing that the matter might be raised at some other time. Indeed, too often opposition members were left with the impression that an emergency debate was permitted only when the government was anxious to have it; thus, the whole purpose of emergency debates was frustrated.

Here, too, the traditional right has been revived. The revised Standing Orders of 1970 specify that, before the Orders of the Day, any member may move to set aside the ordinary business of the House to discuss a matter of urgent public importance, of which he has given written notice to the Speaker two hours prior to the sitting of the House. When the motion is moved, the member may explain his arguments in its favour for not more than five minutes. One member from each of the other parties may state the position of his party with respect to the motion, again in not more than five minutes. The Speaker must then rule on whether or not the motion is in order and of urgent public importance. If he rules in its favour, he will then put the question: "Shall the debate proceed?" to a vote of the House.

This procedure does not, of course, preclude the spokesman, on behalf of the government party, from clearly indicating if the government favours a debate. But whether or not the government party wishes it, the Speaker is free to exercise his independent judgment and accept the motion. If he does accept it, the government party is faced with the embarrassment of voting against the Speaker if it wishes to avoid the debate. The whip-hand still rests with the government majority, but at least the private member's right to an emergency debate has been restored. Most important, the member has the opportunity to outline the issue, so that his initiative cannot be quashed privately, without any public knowledge.

For obvious reasons, one of the most important features of any Legislature is its relations with the media, and through them, communication with the general public. In this connection, the forty-five-minute oral question period which precedes the Orders of the Day has become the highlight of the Ontario Legislature.

By the 1950s the oral question period had virtually disappeared. Written questions could be placed on the Order Paper, but they were rarely answered promptly, and sometimes not at all. But oral questions were deemed to be an unwarranted invasion of the private operations of the executive.

The first step in the evolution of question period was the submission in writing, before noon of each day, of any question which a member proposed to ask. It could be edited, or even rejected, by the Speaker; but if accepted, a copy was passed on to the minister concerned. This procedure resulted in frequent bickering with the Speaker; there was constant pressure for fewer restrictions.

Consequently, the practice evolved to the present where questions are asked without prior notice, where supplementary questions are permitted from the original member, or from others, with the result that a mini-debate can develop on a matter of current concern. The Speaker has tended to be lenient (in striking contrast to the excessive restrictions of earlier years) with the result that the conduct of the House has become lively to the point of being undisciplined. The press gallery is invariably full for this first hour, and tends to empty quickly thereafter, as is also the case with the cabinet benches. It follows, therefore, that the great proportion of the news of any legislative day emerges from question period.

"Obviously," the Camp Commission observed, "the question period is savoured as the daily feast of partisanship and news-making," and it wondered out loud why the Ontario Legislature presents such a contrast in the uproar, free-flow and disdain for formality during this opening period of the day, and then tends to lapse into hours when speakers address small and usually inattentive colleagues. Certainly, the question period has given most justification for the Ontario Legislature being dubbed "the most unruly House in Canada."

But with all its faults the question period represents the greatest single improvement in legislative procedures during recent years. There is need for more rigid application by the Speaker of the rules regarding argumentative, opinionated, rhetorical or excessively long questions. There is need for greater self-discipline by the members themselves. Such improvement can, and should, be made. But the question period has revived the cut-and-thrust which is generally lacking in the Ontario Legislature. During those forty-five minutes of each sitting day, the operations of government and the inadequacies of its policies can be ruthlessly, even if briefly, brought to public attention. Cabinet members' reputations can be made, or unmade, more quickly than at any other time. The question period has become the most effective device for exercising some influence over the executive.

But if question period has provided the media with the most prolific point of contact with the Legislature in its communication with the public, when will that communication become direct through the live broadcast of legislative proceedings? The Government of Ontario has coyly considered this possibility for more than a decade.

During the Robarts regime, the first tentative steps were taken to provide access to the Legislature for both radio and television. The process began (and has been continued each year) with broadcasting of the formal proceedings of opening day, including the reading of the Speech from the Throne by the Lieutenant-Governor. The public is thereby provided not only with live television coverage, but radio stations can use excerpts from the Throne Speech in reporting the government's program for the ensuing session.

Later, for two years, the television networks carried the Provincial Treasurer's presentation of the budget, and on subsequent days, one hour of the reply by the financial critic of each of the opposition parties. But the government was not enthused with the experiment, and the networks were not happy with the piecemeal approach, so the project simply died.

The key to the government's reluctance was the attitude of Premier Robarts. As we have seen, he was open-minded on legislative reform, but the media represented a real personal hang-up. His attitude ranged from unease to distrust, even disdain, and nowhere more so than with television. As he stated on many occasions, it was possible for film to be edited so as to give a false impression of what was said or done.

Perhaps so, but that is a daily risk of persons in public life. For years all media have had complete access to press conferences where important political pronouncements are often made. Reporters and editors in both the print and electronic media have exercised their professional (or personal) judgment in choosing excerpts from speeches delivered inside and outside the Legislature. That is the essence of freedom of the press; and it is unlikely such freedom will be any more, or less, abused if direct access to the Legislature is given to the electronic media.

Significantly, resistance to legislative broadcasting is breaking down elsewhere and the Ontario government will soon have to fall in line. In Ottawa, televising the House of Commons is being actively reviewed. In Alberta, where televising of legislative proceedings has now taken place for a number of years, everybody concerned—the government, opposition parties and the Speaker who has to cope with all the arrangements—agrees the experiment has been an unqualified success. There has been none of the much-feared grandstanding before the cameras; rather, the equipment has simply become part of the legislative furniture. The great beneficiary, of course, has been the public of Alberta, and of Canada through national newscasts.

The Camp Committee has recommended that broadcasting of the Ontario Legislature should be permitted by both radio and television. Once access is granted, the rest is a matter of mechanics. As with everything else in the Legislature, arrangements will have to be made with approval of the Speaker. Hopefully, not many years hence, all Ontarians will be able to see their MPP's in action no matter how distant from Queen's Park they may live. That could have a subtle, but perhaps far-reaching, impact on both the government and politics of the province.

SELECTED BIBLIOGRAPHY

SCHINDELER, F. F. *Responsible Government in Ontario.* Toronto: University of Toronto Press, 1969.

Ontario Commission on the Legislature
First Report, May, 1973—The Member and the Legislature

Second Report, December, 1973—The Legislature and Its Administration

Fourth Report, Spring, 1975—How the Legislature Works and How It Should Work

Fifth Report, Spring, 1975—The Legislature in Relation to the Electronic Media, the Press Gallery, Information Services and Constituency Offices

8
GEORGE J. SZABLOWSKI

Policy-Making
and Cabinet:
Recent
Organizational Engineering
at Queen's Park

I T IS apparent that we are entering into a new era in public policy-making and public administration. It is a period characterized by a high degree of optimism at the elite level, a conviction that powerful analytic and technological capabilities can transform the decision-making process and thus vastly improve the quality and the effectiveness of the decisions themselves. For the first time, optimists argue, governments have the tools to do the job. It is, therefore, their moral duty to use them to the fullest. This normative imperative is dictated by increasing interdependence and complexity of issues and problems which, many believe, impose progressively heavier burdens on governmental decision-makers and administrators. If we do not begin now, if we do not anticipate and plan comprehensively, we may permanently eliminate many of the desirable "possible futures," leaving only the second-rate alternatives for our children and our children's children to pursue and experience.

The ideas of abundance and growth and, therefore, of a relatively unrestricted freedom to pursue diverse and conflicting social and economic goals without prior calculation and ongoing controls appear to be no longer accepted. In their place emerge the ideas of scarcity and rationality as currently dominant themes preoccupying those concerned with the political and economic future of post-industrial society. "Scarcity," writes Edward Shils, "combined with rationality and efficiency imposes the notion of priority and leads to a decisional technique called the 'optimal allocation of resources among preferred objectives'." Superenthusiasts have already begun to think in terms of Promethean aspirations.

> The notion that a whole society could be planned deliberately in a way that could shape it for a long time to come presupposes not only a pervasive knowledge of the present state of society but also the ability to forsee the subsequent behaviour of its component parts.[1]

The challenge of this new normative thrust has been openly accepted by governmental leaders in Ontario. Its unmistakable expression may be found in the description

1 Edward Shils, ed., *Criteria For Scientific Development—Public Policy and National Goals* (Cambridge, Mass.: M.I.T. Press, 1968), Introduction.

of the "new management style" proposed for the government of Ontario of the 1970s.

This new style will demand that government's approach to problems will be universal rather than narrow or parochial; that government will anticipate change rather than merely react to it; that the organization of government will be flexible rather than rigid; that more productive use will have to be made of human, financial, and material resources; that choices between conflicting programmes will have to be made on the basis of information which has been probed deeper and been more thoroughly analyzed; that programmes are placed in a proper order of priorities; that the decision to eliminate programmes which can no longer be justified can be arrived at rationally; and that policies can be developed which ensure the most economical distribution and use of common services which today represent a significant proportion of government costs.[2]

These words strongly support the belief that "government must become bigger and involved in problems of increasing magnitude." They were written and published in the name of a committee composed of five prominent business executives, five senior public servants, and one highly successful entrepreneur with first-rate academic credentials.

The Committee on Government Productivity (COGP) was created by Premier Robarts in December of 1969 and instructed

to inquire into all matters pertaining to the management of the Government of Ontario and to make such recommendations as in its opinion will improve the efficiency and the effectiveness of the Government of Ontario.[3]

J. B. Cronyn, a well known industrialist, became chairman of the committee; and in March 1970, James D. Fleck, associate dean in the Faculty of Administrative Studies at York University, was named executive director. He assembled and directed the central staff, the working arm of the committee, which consisted of some thirteen full-time project analysts and research officers with professional and academic backgrounds ranging from law, business administration and economics to political science, philosophy and

2 COGP, Interim Report No. 2, p. 7.
3 Order-in-Council 4689/69, dated December 23, 1969.

journalism. Additional individuals joined the central staff
for specific assignments. The committee and its staff relied
extensively on outside advisers numbering over one
hundred persons drawn from the Ontario public service,
the professions, the business community and the academic
community. The advisers and consultants were grouped
into project teams, each charged with a specific and well-
defined area of inquiry. In addition, special advisory committees were formed, and a number of individuals and
organizations were invited to present written and oral
submissions. During the fall of 1970 and the spring and
summer of 1971, members of the committee visited Britain,
Sweden and the United States and held discussions with
governmental officials there. Collaboration with Ottawa involved primarily public officials from the Prime Minister's
Office, Privy Council Office, and the Treasury Board
Secretariat.

COGP's central aim was to pave the way for the fullest
adoption and implementation of the new management
style. This could not be accomplished without a frontal
attack on the traditional structure of government: the
cabinet, the Premier's office, the ministry, and the departmental and agency organization. Innovation was to begin at
the top and proceed down throughout the governmental
apparatus. But to deal with formal structure without an
examination of the remaining key governmental resources
was clearly unrealistic. Organizational engineering would
not be effective unless at the same time new and congruent
ways of dealing with manpower, knowledge and money
were also adopted. Thus, the scope of the inquiry was
extended to cover such additional subjects as: automatic
data processing (Report No. 5, February 1972); utilization
of human resources (Report No. 6, April 1972); communications and information services (Report No. 7, June
1972); real property management (Report No. 8, November
1972); and other studies including the ministry concept,
agencies, decision-making and PPBS, management information systems and management science, statistics as a future
social barometer (Report No. 9, March 1973).[4] The citizen
involvement study originally sponsored by COGP became the

4 Other contributors to this volume comment on these additional
recommendations within their respective terms of reference.

only aborted project. The committee rejected the working paper prepared by the central staff and called its recommendations inappropriate.[5]

In order to understand fully the significance of COGP's innovations, one must reconstruct the guiding assumptions that served as its modus operandi.

First, the government of Ontario including its bureaucratic establishment is a production enterprise which transforms political and economic resources into collective goods and services to be distributed to the public.

Second, policy-making is the strategic task of that enterprise to be pursued along three paths: *meta-policy* concerned with the over-all determination of objectives, priorities and the allocation of resources; *substantive policy* concerned with solutions to concrete issues and problems; and *management and operations policy* concerned with the control of the allocated resources and the delivery of collective goods and services to the consuming publics.

Third, cabinet ministers and senior bureaucratic officials engaged in policy-making behave rationally in the sense that, when acting in the performance of their functions, they consistently choose the optimal or best policy alternatives on the basis of available information and analysis.

These assumptions clearly reflect a conceptual/prescriptive rather than a pragmatic/empirical approach to government. Yet none of the ten reports published by the committee contains a serious, in-depth examination of the theoretical propositions on which this conceptual view hinges. The authors of the final report merely acknowledge that in the Structure of Government Study the committee relied on "the latest works in organization research and theory for government" and that "the concept of differentiation and integration as propounded by Professors Lawrence and Lorsh (of the Harvard School of Business Administration) and the principles of other experts such as Peter Drucker (of Claremont Graduate School) in organization and public administration were accepted by the study team as valid for the Government of Ontario."[6]

5 COGP Report No. 10, pp. 60–61. However, the paper was published "in order to stimulate debate and discussion."
6 COGP Report No. 10, p. 49.

In fact, most of the COGP staffers were ambitious men of action primarily interested in introducing and implementing as many innovations as political feasibility permitted. They knew that a long and thorough academic-type study would diminish rather than increase the likelihood of successful reform. As individuals, they were anxious to move into the government and to assume positions from which they could observe their innovations in the reality of political life. They thus devised a highly effective, direct method of executive approval and implementation. Recommendations considered by the committee were drawn up by the central staff and discussed with the project team members, and then swiftly submitted to cabinet for approval. Although the cabinet minister nominally responsible for the work of the committee was the Treasurer of Ontario and Chairman of the Treasury Board (Charles MacNaughton), Mr. Cronyn and Dr. Fleck managed to develop quickly a direct link to Premier Davis and to one or two key ministers keenly interested in COGP's work (notably Darcy McKeough). Once approved by cabinet, the recommendations became the responsibility of the implementation team headed by T. M. Eberlee, a deputy minister. Thus, a chain of events commencing with the articulation of specific innovations and ending with their practical application became an ongoing process embracing one project after another. However, the Structure of Government Study remained at the centre of COGP's work. It was divided into three separate projects: two of them, the Apex project and the Ministry Organization project, were personally supervised by Fleck; the third, concerning an examination of provincial agencies, boards and commissions, received a lower priority and was not reported on until March of 1973. Most of the recommendations in this last area still remain to be implemented.

The Apex project dealt with "the top of the management pyramid": the provincial cabinet, the Department of the Premier, the Department of the Treasury and Economics, and the Treasury Board. This study, conducted by two COGP staff analysts, John Graham and Malcolm Rowan, under the direction of James Fleck, was nominally completed in December 1970. Two short interim reports summarize the results. The project on the Ministry Organization became in fact a continuation of the Apex project. The initially formulated concepts and ideas were integrated into a larger comprehensive framework. Interim Report No. 3 finally discloses the shape of the new governmental structure designed and proposed by COGP. Premier Davis and his cabinet approved the recommendations in December 1971. All these reforms can be most usefully examined under three descriptive headings:

1. the transformation of the provincial cabinet into a cabinet committee system;
2. the transformation of the relatively autonomous, vertical departments into a semi-horizontal, policy field structure of ministries;
3. the transformation of informal, uncoordinated and frequently highly personal activities leading to policy decisions into a formal policy process.

The history and tradition of cabinet government in Ontario has been admirably dealt with by F. F. Schindeler in his study, *Responsible Government in Ontario*. For our purposes, it is important to stress that no one had designed cabinet or engineered its existence in accordance with some prior plan or conception of what the political executive ought to be. Rather, practical arrangements adopted by political men at the apex of power and followed by their competitors and successors have evolved into this authoritative political institution. It is thus strictly a creature of constitutional practice and convention. The internal cohesion of cabinet is maintained by the collegiality and solidarity of its members sworn to secrecy. The highest constitutional objective of cabinet is to assure continued, stable government within the conventional strictures of responsibility and accountability. Because cabinet government has grown out of political experience rather than conceptual design, it reflects admirably the fundamental belief of constitutionalism that means are more important than ends, and that only the latter may be compromised.

The present Ontario cabinet numbers twenty-four men and one woman who possess varied educational, intellectual, professional and business backgrounds. They hold the most politically demanding and responsible jobs in the province. Their collective and individual decisions significantly affect the lives of all those who reside in Ontario, and they are not without consequence for everyone else in Canada. To a large extent, they owe their fortunes to one

man: the Premier. As the leader of the electorally successful political party, he alone selected them and gave them
their jobs which carry the attributes of political power,
prestige, and a place in Ontario's history. Traditionally,
members of cabinet form a privileged inner circle protected by constitutional convention and the rules of secrecy
and solidarity. In theory, they alone are competent to
formulate governmental policies for Ontario. The Cronyn
Committee recommended the transformation of cabinet
into a cabinet committee system designed to handle more
effectively the task of policy-making along clearly defined
functional lines. The system which was introduced consists
of two senior committees (the Policy and Priorities Board
and the Management Board), three policy field committees,
a coordinating committee, and a legislation committee.[7]

The Policy and Priorities Board of cabinet was established by statute. Its formally designated duties include the
determination of long-term and short-term governmental
objectives in social and economic policy, the determination
of budgetary, fiscal and tax policies and priorities in expenditures, the conduct of intergovernmental relations,
and the consideration of policy recommendations submitted by policy field committees. The board is chaired by the
Premier and it occupies the top spot in the hierarchy of
cabinet committees. In addition to the Premier, its membership is composed of the Treasurer of Ontario and the
Minister of Economics and Intergovernmental Affairs; the
chairman of the Management Board, three policy field
ministers (Provincial Secretaries); and last but certainly
not least, Mr. Darcy McKeough, the Minister of Energy.
Robert Welch described the meetings and the work of the
Policy and Priorities Board as follows:

> Its agenda to a large extent is dictated by the matters
> which have come up through the system. The Minister of
> Health, for instance, decides that there is a need for inte-
> gration of all of the health delivery systems with a decen-
> tralized focus at the local level, and so he feels that we
> should have district health councils. This proposal coming
> from the Minister of Health would go before the Social
> Development policy field committee, at which time its

7 See Appendix I on pp. 130–31 entitled "The Cabinet Committee Organization and Membership as of July 1974."

policy implications would be discussed in some detail. The policy field committee would come to some decision and would send its recommendation to the Policy and Priorities Board. Financial implications with respect to this proposal would find their way to the Management Board. The Board would examine how it fits into the present budget structure. The Policy and Priorities Board would look at this proposal from the standpoint of general policy. One couldn't talk about decentralization in the delivery of health services without taking into account the whole question of the place of special purpose bodies in so far as they relate to local governments. Obviously the Treasurer and Minister of Intergovernmental Affairs would have something to say about that. The interesting thing about this process is the fact that over two thirds of the cabinet would have got a crack at that particular issue before it got to the cabinet table; and that's awfully important to keep in mind when one thinks in terms of the functioning of the cabinet. However, there are exceptions, and in some instances matters can go directly to the Policy and Priorities Board. For example, the Comay Housing Report was sent straight to the Policy and Priorities Board. Also, proposals originating from Treasury, Economics and Intergovernmental Affairs don't go through a policy field first; so in effect, Policy and Priorities Board is their policy field.[8]

The Management Board of cabinet was also established by a special statute. It is chaired by a cabinet minister with no other responsibilities. Its duties include the coordination of existing programs, the control of expenditures, the management of the public service, and the analyses of effectiveness and efficiency of existing and proposed programs.

The term "management" of course carries with it the responsibilities of managing the allocation of the resources; but keep in mind the quantum has been determ-

8 This text consists of edited selections from an interview with Robert Welch taped on September 14, 1973. Mr. Welch, currently Minister of Culture and Recreation, held at the time of the interview the portfolio of the Provincial Secretary for Social Development. I would like to thank him for expressing his views to me so frankly and allowing me to publish them.

ined before Management Board gets at it. In other words, decisions taken by the Policy and Priorities Board and confirmed by cabinet determine what the financial guidelines will be. We have what is called a multi-year planning process, whereby my policy field is allocated a gross amount for the needs of all the ministries in the field for a period of three fiscal years. Then the gross amount is broken down into the separate budgets of individual ministries. Those determinations are not made by Management Board. Management Board then takes a look at a ministry's budget and comes to a conclusion that, say, for the delivery of that particular program you really don't need 206 public servants, you can do it more efficiently with 183. To that extent the Management Board is engaged in a management function. But, I think the Board will have to get into a little more cost-effectiveness work in the future. You see, then, that we don't go to the Management Board pleading for our budgets, but we do have to satisfy them later that it requires that much money to function.[9]

Each policy field committee (Social Development, Justice, Resources Development) is chaired by a Provincial Secretary. The coordinating committee constitutes, in effect, a fourth policy field; it includes ministries whose responsibilities are related to the activities of the Ministry of Treasury, Economics and Intergovernmental Affairs (TEIGA), whose minister chairs the coordinating committee.

Finally the committee on legislation develops the government's legislative strategy and is generally responsible for the introduction and piloting of government bills in the Legislative Assembly of Ontario.

Each cabinet committee is supported by a secretariat. The policy field secretariats are still relatively small; the TEIGA secretariat is by far the largest and most influential. The Premier's office and the cabinet office provide support to the Policy and Priorities Board. The Management Board is developing its own secretariat which is rapidly expanding.

The new ministry organization as originally conceived was based on the concept of a policy minister. There were to be three policy ministers officially called Provincial

9 Ibid.

Secretaries. The choice of this unglamorous title was clearly unfortunate and it may have sealed the fate of the idea developed and nourished by COGP. In one of its early reports COGP called policy ministers "a key element in our proposed policy-making system."

As members of the Policy and Priorities Board of Cabinet, Policy Ministers would assume a leadership role in initiating, developing, assessing and modifying new policies and programs. It would also be part of their function to attempt to anticipate emerging issues within their policy field. Policy Ministers would announce major new policy proposals for their policy fields and would answer questions in the Legislature relating to these proposals. . . . The second major aspect of a Policy Minister's role affects his relationship with the general public. Once freed from the administrative responsibilities of a portfolio, a Policy Minister would be in a position to devote considerably more time and thought to achieving improvements in the linkages between government and citizens.[10]

In contrast to the express intention of COGP that each Provincial Secretary should be responsible before the Legislature for new policy proposals, Mr. Welch assessed his role as follows:

There's no doubt that this is creating a great deal of problems for the members of the Legislature. We're talking now of course about the accountability to the Legislature and the right of a member to get an answer with respect to certain matters. I would think that the present system is such that there are really very few questions that can be directed to a policy minister. He is obviously accountable for the budget of the secretariat which is his support staff. So, at the time he asks the Legislature to vote him so much money for the operation of his office (that is, his own salary and the salaries and supplies of the small secretariat), he should be expected to answer all of the questions that are relevant to the appropriation. But some members try to simplify their approach to the new structure by saying, "I guess any questions which have to do with policy, I'll ask the policy minister; and any questions with respect

10 COGP Report No. 3, p. 16.

to the day-to-day operations of a ministry, I'll ask the operating minister." Such an approach ignores the fact that to try to find out what I may be presiding over at any particular time is really trying to find out what's on the cabinet agenda—which is, as you know, privileged information until the government reveals the decision. So, all I'm pointing out is that, when you really go into it, there's very little you can ask a policy minister.[11]

Early in 1972, Allan Lawrence, Bert Lawrence and Robert Welch, all former contenders for the leadership of the Ontario Progressive Conservative party, were named Provincial Secretaries for Justice, Resources Development and Social Development, respectively. They were given no operating responsibilities, and their formal duties were not spelled out in legislation but simply adopted as a matter of executive practice. Unlike all their cabinet colleagues (with the exception of the ministers without portfolio), the Provincial Secretaries have no fixed, statutory authority and the scope of their responsibilities depends entirely on what the Premier may from time to time determine. Clearly, this does not give the policy ministers the kind of status and position which the COGP had envisaged for them. Their inability to answer questions in the Legislature on matters of policy within their own fields further decreases their political weight and importance. Thus, COGP's desire to create ministers who would be leaders in their respective policy fields failed to take into account the principle of equality of all cabinet ministers and the principle of individual ministerial responsibility before the Legislature for the operations of their departments.

In February 1974 Premier Davis announced a major cabinet shuffle. He appointed Margaret Birch Provincial Secretary for Social Development and Allan Grossman Provincial Secretary for Resources Development. However, a third Provincial Secretary, Robert Welch, became Attorney General at the same time as Provincial Secretary for Justice, thus openly challenging one of the fundamental principles advocated by COGP—that policy field ministers must not hold operating portfolios. The *Globe and Mail* in a front page article commented as follows:

11 Welch, *op. cit.*

Yesterday's move also makes it very clear that Mr. Davis has decided to downgrade the policy secretaryships established just two years ago. The people holding these posts have no departments to run, but rather coordinate policies in their fields and supposedly spend their time thinking of the big picture. However, the Tory stars initially given the posts found that they had been handed fast tickets to political limbo. It was the operating ministers who got the headlines and credits, while the ironically named superministers went almost unnoticed. Both privately and publicly they spoke of their unhappiness. Mr. Davis has made it clear that the posts are henceforth of only middling importance.[12]

Unwilling to tarnish the purity of its new management style and the intellectual elegance of its conceptual/prescriptive approach to governmental reform, COGP clearly ignored the reality of political self-interest as a powerful motivating factor in ministerial behaviour. Policy-making is not a one-dimensional activity. The actors who participate in it do not subscribe to a single, uniform idea of public good; rather, they pursue diverse and often conflicting conceptions of socio-economic objectives. In addition, and with varying degrees of perserverance and success, they act to maintain and enhance their own positions of influence, prestige and power in the face of an ongoing competition and rivalry.

A provincial cabinet minister, for example, may want to develop and maintain his own political following. He must, therefore, be able to secure benefits for his clients and supporters, and must attempt to prevent criticism, embarrassment or failure which might destroy his image in the eyes of his followers. To the extent that his pursuit of self-interest coincides with the interests of his colleagues, he may join with them to achieve a tactical advantage. Such temporary coalitions, however, may cross the artificial boundaries of the policy fields and inject an unanticipated amount of disturbance into the carefully designed formal relationships of ministers and officials. It is thus apparent that the remaining uncertainty and ambiguity about the role of the policy minister can be directly ascribed to

12 *Globe and Mail*, February 27, 1974.

COGP's neglect of the political variables which impinge upon the behaviour of ministers and officials.[13]

The second major fallacy committed by the Cronyn Committee was the assumption that the so-called "inputs" into the policy process originate exclusively from within the governmental sector. The logical, sequential steps in the formal policy process designed by COGP exclude any reference to the role of organized, private interests which exert their influence on governmental decision makers. Robert Presthus' recent study, *Elite Accommodation In Canadian Politics*, demonstrates the strength of the symbiotic relationship between the functionally defined departments and agencies and the specialized interest groups in Canada and in Ontario. A formal, comprehensive process of policy and program formulation, such as was developed by COGP, permits private interests to establish points of entry and access at different stages of the flow and to adjust the strategy of pressure to the particular conditions prevailing at each stage. Thus, although the opportunities and requirements for successful external inputs (more commonly known as lobbying) may differ, for example, from the Management Board Secretariat or TEIGA's office of intergovernmental affairs to a policy field cabinet committee, the size and complexity of the new system increase the number of possible entry points through which effective pressure can be applied. These advantages are not likely to remain unrecognized by interest group directors and representatives.

The new formal policy process at Queen's Park may be viewed as a set of nine sequential steps. The duration of each sequence may vary greatly depending on the particular circumstances. Moreover, some steps may be omitted or

13 See Appendix II on pp. 131–32 entitled "The Ministry Organization as of July 1974." In political terms, the distinction between policy ministers and operating ministers is not very meaningful. For example, the Minister of Energy undoubtedly exerts more influence on policy formulation than the Provincial Secretary for Resources Development. However, the three Provincial Secretaries, the Treasurer and Minister of Economics and Intergovernmental Affairs, and the Chairman of the Management Board share in common much broader and more pervasive responsibilities within their respective areas of policy-making. But political effectiveness and influence do not always coincide with formal responsibility.

postponed; and in general no one should be deluded into a belief that real-life decision-making is as neat, logical and rational as it can be represented on paper.

First stage: policy development or initiation. In this function the problem or issue to be dealt with must be identified, it must be related to the priorities and guidelines established by the Policy and Priorities Board of cabinet, and it must be channelled through one of the three policy fields (Justice, Social Development, Resources Development) or TEIGA (which is primarily concerned with economic policy, intergovernmental affairs, fiscal and tax policy, and urban and regional affairs). Normally, a policy development unit in an operating ministry or in TEIGA secretariat will initiate a policy and put it on course.

Second stage: study and report. This stage may consume very little or a great deal of time depending on the scope and depth of the study. The unit conducting it may be an intra- or an inter-ministry committee, a special task force, or a royal commission. However, the problem or issue must be examined comprehensively (within its defined scope and depth) and in relation to the existing policies and programs which may impinge upon it. The report when completed will be referred to the appropriate policy field committee, and in addition to the TEIGA secretariat and to the Management Board secretariat.

Third stage: examination of the economic, fiscal and intergovernmental consequences that the proposed policy or program is likely to produce. This assessment will be carried out by a specific unit of the TEIGA secretariat. It must include the probable impact of the proposed policy on the political relations between Ontario, Quebec, the other provinces and Ottawa, and in particular on the federal-provincial fiscal arrangements. The conclusions reached by TEIGA are reported to the Policy and Priorities Board.

Fourth stage: examination and estimate of the necessary resources which will have to be allocated if the proposed policy is approved and implemented. These will normally include a budget, sufficient executive and professional manpower, creation of a new organizational unit, and specialized knowledge required for the ongoing successful administration of the program. The budgetary estimate must be projected at least three years into the future under the multi-year planning process adopted by the Ontario government. The necessary resource calculations will be done by the Management Board secretariat and the final recommendations of the board will be reported to the Policy and Priorities Board.

Fifth stage: substantive examination of the proposed policy within the terms of reference and priority perspective of the appropriate policy field committee. It is the committee's responsibility to accept or reject the proposed policy or program and to make a recommendation accordingly to the Policy and Priorities Board. The aim at this stage is to examine the proposal in the context of the policy field requirements and priorities as they are seen by the participating operational ministers.

Sixth stage: strategic examination and final approval. This function belongs exclusively to the Policy and Priorities Board which takes into account all three preceding assessments: the economic-fiscal-intergovernmental focus, the resource allocation focus, and the substantive policy field focus. If the proposed policy is approved, the board issues implementing instructions to the Management Board to allocate the needed resources, and instructions to the designated operating ministry for the administration and implementation of the program.

Seventh stage: formal confirmation by full cabinet. The main purpose at this stage is to reaffirm the principle that all members of cabinet are collectively responsible for the new policy. The exhaustive nature of earlier deliberations makes any further discussion at this level unlikely, except in highly contentious matters where political conflict was not resolved earlier.

Eighth stage: policy and program evaluation. The Management Board is authorized to conduct studies intended to measure the performance and success of existing policies and programs. This task, although generally regarded as essential for comprehensive and systematic policy-making, is plagued with immense conceptual and political difficulties. The results of such studies will be reported to the Policy and Priorities Board of cabinet for discussion and action.

Ninth stage: termination of ineffective, unnecessary, dysfunctional or outdated policies and programs. Because of the highly contentious nature of this task, decisions to terminate major programs, if at all politically feasible, may have to be taken by full cabinet.

It is most important to keep in mind that decision-making at each of the nine stages occurs in the atmosphere of more or less intense struggle among the competing interests and claims represented by the participating actors. The new management style and the organizational reforms introduced by COGP have not removed politics from policy-making. What then has been accomplished?

It is still too early for a firm, comprehensive assessment, but some tentative conclusions are in order. At the beginning of this essay I have suggested that the COGP-inspired reforms fall under three headings: 1. the transformation of the provincial cabinet into a cabinet committee system; 2. the transformation of the relatively autonomous departments into an integrated policy field structure of ministries; and 3. the transformation of the informal, uncoordinated activities leading to policy decisions into a formal, systematic and comprehensive policy process.

Full cabinet no longer serves as the principal decision-making unit in either Britain or at the federal level in Ottawa. To this extent, Ontario has simply followed the lead of other governments which have recognized that the tradition of cabinet collegiality cannot be a bar to increased functional specialization. Cabinet committees are more effective decision-making units precisely because their terms of reference are narrower and more specifically defined, and because they follow routinized procedures. Greater decisional effectiveness cannot be achieved without a price: ministerial relationships characterized by collegiality and transactional ties are likely to change into a pattern resembling bureaucracy.

Autonomy of bureaucratic institutions cannot be broken easily. Grouping of several ministries into a policy field may produce some integrative results, provided the policy field secretariat becomes sufficiently influential so that its co-ordination role is fully accepted by each ministry. In my view, none of the three policy field secretariats (Justice, Resources Development, Social Development) has reached that degree of influence and legitimacy. Moreover, the political status of each Provincial Secretary (except the present Secretary for Justice who is also Attorney General) remains wrapped in ambiguity. There is little evidence that the new ministries perceive their roles differently from the old departments.

The policy process has become longer, more demanding, more technical, and more expensive. A greater number of individuals, both elected and appointed, are routinely engaged in the examination of policy issues and problems which concern the government of Ontario. At the same time, the competition inside the provincial executive/ bureaucratic establishment waged over highly valued and scarce resources (strategic knowledge, highly skilled and specialized manpower, latest organizational models, and budgets) is becoming more intense. Ontario's political and technical capability to bargain with Ottawa and with the other provinces for increasingly scarce natural resources has been greatly improved, and correspondingly the provincial government's readiness for compromise and accommodation has diminished. Only time can tell whether these conclusions will be ultimately borne out by the events.

APPENDIX I

*The Cabinet Committee Organization
and Membership as of July 1974*

STRUCTURE	MEMBERSHIP
Full cabinet	Premier, twenty-five cabinet ministers and the Progressive Conservative party whip (Kennedy)
Policy and Priorities Board	Davis (chairman) Birch Grossman McKeough Welch White Winkler
Management Board	Winkler (chairman) Auld Birch Grossman Irvine Potter Snow
Social Development Policy Field Committee	Birch (chairman) Auld (Colleges and Universities) Brunelle (Community and Social Services) Millar (Health) Timbrell (Youth) Wells (Education)

STRUCTURE	MEMBERSHIP
Justice Policy Field Committee	Welch (chairman and Attorney General) Clement (Consumer and Commercial Relations) Kerr (Solicitor General) Potter (Correctional Services)
Resources Development Policy Field Committee	Grossman (chairman) Bennett (Industry and Tourism) Bernier (Natural Resources) MacBeth (Labour) McKeough (Energy) Newman (Environment) Rhodes (Transportation and Communications) Stewart (Agriculture and Food)
Coordinating Committee	White (chairman) Handleman (Housing) Irvine (Municipal Affairs) Kennedy (PC party whip) Meen (Revenue) Snow (Government Services) Winkler (chairman of the Management Board)
Committee on Legislation	Clement (chairman) Auld Kerr MacBeth Meen Snow Winkler

Note: Minister without portfolio, Jack McNie, is not a member of any committee.

SOURCE: Teachers' Guide to the 4th Session of the 29th Parliament of Ontario, published by the Education Action Committee, OTF.

APPENDIX II

The Ministry Organization as of July 1974

Premier	Cabinet office Premier's office Political office
POLICY MINISTERS	
Chairman of the Management Board	Management Board secretariat
Treasurer of Ontario and Minister of Economics and Intergovernmental Affairs	TEIGA secretariat
Provincial Secretary for Justice	Justice Field secretariat
Provincial Secretary for Resources Development	Resources Development Field secretariat
Provincial Secretary for Social Development	Social Development Field secretariat

OPERATING MINISTRIES

Justice	Resource Development	Social Development	TEIGA
Attorney General	Agriculture and	Colleges and	Government
Consumer and	Food	Universities	Services
Commercial	Energy	Community and	Housing
Relations	Environment	Social	Municipal
Correctional	Industry and	Services	Affairs[1]
Services	Tourism	Education	Revenue
Solicitor General	Labour	Health	
	Natural	Youth[1]	
	Resources		
	Transportation		
	and Com-		
	munications		

1 These responsibilities are assigned to ministers without portfolio.

SOURCES: Reports of the Committee on Government Productivity; Teachers' Guide to the 4th Session of the 29th Parliament of Ontario published by the Education Action Committee, OTF.

SELECTED BIBLIOGRAPHY

BAILEY, F. G. *Stratagems and Spoils.* Oxford: Basil Blackwell, 1970

CROSSMAN, RICHARD H. S. *The Myths of Cabinet Government.* Cambridge, Mass.: Harvard University Press, 1972

DOERN, BRUCE. "Horizontal and Vertical Portfolios in Government," in G. B. Doern and V. S. Wilson, eds., *Issues in Canadian Public Policy.* Toronto: Macmillan of Canada, 1974

FLECK, JAMES D. "Restructuring the Ontario Government." *CPA,* vol. 16 (Spring 1973), p. 55

HOCKIN, T. A. *Apex of Power.* Toronto: Prentice-Hall, 1971

JOHNSON, A. W. "Management Theory and Cabinet Government." *CPA,* vol. 14 (Spring 1971), p. 73

KEELING, DESMOND. *Management in Government.* London: Allen and Unwin, 1972

KERNAGHAN, KENNETH. "Responsible Public Bureaucracy: A Rationale and a Framework for Analysis." *CPA,* vol. 16 (Winter 1973), p. 572

MALLORY, J. R. "Cabinet Government in the Provinces of Canada." 3 *McGill Law Journal* (1957), p. 195

———. "Restructuring the Ontario Government—A Comment." *CPA,* vol. 16 (Spring 1973), p. 69

MCKEOUGH, DARCY. "The Relations of Ministers and Civil Servants." *CPA*, vol. 12 (Spring 1969), p. 2

MOSHER, F. C. *Government Reorganization.* New York: Bobbs-Merrill, 1967

ROWAN, M. "A Conceptual Framework for Government Policy-Making." *CPA*, vol. 13 (1970), p. 277

SZABLOWSKI, G. J. "The Optimal Policy-Making System: Implications for the Canadian Political Process," in T. A. Hockin, ed., *Apex of Power.* Toronto: Prentice-Hall, 1971, p. 135

————. "The Public Bureaucracy and the Possibility of Citizen Involvement in the Government of Ontario." Working paper prepared for the Committee on Government Productivity. Toronto: Queen's Printer, 1972

————. "The Prime Minister as Symbol—A Rejoinder." *CJPS*, vol. 6 (September 1973), p. 519

THAYER, FREDERICK C. "Regional Administration: the failure of traditional theory in the United States and Canada." *CPA*, vol. 15 (Fall 1972), p. 449

WALKER, PATRICK GORDON. *The Cabinet.* London: Jonathan Cape, 1970

WILDAVSKY, A. "If Planning is everything, maybe it's nothing." *Policy Sciences*, vol. 4 (1973), p. 127

Committee on Government Productivity: Reports No. 2 (March 1971), No. 3 (December 1971), No. 9 (March 1973), No. 10 (March 1973). Toronto, Queen's Printer

The Institute of Public Administration of Canada (Toronto Regional Group). *People and Government.* Papers presented at a symposium on February 11, 1972. Toronto, Ontario

9
PETER SILCOX

The ABC's of Ontario: Provincial Agencies, Boards and Commissions

THE BUREAUCRATIC structure of any government is shaped by its political philosophy, its understanding of administrative theory and the practical political problems it has faced. The prevailing political philosophy of Ontario governments has been to stress the importance of free enterprise and to view governmental expansion with great suspicion. Despite the interventionist activities of successive Ontario governments, particularly in the postwar period, the conventional wisdom of the politicians has been that an enlarged centralized bureaucracy poses a threat to individual freedom, is likely to perform with less than desired efficiency and is rarely capable of undertaking a creative role in society. The political philosophy and the actual conduct of the politicians are sharply at variance. However, the philosophy cannot simply be dismissed as empty rhetoric for it has had a substantial effect on the choice of administrative structures to manage newly acquired and expanded functions.

Administrative theory has long been concerned with the need to promote flexibility and accommodate expert and specialist input in the structure of large-scale organizations. The decentralization of power and the recognition of the need for some variety in the forms of organization have been powerful elements in administrative theory, often in conflict with the values of coordination and the need for clear lines of public responsibility for all administrative activities.

The expansion of government activities in Ontario has brought the provincial government in contact and often into conflict with well-organized interest groups. While on many occasions these groups have had to give ground by accepting government involvement in activities of concern to them, the provincial government has sought to accommodate their preferences and prejudices, in an obvious attempt to minimize their hostility. In many cases the government realizes that certain functions can only be adequately fulfilled with the active advice and participation of such groups.

It must be remembered that the creation of administrative structures is a political activity. Just as in policy-making governments seek to satisfy the desires of most of the electorate most of the time, so a similar aim guides the politician in shaping the administrative structures he creates. As the Ontario government has assumed new responsibilities it has assigned many tasks to an expanded range of traditional departments. But the influence of political philosophy, the imperatives of administrative theory and the practical question of maintaining political support for the government have led to the assignment of many new functions to a variety of agencies, boards and commissions. Although the numbers of these have grown rapidly in the postwar period, the forms themselves are very old. Such organizations are public bodies and part of the provincial administration; they exercise executive functions but stand outside the traditional departmental structure. In theory such bodies have a clearly defined role and relationship to the provincial administration; in practice this conventional theory hides great complexity and confusion.

The provincial semi-independent agency, the term I shall use for agencies, boards and commissions, has a long history in Ontario, as it has at local and federal levels. It was the form of organization used to reclaim from the forces of crass commercialism one of the province's most beautiful natural features with the creation of the Niagara Parks Commission in 1887. A major project for northern development, the construction of a provincial railway, was given to the Temiskaming and Northern Ontario Railway Commission, predecessor of the present Ontario Northland Transportation Commission, in 1902. The Ontario Hydro-Electric Commission was established, following a Commission of Inquiry, in 1906. A lengthy inquiry by Chief Justice Meredith also preceded the formation of the Workmen's Compensation Board in 1915.

The continuing appeal of this form of organization can be seen in its use by the United Farmers' government at the end of the First World War. That government was based on a movement which developed as a reaction against bureaucracy and the partisan political system. Not surprisingly, it sought to establish public bodies insulated from political pressures. The criticism of that approach, voiced at the time by such traditional party figures as the Conservative leader Howard Ferguson, has often been echoed in more recent times by politicians unhappy at the fragmentation of the provincial administration. During the Great Depression the semi-independent agency had a renaissance. The financial collapse of a number of municipalities led to the establishment of the Ontario Municipal Board in its present form, charged with the financial supervision of Ontario municipalities. The Depression also led to the collapse of the securities industry and brought to light a variety of scandals. The Ontario Securities Commission was created to regulate the industry in an attempt to restore public confidence in it. The first provincial marketing boards were also established in this period to impose some order on the chaotic state into which the marketing of agricultural products had fallen during the economic collapse. It should, therefore, come as no surprise that since the rapid growth of the provincial administration in the early nineteen fifties agencies, boards and commissions proliferated at an alarming rate. This rapid growth aroused controversy which concentrated mainly on two questions: the procedures used by such bodies in examining individual cases, and, to a lesser extent, the difficulty of defining political responsibility for their operations. Premier Frost established a Committee on the Organization of Government in Ontario headed by Walter L. Gordon. The resulting report (1959) placed major emphasis on the legal form of such agencies and failed to relate their operations to the political and administrative structure in which they operated. Its recommendations largely concerned the question of the separation of quasi-judicial functions from investigative and administrative ones and the assumption of the latter by government departments. The report threw little light on the actual performance of government agencies; it contented itself with classifying them according to criteria, type of functions performed and apparent formal political responsibility, which did little to increase the understanding of their operations. The report almost completely ignored the major questions of public policy involved in the fragmentation of the administrative structure, the problems of coordination of government activities, the responsiveness of such agencies to public opinion and the dangers to the larger public interest inherent in a system where special agencies were deeply involved with powerful pressure groups.

The relationship between the individual citizen and the semi-independent agency continued to be the main focus of interest among those concerned with the latter's growth in numbers. This was the natural outcome of a situation in which scrutiny of a cross-section of these bodies was left largely in the hands of lawyers. The McRuer Royal Commission of Inquiry into Civil Rights paid particular attention to semi-independent agencies in the first volume of its report (1968). The passage of the Statutory Powers Act three years after the report's publication was a comprehensive response to these long-time concerns. The scheme laid down in that Act sets out in very substantial detail a series of procedural safeguards for the private citizen in his dealings with semi-independent agencies.

The rapid expansion of government programs in Ontario in the nineteen sixties absorbed the energy of both politicians and civil servants. As a consequence there was an enormous growth in the size of the provincial civil service; a budget, elements of which appeared to be out of control; and an administrative structure developed in an ad hoc manner in response to immediate political circumstances. In 1970 the provincial government created the Ontario Committee on Government Productivity (COGP) to review the structure of the administration. In the changes it proposed to the provincial government the committee emphasized that its attitude to the semi-independent agency was essentially skeptical. It was concerned with the fragmentation of authority and the lack of policy control exercised by the provincial cabinet over the work of such agencies. While the committee recognized that a case could be made for the continued existence of certain semi-independent agencies, it proposed that a regular review of such bodies should be undertaken to ensure that this form was the most appropriate one in each particular circumstance. It stressed the need for the political executive to retain a firmer grip of the policies under which agencies function and for the improvement of mechanisms to coordinate the agencies' activities with the work of government departments. The committee proposed a system of classifying agencies by reference to the nature of the main function they performed. In the interests of clarity in describing their work it proposed a change in the names of boards, commissions and agencies which would have the effect of clearly labelling and distinguishing between the various groups. The major change suggested, and shortly implemented, to improve coordination between such bodies and departments was the creation of ministries. Each ministry would consist of a department and associated boards, commissions and agencies under centralized political and administrative control.

Ironically, the special task force of the committee assigned to deal with Ontario Hydro made proposals, later put into effect, which moved in the opposite direction from these recommendations. A clearer formal separation between this, the most important of provincial semi-independent agencies, and the rest of the provincial administration was to be achieved by establishing Ontario Hydro as a public corporation. The practical consequences of such a change are open to question, but it seems odd that in a period when closer coordination and unity in government policy is stressed the largest operating agency in the energy field should be more completely separated from the rest of the provincial administration concerned with energy questions.

The opposite direction was taken a short period before this with the integration of two important semi-independent commissions into their associated departments. The Ontario Water Resources Commission had been established in 1956 to work with municipalities in improving and enlarging their water systems and in developing sewage collection and treatment. The commission had had a great deal of success in accomplishing both these tasks but by the early nineteen seventies it was clear that the separate existence of the commission stood in the way of a more comprehensive and coordinated attack on pollution and the threat to the environment that it posed. The commission was abolished in 1972 and its functions assumed by the new Ministry of the Environment. The Ontario Hospital Services Commission had also been created in 1956 to set up and manage the new government hospitalization scheme. By the mid nineteen sixties, with the scheme well established, the need for its separate existence came into question. What is more, as the range of government activities in the medical services field expanded the need for closer coordination became clear. The abolition of the commission and the assumption of its functions by the Ministry of Health in 1972 was very much in line with the thinking of the Committee on Government Productivity. The effect of the work of this latter body seems to have been to call into question the wisdom of further proliferation of boards, commissions and agencies and to promote a movement for the consolidation of government activities. ⁃ Semi-independent agencies are set up by provincial statutes which provide for the creation of a directing board, detail its powers, and prescribe the manner in which it is to be related to other parts of the provincial administration and by which it is to render public account of its activities. The internal organization of the agency is rarely touched on in any detail in the legislation; such matters are a primary concern of the board. The board itself is a collective executive and, in theory at least, it is to be made up of those with a special understanding or competence in the field of the agency's operations. The general parameters within which the agency is to be operated are to be set out in policy directives established by the provincial government.

It is clearly necessary for provincial government agencies not to do things which would conflict with policies of the elected political executive acting on behalf of the people of the province. There is to be a clear separation between the general policy under which the agency is to operate and the direction of its day-to-day activities. While the former is the responsibility of the provincial cabinet, the latter is the exclusive preserve of the directing board of the agency. Responsibility to the public for the semi-independent agency's operations is likewise divided. While the minister of the crown attached to the agency answers on behalf of cabinet for the overall policy guiding the agency's work, he merely reports to the Legislature on its day-to-day operations. Final responsibility for these rests with the directing board who themselves hold the position of public trustees and interpreters of the public interest in relation to matters within their control. This is an absolutely vital element in the conventional theory. Unless the directing board has significant areas in which it is independent and is effectively insulated from covert or overt political pressure, then the raison d'être for a semi-independent board disappears. If the agency is a tool, or potentially a tool, of the present political executive there is no reason why the agency should not be simply a part of the departmental structure. This vital distinction was recognized in the Gordon report in which semi-independent agencies were identified as ministerial agencies and distinguished from a large class of departmental agencies. The latter were simply a collection of, in effect, branches of government departments which for greater administrative convenience had been given a somewhat different form from that of the ordinary departmental branch. Examples of departmental agencies were the Ontario Telephone Authority, Public Trustee, and the Industry and Labour Board. These were contrasted with such ministerial agencies as the Ontario Food Terminal Board, the Ontario Research Foundation, and the Board of Censors.

The conventional theory of the semi-independent agency clearly requires of both the minister concerned and the directing board some sophistication in managing their relationship. The minister is required to exercise restraint in his dealings with the agency. He must confine himself to general policy direction and respect the independence of the board in exercising its discretion. The board must insist on its right to exercise its discretionary power and must be prepared to face public scrutiny and criticism. It can perhaps best protect its own independence by being responsive to the general public and in particular to the organized groups with which it has to deal.

It is, of course, possible to promote the situation described above by shaping the legislation establishing an agency to provide at least formal protection of its independence. Such devices as protected long-term tenure for board members, the precise delineation of the matters to be classed as public policy, the publication of explicit public policy guidelines and a large measure of financial freedom for the board, would serve this end.

The central element of the theory is a distinction between general policy and the management of day-to-day affairs. In practice such a distinction is hard to recognize, particularly in a situation where decisions taken by a board may have political consequences of real significance for the government in power. In Ontario the line between matters of public policy and matters of day-to-day management is certainly not drawn with any precision. In a large number of cases it is extremely difficult to find any comprehensive statement of policy guidelines for any particular agency. Far more typical is a situation in which the Act creating the agency contains a rather vague statement guiding the board in the exercise of its powers, the interpretation of which is left to the board in making concrete decisions. Thus the Ontario Highway Transport Board has the power to issue certificates of "public necessity and convenience" which allow commercial truckers to operate a service between two centres of the province. The criteria for judging when a situation of "public necessity and convenience" exists are established in practice by the board and are implicit in its records of decisions in individual cases. Among a large array of powers, the Ontario Municipal Board has the authority to consider bylaws governing the borrowing of funds by local municipalities and also to consider zoning bylaws passed by municipal councils. One can search long and hard for any explicit statement by the provincial government on the criteria which the board should use in establishing the acceptability of such bylaws.

On the other hand it is quite possible for the government to decide that quite minor questions before a board are matters of public policy and to set out a specific policy on the matter concerned. One example of this is the decision to introduce night racing in Ontario in 1960. This matter, which is surely one of minor significance in the overall regulation of the industry over which the Ontario Racing Commission has very wide-ranging regulatory authority, became a subject of political controversy. The Minister of Agriculture responded by making a formal statement specifying the circumstances in which night racing would be allowed. This involved an even greater departure from the prescriptions of theory than might be imagined in that the Minister of Agriculture had no formal contact with the commission at all. Presumably his involvement arose from the fact that the pressure groups concerned with the decision were mainly in the agricultural field. In fact the Treasurer of Ontario was at the time the minister responsible for the commission.

Considerable emphasis is laid on the special character and the independence of the directing board of the agency. Yet in the Ontario experience one can find little which is internally consistent in the process of selecting board members. Many members appear to have little in the way of special qualifications, and the practice of appointing civil servants and current members of the government party in Legislature to many boards seems to undermine the model of the non-partisan independent board. Many board members appear to be chosen to represent specific interest groups, but this hardly seems appropriate in bodies whose apparent mandate is to act as guardians of the public interest in regulating the activities of private individuals and organizations. It is, of course, perfectly natural that a government will seek board members from amongst those who are likely to be sympathetic and sensitive to government policy, but this is surely quite different from the selection of members whose sole apparent qualification is adherence to the party in power. One should note here that Ontario practice is not markedly different from that in other jurisdictions and cynics have some grounds for arguing that a major reason for having semi-independent agencies at all is that they provide jobs for the current government's "boys."

The conventional theory has relatively little to say concerning public accountability. The minister is publicly accountable for the appointment of board members, the general policies governing the agencies and for the exercise of any other powers of supervision given to him in the statute establishing the agency. These latter powers usually relate to the approval of regulations made under the statute and such financial matters as the issue of debentures involving a guarantee by the province. The minister is, of course, accountable for his actions to the people through the Legislature. The problem area is that of the board's exclusive discretionary authority. Under the present procedure each agency files an annual report, which is laid before the Legislature and is available to members of the general public who have the patience and tenacity to seek it out. The Legislature may then review this annual report either in the House or in committee. The Legislature also has power to review the work of the agencies when amendments to the enabling statute are proposed and when estimates concerning the agency's budgets are presented.

The capacity of the Legislature to carry out these tasks in any meaningful way has long been open to serious question. In the absence of legislative involvement in the field there exist no other structures to undertake a continuing review of an agency's work or to ensure that the agency is responsive to the general public or even its clientele. The problems encountered in this area are well illustrated by

144 / Peter Silcox

the case of the Ontario Workmen's Compensation Board described earlier in this volume. The Legislature's inability to be an effective watchdog is the result of a number of factors: domination of the House by the party in power; the prior concerns of a relatively small group of opposition members who must devote a large part of their time and energy to political matters of greater political visibility than detailed administrative scrutiny of sometimes relatively obscure specialist agencies; the limitations on time in the House and committees, and the lack of independent research support necessary for such scrutiny. Whenever administrative scrutiny is discussed in this context, suggestions are almost always made for improvement in the Legislature committee system. In the past twenty years the arrangements for committee review of the work of agencies, boards and commissions have been regularly reshuffled in an attempt to increase the quantity and quality of review. The problem is now more clearly understood and the situation is better now than in the past. However, the inherent difficulties are unlikely to be overcome. Legislative committees in Ontario are dominated by government members who can limit the scope of inquiries. The demands made on members are so large that even with far more substantial research assistance than presently exists it seems very unlikely that more careful scrutiny—which, to be effective, must be informed—is possible. Then, too, the restriction of the work to the Legislature and its committees is to force public scrutiny into a narrow channel dominated by parties and considerations of party interest.

Some reference should be made at this point to periodic investigations of the work of semi-independent agencies by legislative committees, task forces, royal commissions and other investigating bodies. Much of our knowledge and understanding of the work of semi-independent agencies is based on the reports of such investigations and the impetus for change and improvement in their work has often been due to such reports. Such inquiries have, however, serious defects. Often they have a limited purpose and mandate; to investigate the process by which Ontario Hydro went about making the arrangements to construct a new building is one recent example. They are normally conducted only when some potential political scandal is in the offing or when the government itself believes that it would benefit from a review of some aspects of an agency's work. This kind of review's limitations are obvious: the investigation may be narowly confined, it is episodic rather than continous and governments are normally in a position to affect the outcome of the review by their ability to set terms of reference and to dictate personnel.

If asked to explain why a particular governmental function is carried out by a semi-independent agency rather than a traditional government department the provincial politician or agency head will defend the decision by reference to the conventional theory we have described. The attractions of the model can best be summed up in one word: flexibility. The politicians and public servants who create and operate semi-independent agencies lay greatest emphasis on what one might describe as the administrative case for flexibility. They argue that certain government functions have a special character which requires a special form of organization.

The entry of government into a new field means that within the provincial civil service few people have either the expertise to manage the new programs or even to anticipate the unique problems likely to occur in launching the program. A new organization created to concentrate its whole attention on the innovation seems appropriate. This type of case was made out when Ontario entered the hospital insurance field in 1956–57. Along with it went arguments based on the need for flexibility and freedom from the normal central control systems in the personnel and financial fields. The recruitment of new specialist and professional staff, some on contracts for short periods, from existing private agencies was more easily managed by a board expert in the field. Then, too, the complexity and uncertainty of the financial arrangements in launching the massive hospitalization scheme simply cried out for flexibility.

A similar argument is often made when the government contemplates the operation of an essentially commercial enterprise; or to be more precise, when it wishes to restrict the commitment to provide a certain service by deciding to operate it on business lines. The distinction made here is an important one. There is nothing inherent in the nature of operating a railway, a bus line or the provision of electric power which requires it to be operated on a market basis.

For the government to adopt market criteria and to provide service on a commercial basis is a specific policy decision. Having taken this decision it can then be reasonably argued that the semi-independent form best enables the government to use the model of the private business corporation to provide the service.

The desire for administrative flexibility is also understandable when a government seeks to provide services or fulfill functions in partnership with other governments or organized groups. In this instance the agency must attempt to accommodate more than one set of aims. In its early years the partnership argument applied to Hydro, created with the support of and participation by municipal bodies. The Hydro model was specifically referred to when the Ontario Water Resources was established in 1956. This organization was to work with municipalities to improve water supply and sewage disposal and treatment systems.

One large group of semi-independent agencies owes its existence to a desire for a different type of flexibility. These agencies are tribunals which make decisions concerning the application of laws to individual cases. Often described as quasi-judicial agencies, their functions are similar to those of the courts. However, their creation represents an attempt to allow for the disposition of cases in a simpler, cheaper and speedier manner by more knowledgeable people than would be possible in the courts. Typically they exercise jurisdiction in areas where there is a greater policy discretion than is normal in the courts. The importance of the maintenance of public confidence in their decisions is, however, of prime importance. This is achieved by imposing a barrier to partisan political influence over their decisions by the deliberate separation of the agency from the direct line of ministerial authority and responsibility. The existence of such bodies as the Ontario Energy Board and the Ontario Labour Relations Board is explained largely on these grounds.

The discussion of these agencies raises the question of political motives for creating semi-independent agencies. With the exception of a case for insulating certain quasi-judicial functions from partisan pressures these are rarely discussed in public by those who create and operate such agencies. On the other hand opposition politicians usually explain the creation of virtually all such bodies largely in partisan political terms. This is scarcely surprising and, given the fact that decisions on the shape of the public administration are first and foremost political ones, such comment is highly relevant in understanding why such bodies are created and are allowed to continue in existence.

The insulation of the performance of a particular government function from partisan political influence can be based on factors other than a desire to create public confidence in its impartiality. The limitation of formal political control may also be a device by which governments can seek to avoid the full political responsibility for the performance of public business. As was pointed out, the decision to carry out a particular function through a body closely resembling a private business corporation may be the result not only of a desire for technical efficiency but also a device by which the government can seek to legitimize the limitation of its commitment to provide financial support for certain services. The Ontario Northland Railway was intended to be a development project for northern Ontario. While its commercial viability has always been open to serious question, the pressure on governments to use it as a development tool has been limited to some extent by the particular form of management given to it.

There are some functions of government which are inherently difficult to deal with from a political point of view. The sale of liquor and the licensing of premises for this purpose are beset with political difficulties. Powerful lobbies have long done battle in this field in Ontario. By assigning the detailed administration of general policies to semi-independent agencies, the Liquor Control Board and the Liquor Licence Board, the provincial government can avoid direct involvement and responsibility in a difficult political field.

The increasing interventionist role of the provincial government brings it into contact with more and better organized interest groups. The political accommodation of such groups is a major means by which parties gain and hold power. Interest groups naturally feel that their concerns are matters of a special importance and wish to have their contacts with government carried on with public servants with particular knowledge and understanding of their interests. In fact they often seek the position of partners with the provincial government in the making both of public policy and of administrative decisions. The creation of a special agency at least formally insulated from direct political control and under the direction of professionals increases the confidence of such groups in the potential sensitivity of government to their special concerns. A further step in developing this relationship is the deliberate ministerial appointment of representatives of the groups to the directing board of the agency. One should also note that included in such special interest groups are local communities.

In discussing the reasons for the choice of the semi-independent form it is of vital importance to take into account the aims of those who created a particular agency. It must, of course, be obvious that a number of the factors mentioned above are considered. There has, however, been a tendency to classify semi-independent agencies in terms of "objective" administrative criteria: to divide agencies into groups by reference to such factors as who audits their accounts, the extent to which they finance their operations from internally generated revenues, and the type of decision-making undertaken by the agency. Such classifications are of interest to certain people who have specific responsibilities for part of government activities but they are of little interest in understanding the political process in Ontario. Take, for example, the question of financing. A number of quasi-judicial agencies which have the greatest independence in actually making decisions are almost entirely dependent on the provincial cabinet as government departments in obtaining funds for their operations.

The attempt to classify agencies by reference to the type of decision-making appears at first glance to make some sense. Yet, as the McRuer Commission discussed at length, in practice it is extremely difficult to clearly distinguish the character of decisions when real cases of decision-making are studied and, even when this is possible, most government bodies can operate efficiently only when they make a number of different type of decisions which may be distinguished analytically but in administrative practice cannot be separated.

The most relevant way to distinguish groups of semi-independent agencies is to pay attention to the purposes for which they were created. In addition attention must be paid to the political balance of forces in the field in which the agency operates. Where the agency operates in concert with other governments or is surrounded by powerful client groups, the freedom of the agency to operate as an independent body is significantly enhanced. Agencies not in one of these two situations are at least potentially in a clearly subordinate position to the provincial cabinet. Some idea of how this approach to classifying agencies can work is illustrated by the following examples. The Niagara Parks Commission and the St. Lawrence Parks Commission both manage elements of a large provincial parks system. While both were heavily involved in large-scale land assembly and construction in their earlier years, which had a major impact on local communities, their task now is of routine management and maintenance of existing park systems. While their significance to the local economy justifies the involvement of local interests in these tasks, neither is now the focus of important local interest groups. As a result they are local subordinate agencies.

In contrast, the Ontario Northland Transportation Commission, despite its long history, is of such significance to the economic and social life of northern Ontario that local interest groups of political significance are still vitally concerned with its activities. It is a local partnership agency created primarily to serve the interests of a particular community. Potentially, it should be in a position to operate with considerable independence.

There are numerous examples of agencies whose form is the result of a desire to create a picture of non-political decision-making—for example, the Ontario Highway Transportation Board, the Ontario Securities Commission, and the Ontario Energy Board. All these operations work in areas where important special interest groups are involved and these have a very substantial interest in the form and operations of the agency. These agencies could be described as quasi-judicial partnership agencies.

The division of agencies into groups by such a scheme of classification as the one proposed here is not simply a sterile academic game. It is a means by which one can identify the function of an agency in the political and administrative structure. It also provides the starting point for any consideration of the way in which the arrangements for the coordination of the work of government can be improved and public responsibility and accountability assured. Any discussion of reforms aimed at a significant improvement in these two fields of major importance must be based on a real understanding of the place of any given agency in both the bureaucratic structure of the provincial administration and also the political life of the province. As the reader will have observed, the variety of boards, commissions and agencies is so great that general discussion of them is extremely difficult. There is a dearth of studies of individual agencies. Only when such work is completed will it be possible to really appreciate their role in the political life of the province. Such detailed work is, of course, also the necessary prelude to continuous and effective scrutiny of these vital elements in the provincial administration. At present there are suspicions that such agencies do not always work in the larger public interest or work closely with other parts of the provincial administration. In the absence of detailed studies either confirmation of or the quieting of such suspicions is impossible.

SELECTED BIBLIOGRAPHY

The sources listed here deal with agencies, boards and commissions in general. For information on specific organizations, students should begin with their annual reports. The reports of select committees, commissions of inquiry and royal commissions are valuable sources of information. The student will find it most useful to contact agencies directly and ask for published material on their work.

Ontario, Committee on the Organization of Government in Ontario (W. L. Gordon, Chairman). *Report.* Toronto, 1959.

Ontario, Royal Commission of Inquiry into Civil Rights (McRuer, Chairman). *Report*, vols. 1–3. Toronto, 1968.

Ontario, Committee on Government Productivity. *Report*, vol. 9. Toronto, 1973.

SCHINDELER, F. F. *Responsible Government in Ontario.* Toronto, 1969.

SILCOX, P. "The Proliferation of Boards and Commissions," in J. T. McLeod and T. Lloyd, eds. *Agenda 1970.* Toronto, 1967.

LIST OF ONTARIO AGENCIES, BOARDS AND COMMISSIONS

Volume nine of the report of the Ontario Committee on Government Productivity contains a very extensive list of special purpose bodies. The list includes a large number of bodies, such as advisory committees, regional municipalities and university boards of governors, which cannot reasonably be regarded as provincial agencies, boards and commissions. I have selected a number of organizations from this list to give some idea of the number and variety of important government agencies. They are listed under the title of the ministry which has nominal responsibility for them.

AGRICULTURE AND FOOD
  Agricultural Research Institute of Ontario
  Crop Insurance Commission
  Farm Products Marketing Board
  Ontario Food Terminal Board
  Milk Commission of Ontario
  Ontario Stock Yards Board

ATTORNEY GENERAL
  Criminal Injuries Compensation Board
  Land Compensation Board
  Ontario Municipal Board

COLLEGES AND UNIVERSITIES
  Archaeological and Historic Sites Board
  Ontario Council for the Arts
  Ontario Educational Communications Authority
  Ontario Heritage Foundation
  Board of Trustees, Centennial Centre of Science and
    Technology

COMMUNITY AND SOCIAL SERVICES
  Athletics Commissioner
  Day Nurseries, Board of Review
  Family Benefits Act, Board of Review
  Soldiers' Aid Commission

CONSUMER AND COMMERCIAL RELATIONS
  Board of Censors
  Commercial Registration Appeal Tribunal
  Liquor Control Board of Ontario
  Liquor Licence Board of Ontario
  Pension Commission of Ontario

Ontario Racing Commission
Ontario Securities Commission

CORRECTIONAL SERVICES
Board of Parole

EDUCATION
Teachers' Superannuation Commission

ENVIRONMENT
Environmental Appeal Board
Environmental Hearing Board
Hydro-Electric Power Commission of Ontario

HEALTH
Alcoholism and Drug Addiction Research Foundation
Ontario Cancer Treatment and Research Foundation
Hospital Appeal Board
Ontario Mental Health Foundation

INDUSTRY AND TOURISM
Northern Ontario Development Corporation
Ontario Development Corporation
Ontario Place Corporation
Ontario Research Foundation
Sheridan Park Corporation

LABOUR
Ontario Human Rights Commission
Ontario Labour Relations Board
Workmen's Compensation Board

NATURAL RESOURCES
Ontario Energy Board
Mining Commissioner
Niagara Parks Commission
St. Lawrence Parks Commission

REVENUE
Ontario Housing Corporation

SOLICITOR GENERAL
Ontario Police Commission

TRANSPORTATION AND COMMUNICATIONS
Ontario Highway Transport Board
Ontario Northland Transportation Commission
Ontario Telephone Service Commission

10
ALLAN O'BRIEN

Father Knows Best:
A Look at the
Provincial-Municipal
Relationship in
Ontario

WHEN the Fathers of Confederation gave the provinces exclusive responsibility for municipal institutions, they provided for a kind of guardianship. In the next hundred years the provinces were both restrictive and neglectful as their "children" struggled for a life of their own. Ontario was no exception.

Ontario law provided for municipalities in the form of cities, towns, villages, rural townships and counties. The counties are upper-tier municipalities carrying out limited functions on behalf of the townships, towns and villages within their boundaries. Northern Ontario does not have counties and most of its vast non-urban areas are not part of any kind of municipality. In 1965 Ontario had 977 municipalities to regulate, support, restrict and confront. These included Metropolitan Toronto, with its two million people, 32 cities, 157 towns, 572 townships with populations averaging 2,500, and 159 villages averaging about 1,000. Townships usually had dimensions of about nine miles one way and twelve the other. Most municipal units were too small to be given much power. They were also too small to cope with industrialization and urbanization, which require regional planning and widespread municipal services.

These historic municipalities had only part of the local government function. Separately elected boards of education, public utilities, and sometimes hospitals were like single-purpose separate governments. Appointed library boards and transit commissions enjoyed enough autonomy to be outside effective municipal control. Authority to plan was meaningless because authority to act on plans was divided so many ways. Even when decisions could be made locally they were subject to ratification or reversal by the Ontario Municipal Board, a provincially appointed tribunal enjoying relative independence. Thus local government decision-making has become fractured horizontally (at the local level) and vertically (between levels of government). It has also been frustrated by lack of adequate financial resources free from provincial restrictions on their use. Together the jurisdictional and financial problems of the municipalities have made them unresponsive and very conservative.

The municipalities have banded together over the years in a number of associations through which they have sought from the provincial government access to greater financial resources without strings attached. One response of the province was the Ontario Committee on Taxation which during the 1960s produced what is known as the Smith Report. This report drew attention to the link between municipal financial problems and the fragmentation of local government. It led to an increased public awareness of the need to reform municipal government structures in a variety of fundamental ways.

Students of the local government scene have concluded that if there is to be effective local democracy, many of these out-moded structures will require attention and action. Since 1965 the government of Ontario has made an attempt to tackle several of these problem areas. We will look at government policy in a number of areas in turn, and attempt to assess how far such policy has succeeded.

LARGER UNITS OF GOVERNMENT

The important decisions affecting local communities have to do with housing, urban transportation, the environment, social policy development, education, work and recreation opportunities, and local tax rates. Small governmental units cannot expect to have the jurisdiction, the tax base or the professional staff to solve these interrelated problems. The chapter by Norman Pearson and the case study by Henry Jacek contain descriptions and analyses of regional developments in Ontario and of the provincial decision-making as illustrated in Hamilton-Wentworth. Clearly, progress has been made in establishing regional governments covering more than 60 per cent of the province's population, and in amalgamating many of the smaller units in the lower-tier area municipalities.

FEWER SEPARATE BOARDS

The fracturing of local authority among a number of elected and appointed bodies leaves no one of them able to act like a responsible and responsive government. Solutions to urban and regional problems require the integration of physical, social and financial planning. The implementation process must also be integrated. The absence of unified government at the local level makes this virtually impossible. Citizen confusion is guaranteed by the multiplicity of choice in civic elections. In London, for example, voters regularly have to consider more than one hundred candidates at once in order to choose one for mayor, four for board of control, two for alderman, twelve for school board, and four for public utilities commission.

In 1968 Darcy McKeough, then Minister of Municipal Affairs, announced in the Legislature that "Municipal councils will be strengthened by removing the powers from many special-purpose bodies and turning these powers over to Regional or Local Municipal Councils" (Design for Development, Phase Two). In 1972, speaking as Ontario Treasurer, he developed the rationale this way:

> As a general observation about local government, I think it is fair to say that over the years there has been a pre-occupation with something called "service delivery." A vast array of municipalities and special purpose bodies, boards and commissions have grown up to deliver services. Surely, however, government is more than an instrument through which to deliver services. Its central role must be to deal with issues. One of the major and insistent issues of our time is the quality of life and conservation and preserva-tion of our environment. Taken as a whole our "system" of local government is unsuited to providing the broad poli-cies and priorities to tackle this issue. It is virtually im-possible to deliver services through thousands of local government bodies and provide for the rational manage-ment of resources at the same time. . . .
>
> Essentially, the circumstances that inhibit local govern-ment's effective participation in meeting modern problems can be summed up in a single word—fragmentation. . . . There are far too many special-purpose boards and com-missions. They obscure the accountability of councils, and impede comprehensive priority setting. . . . The lack of co-ordination of land-use planning, for example, can only lead to very costly servicing problems and the waste of our resources. (Design for Development Phase Three)

By 1974, the action implementing the 1968 announcement was limited to the abolition of a few elected public utilities commissions and a few appointed planning boards, steps taken mainly as part of the process of creating regional governments. The conservation authorities, school boards, transit commissions and most planning boards and public utilities commissions still operated with their varying degrees of autonomy from municipal councils.

The school boards are a special case. In their present consolidated form, they cover mainly the area of a city or county. They spend approximately half of all local government revenues and do so free from any decisions taken by municipal councils. As elected bodies, school boards are accountable directly to their own electorate and to the provincial Department of Education. They are in no sense accountable to city hall. And yet school boards own and control some of the most valuable public property. As the older parts of our cities lose population, particularly school-age population, school boards have been free to close schools and sell the property. In many cases these school properties are an essential element in the official plan adopted at city hall. Thus the autonomy of school boards "impede(s) comprehensive priority setting."

Similarly, public transit commissions make all sorts of decisions affecting land use and traffic patterns. They could be used by municipal councils as an aid to effective land-use planning in the pursuit of environmental and social goals if they had less autonomy or were integrated into city hall policy-making and administration.

In counties where regional government is not an immediate prospect, there is a tendency to proliferate joint or regional boards with single-purpose responsibilities. These include planning, health and welfare. Conservation authorities are a long-standing example of regional bodies not accountable to any one government and therefore virtually not accountable at all. Even where regional governments have been established, conservation authorities continue with their autonomy and their own boundaries, appropriately related to watersheds. In 1974, the government created a new single-purpose body for an area which has four regional governments, the Toronto Area Transit Operating Authority, thus moving farther from the idea of stronger general purpose local government.

LESS PROVINCIAL REGULATION

All Canadian provinces exercise some regulatory role with respect to their municipalities. The absence of such supervision would, for example, permit municipalities to borrow excessively, thereby adversely affecting the province's credit rating and usurping the right of future municipal councils to make expenditure decisions.

In Ontario this supervisory role, carried out mainly by the Ontario Municipal Board (OMB) has been detailed in the extreme. The OMB is an independent tribunal composed of fifteen persons appointed by the province. In 1972 a select committee of the Legislature on the OMB reported as follows:

> In matters of finance and planning, the Legislature has delegated some of its legislative powers to the elected municipal councils, thus empowering them to enact bylaws. It has meanwhile retained a degree of control by the Provincial Government by providing that many of these bylaws cannot become effective without the approval of an appointed body (i.e., the OMB). This appointed body is not directly responsible to the people and may interject its own views on what the municipal legislation should be. An OMB decision can be appealed to the Lieutenant Governor in Council. In practice, however, most matters stop at the Board level.
>
> This is an important question because the OMB can thus shape or control matters of much greater breadth and magnitude than those dealt with by the courts. Furthermore, the courts are obliged to decide cases in strict accordance with the law, while the OMB decides cases within much broader terms of reference. Its decisions are based on government policy, where known, but otherwise on its own policy formulated according to its interpretation of the facts and the sentiments of people.

This broad overriding power, combined with detailed approval procedures and a heavy caseload, has the effect of burdening the municipalities with interference in their jurisdiction, constant delays, inefficiencies and frustration. The select committee made a number of recommendations designed to restore some of the individual decision-making to municipal councils while retaining protection against excessive total borrowing. The committee also saw fit to recommend that a municipality with an official plan should have the power to bring relevant by-laws, consistent with the plan, into force without OMB approval. It further recommended that the power to create or dissolve wards be transferred from the OMB to municipal councils, subject to an appeal to the OMB.

During the latter part of 1973, John White, Ontario Treasurer, made a number of statements indicating that the province would delegate a number of powers to the municipalities as part of a policy of strengthening local government. He forecast legislation to "eliminate, as much as possible, the approval and consent that municipal councils are now required to obtain from the Province on a variety of by-laws, special undertakings, license fees, laying out of highways, sale of land acquired for nonpayment of taxes, tax registration procedures, disposition of funds received during the subdivision of land and various other planning matters" (*Municipal World*, October 1973).

In December the minister referred to "the provincial government's proposal for delegating many of their responsibilities to the municipal level of government" and suggested that "this extensive transfer of money and power to local government is a revolutionary process" (*Municipal World*, February 1974). Some of the powers being delegated are given only to the new regional municipalities. Such discrimination would make more sense if the province had not abandoned its policy of completing the restructure of local government as put forward in 1972 in *Design for Development, Phase Three*.

The decentralization of a number of very minor powers must be seen in the context of the centralization at Queen's Park of major planning powers through the Ontario Planning and Development Act, 1973. For a clear perspective on this important change, the reader is referred to Chapter 11 by Norman Pearson.

THE LOCAL GOVERNMENT REVENUE BASE

The most common complaint the province hears from mayors and councillors is that their sources of revenue come nowhere near their expenditure responsibilities. The only significant tax they have is the tax on real property. While expenditure requirements for services related to urbanization, the environment and social considerations exhibit a rapid growth rate compounded by inflation, the property tax cannot be increased at anything like the same rate.

Unlike the federal or provincial tax base when it is incomes or purchases, the property tax base in the form of the assessed value of real properties does not rise automatically with inflation. The reassessment of each piece of property is an individual, often arbitrary, act by an assessor using substantial discretion. It requires notification and the opportunity for appeal to an Assessment Review Court, to the county or district court and to the Ontario Municipal Board. Though actual property values may be in a state of constant change, assessed values are altered at such infrequent intervals that a consequent significant rise brings an expectation of a proportionate reduction in tax rate. In any case, the non-response of the tax base to inflation or to growth in the economy means that any significant increase in tax revenue must be determined in the annual public rate-setting ritual at the end of municipal budget discussions. The visibility of the process combined with Ontario's legislated short terms of office (two years) makes raising the mill rate to any substantial extent a political improbability easily understood.

The chief weakness of the property tax, however, is its regressive nature. Assessment is not a reasonable indicator of ability to pay. Research reported in the 1972 Ontario Budget papers shows that the impact on low-income earners averages about 9 per cent and on high-income earners about 3 per cent of income. One effect of the fiscal squeeze has been the passing on to developers of costs of servicing land. They, in turn, pass them on to the occupiers of housing, whether owner-occupiers or tenants. This further exacerbates the housing problem while continuing the tax regressivity.

The major provincial response until very recently has been a substantial hike in transfer payments to municipalities. This is illustrated by the following table from the 1974 Ontario budget.

Local Government Financing Overview: 1968–73

	$ MILLION				% GROWTH
	1968	1970	1972	1973	1973/1968
Spending	2,901	3,505	4,185	4,469	54
Own-account revenues	1,972	2,229	2,519	2,594	32
Ontario transfers	929	1,276	1,666	1,875	102

The same budget shows that less than 10 per cent of the
provincial transfers in fiscal 1973–74 were unconditional.
The other 90 per cent were paid with firm strings attached,
saying how the money must be spent. Not only that, they
also tied strings around much of the property tax revenues
which had to be spent jointly with the conditional grants
for specified programs of education, welfare, public works
and police protection. The municipalities, through their
associations, have made clear their unhappiness at having
so little right to decide how their revenues will be spent.
They demand a new tax base or a large increase in unconditional grants.

Queen's Park has heard the call. John White announced
the deconditionalization in 1974 of nine grants totalling
$3,237,000. That gets the unconditional grants up from 9.85
per cent of the total to 10 per cent. He has also put forward
a list of fifteen other grants for possible deconditionalization. They total $56 million and if approved would raise
the percentage to 13 per cent. /

But the municipal leaders press on. They see their independence, self-respect and usefulness to their electorates
as wrapped up in the twin issues of the adequacy and
autonomy of their financial resources. Talk of decentralization of minor powers and deconditionalization of minor
grants is to them so much rhetoric when their fundamental
financial dependence is not altered.

It is clear that the Ontario government knows what the
municipal leaders are saying. And some of its responses go
beyond mere rhetoric. For instance, the provision for
property tax credits from income tax, inversely related to
incomes and with provision for rebates to those who earn
too little to pay income tax, marks the most fundamental
attack on the regressivity of the property tax attempted in
any province. Indeed, it has since been adopted elsewhere
in Canada. At the national conference of the three levels of
government in Edmonton in October 1973, Ontario's
Treasurer announced that in future years total provincial
assistance to local government would "grow at a rate not
less than the growth rate of Ontario's total revenues." This
promise was implemented in the 1974 budget. The provincial total revenue growth rate for 1974–75 was projected at
11.7 per cent. This rate, when applied to local government
transfers, required an increase of $239 million. Existing

grants contained a growth factor amounting to $115 million, so an extra $124 million was paid, split almost equally between conditional and unconditional grants.

Since provincial transfers had increased on an average at approximately 15 per cent per year since 1968, the 11.7 per cent figure for 1974–75 represented both a retrenchment for the province and a kind of minimum guarantee to the municipalities. It may be a more serious retrenchment in future in view of the Ontario Treasurer's warning that revenue growth will drop off due to indexing of personal income taxes.

Treasurer White recognized that his revenue growth rate promise would not meet the municipal need. At Edmonton he committed the government of Ontario "to make available to local governments the full revenue benefits, dollar for dollar, of any new tax sharing made available by Ottawa." In his 1974 budget, the pledge was reworded to read "the Province will pass on to local governments the full benefit of any net gains in new unconditional tax sharing by the federal government." Local government expenditures (combined education and municipal) were projected to grow "by at least 10 per cent per year." Property taxes would increase at 4 per cent and total local own-account sources at 5 per cent. The impact of the province's commitment to increase its total transfers at the rate of its own revenue growth is enough to raise the municipal revenue growth rate to 7½ per cent. To close the gap of 2½ per cent in the years 1974, 1975 and 1976, Ontario proposed that Ottawa transfer five personal income tax points over the three years to the provinces. Ontario would pass the entire yield of the five points on to the municipalities on a basis to be determined following provincial-municipal consultation. According to the Treasurer, "By 1976, Ottawa would relinquish some $800 million to all provinces, out of a tax source which, in that year alone, will grow by $2 billion."

At the Edmonton meeting the Ontario municipal representatives were pleased with the Treasurer's proposal. It has not been accepted by Ottawa, but it is a proposal which shows that Ontario recognizes the municipal claim and is prepared to develop a mechanism aimed at getting unconditional federal money into municipal hands.

INTERGOVERNMENTAL RELATIONS

In today's world many of the issues of public policy require the joint action of two or three levels of government. It is not possible to parcel out the various functional jurisdictions to the federal, provincial and municipal governments and keep them in water-tight compartments. Housing, for instance, requires action from all three levels of government. For appropriate co-operative activity to occur requires new mechanisms, policies and procedures for intergovernmental consultation, program development and implementation.

In 1970 Premier John Robarts convened a public conference of his government and the municipalities of Ontario. Though the Premier began the conference by issuing a call for a provincial-municipal partnership, as the conference developed, there was evidence of a kind of paternalism that denied the spirit of partnership. The Premier had the first and last words; his ministers read lengthy prepared texts; a few municipal leaders were on the agenda to speak. But there was no substantive dialogue. Very little happened apart from the provincial proposal for joint committee activity in preparation for future meetings.

The nine hundred municipalities of Ontario were at that time organized in four separate associations. These were:

The Ontario Municipal Association (OMA)

The Association of Ontario Mayors and Reeves (AOMR)

The Association of Counties and Regions of Ontario (ACRO)

The Ontario Association of Rural Municipalities (OARM)

The first two were predominately urban while the latter two were rural. Representatives of the four associations had met in 1969 and established a joint committee known as the Municipal Liaison Committee (MLC). This committee has continued in existence and now plays a major role in provincial-municipal negotiation and communication. Initially each association had four representatives on the committee, recognizing the equality derived from autonomy, but ignoring the inequality of relative organizational strength or populations indirectly represented.

By 1972 the OMA and AOMR had merged to form the Association of Municipalities of Ontario (AMO). By 1974 the MLC membership was composed of its chairman, Mayor

Desmond Newman, of Whitby, eight from AMO, four from
ACRO, four from OARM and two from Metropolitan Toronto.
The joint committee activity following the Robarts conference was in the form of the MLC joined by a committee
of ministers. The group came to be known as the Provincial-
Municipal Liaison Committee (PMLC). By the latter part of
1973 the PMLC was meeting in public one day a month under
the co-chairmanship of Provincial Treasurer White and
MLC chairman Newman. Mr. White was accompanied at the
meetings by staff support from his Ministry of the
Treasury, Economics and Intergovernmental Affairs and by
other cabinet ministers and senior civil servants as were
appropriate for individual agenda items. Mayor Newman
had with him the entire membership of the MLC plus the
small MLC staff, other employees of the parent associations
and, as required, particular persons borrowed from individual municipalities.

The PMLC is provided with executive secretarial services
by the Provincial-Municipal Affairs Secretariat of the Office
of Intergovernmental Affairs within the ministry. Though
the municipalities prize their relatively independent status
within the PMLC, they have resisted attempts to establish
a secretariat which would belong to the committee rather
than the province. Their fear of an autonomous bureaucracy turning into a separate power between levels of
government is greater than their fear of any unfairness
from officials in the employ of the ministry. The nineteen
members of the MLC are organized in the form of a shadow
cabinet. The shadow ministers are organized in sub-com-
mittees modelled on the policy fields used by the cabinet.

A special MLC committee of unusual importance is the
Fiscal Arrangements Sub-Committee. In 1974 this committee participated in the process of determining how the
increased transfers arising from the Treasurer's commitment (to increase municipal assistance at the rate of provincial revenue growth) would be distributed to municipalities. This meant disclosing figures to municipal officials
in advance of budget day and jointly considering policy
alternatives before the budget was finalized.

On March 7, 1974, Mayor Newman disclosed on a confidential basis some of this information to MLC members
attending their caucus prior to the PMLC meeting of March
8. At the public PMLC meeting the next day Treasurer White

acknowledged the process and said that having regard to traditions, most of which were ill-founded, he could not give the figures before the budget. One month later in his budget address at Queen's Park, the Treasurer said,

> In developing these measures (to share Provincial resources with local governments), I have had the pleasure of extensive discussions with representatives of local government. Particularly, I had many useful meetings with the Municipal Liaison Committee and its Fiscal Arrangements Sub-Committee. These discussions contributed greatly to the Government's revenue-sharing arrangements.

At the May 10, 1974, PMLC meeting, the MLC financial spokesman, Toronto Alderman Arthur Eggleton, said: "I believe that the municipalities of Ontario join with the MLC in saying that the 1974 Budget is a milestone in the development of a co-operative approach to fiscal management in the Province of Ontario."

The MLC immediately pushed on with proposals "to sophisticate the process," as Mayor Newman puts it. This would include a joint technical sub-committee with responsibility for analysis and data base development.

The agenda for PMLC meetings often contains a wide range of items. On March 8, 1974, for example, the following were among those discussed:

1. The relation between conservation authorities and the new regional governments. (The province said no to an MLC request.)
2. How should store hours and Sunday as a day of rest be regulated? (The MLC wanted the province to do the regulating.)
3. Was the proposed Toronto Area Transit Operating Authority a fifth level of government between the regional municipalities and the province? (Mayor Newman probed deftly without disclosing divisions within the MLC.)
4. A provincial program to assist in the improvement of local government management. (The MLC approved.)
5. The composition of the new Municipal Advisory Committee for Northwestern Ontario. (At the request of the Mayor of Thunder Bay and with MLC approval, Mr. White accepted a modification.)

6. A dispute between Ottawa and Ontario on the shared financing of extended health care. (The PMLC co-chairmen agreed to sign a joint letter to federal Treasury Board President Drury.)
7. The Green Paper on Environmental Assessment. (The MLC questioned the need for new policies and Deputy Minister Biggs bristled at Mayor Newman's demand for detailed justification.)
8. Plans and agenda for a meeting of the Federal-Provincial-Municipal Liaison Committee (FPMLC) the following month.
9. A progress report from the Fiscal Arrangements Sub-Committee.

At the conclusion of this item, John White said, "We need a more decentralized system. . . . Minority government is a decentralized system. . . . My best friends go to Ottawa and three months later they think it's the centre of the universe. . . . I have talked to Stanfield and Gillies. . . . Des, I hope you talk to those you know! We must get federal money down to the municipalities. . . ."

Since that meeting, a question period has been added to the agenda. Questions can go either to the minister or to the MLC. The evolution appears to be in the direction of parliamentary forms. Indeed, Mayor Newman once said he could see one strong municipal association some day becoming a provincial policy-making assembly which might rival Queen's Park.

The development of the PMLC as an instrument of formal, public discussion between Ontario and its municipalities has depended on two strong figures, John White and Desmond Newman. Darcy McKeough played an important and constructive role initially, but much of the progress has occurred since White took over Treasury, Economics and Intergovernmental Affairs. White has known his own mind, been willing to grant a point, stand firm, absorb criticism or fight back, and has appeared to enjoy it. His cabinet colleagues have seemed much less enthusiastic when called to the PMLC for an agenda item in their respective bailiwicks. And senior officials have even appeared hostile under close municipal questioning. Mayor Newman is a master of the parliamentary arts, a brilliant cross-questioner, an enthusiastic and articulate spokesman with a constant awareness of the goals he seeks to achieve. His Liberal

affiliation does not appear to reduce his credibility with Tory White.
' The effectiveness of these two leaders makes the observer wonder whether the process is too dependent on their respective skills and commitment to endure the loss of either. Both perform as if they have a mission to perform and with the conviction that the process must prove durable even as it evolves.

The PMLC developed in a national context of the drive to establish talks among the three levels of government. At the first national tri-level conference in 1972, Ontario through then Treasurer Charles MacNaughton, appeared to be dragging its feet more than any other province on federal and municipal requests. At the second such conference in 1972, with White in the Treasury portfolio, Ontario became the friend of the municipalities and put Ottawa on the defensive. This switch has helped solidify the improved provincial-municipal relationship in Ontario.

MUNICIPAL ADMINISTRATION

As the Hickey Report on Decision-making Processes in Ontario's Local Governments pointed out in 1973, the internal structures of most municipalities need major reforms in order that the administrative side of local government can function efficiently. Antiquated legislation does not permit appropriate delegation of power and confuses the roles of elected and appointed people. The board of control system has long since been abandoned in other provinces but remains in Ontario, confusing mayors, aldermen, department heads and the public.

The provincial government appears to understand the issues. For instance, it does not provide for a board of control in the new regional municipalities. It does provide for a chief administrative officer. And yet when it comes to accepting Hickey's advice and abolishing existing boards of control, Queen's Park seems to lose its nerve. As Jacek points out in his case study of Hamilton-Wentworth, the Hamilton board of control issue was the one on which the province was prepared to give ground. On the other hand, the province is prepared to help municipalities improve their management practice and supports programs to educate municipal employees. These are essential, given the increasingly complex nature of urban government.

The advent of active citizen groups demanding a part in government policy development has placed an extra strain on the decision-making process. In the circumstances, structures, processes and personnel all require improvement designed to make local government both efficient and responsive.

MUNICIPAL POLITICS

The penchant for non-partisanship in local government has resulted in an absence of political cohesion, policy consistency and accountability of government to the electorate. The excessive individualism of the system makes for headline hunters who lack the saving political graces of relevance and coherence. The absence of collective responsibility means that the local democracy is government by chance; the character of our cities is daily determined by accident. The individualism also leaves each alderman to face alone the pressures and stratagems of the highly motivated development industry. A system more like our parliamentary form would encourage healthy debate on issues, such as the urban environment, and provide for a responsible, accountable government.

The province could legislate for mayors to be chosen by the councillors from among themselves. The mayor could be given the power to choose his executive and committee chairmen. He would then tend to be the leader of the largest group or party. Instead of facing this one head-on, the provincial parties are often involved surreptiously in municipal campaigns while their non-partisan candidates condemn others who have declared a group or party involvement.

In conclusion, it might be said that while Ontario is far from achieving overall solutions in the area of combined provincial and municipal responsibility, there is a ferment. Some reforms are occurring, but the rhetoric is well ahead of the action. In 1974, among the provinces of Canada, Ontario was among the innovators, as were Manitoba and New Brunswick. The political risks to a provincial government in strengthening local, mainly urban, government are yet to be fully measured. But the risks of not doing so are the risks of centralizing all non-federal power in the provincial capital.

SELECTED BIBLIOGRAPHY

ADLER, GERALD M. *Land Planning by Administrative Regulation* (OMB). Toronto: University of Toronto Press, 1971.

CLARKSON, STEPHEN. *City Lib.* Toronto: Hakkert, 1972.

DUPRE, J. STEFAN. *Intergovernmental Finance in Ontario: A Provincial-Local Perspective.* Toronto: Queen's Printer, 1966.

FELDMAN, LIONEL D. *Ontario 1945–1973: The Municipal Dynamic.* Toronto: Ontario Economic Council, 1974.

Government of Ontario. *Budget* (1972, 1973, 1974). Toronto.

———. *Design for Development: Phase Two.* Toronto, 1968.

———. *Design for Development: Phase Three.* Toronto, 1972.

———. *Municipal Directory* (Annual). Toronto.

———. *Ontario Committee on Taxation* (Smith Report). Toronto, 1966.

———. *Provincial Assistance to Municipalities, Boards and Commissions* (Annual). Toronto.

———. *Select Committee Report on the Ontario Municipal Board.* Toronto, 1972.

Government of Nova Scotia. *Report of the Royal Commission on Education, Public Services and Provincial-Municipal Relations* (Graham Report). Halifax: Queen's Printer, 1974.

HICKEY, PAUL. *Decision-Making Processes in Ontario's Local Governments.* Toronto: Queen's Printer, 1973.

Joint Municipal Committee on Intergovernmental Relations. *Brief to the Joint Committee of the Senate and House of Commons on the Constitution of Canada.* Ottawa: Canadian Federation of Mayors and Municipalities, 1971.

———. *The Municipality in the Canadian Federation.* Ottawa: CFMM, 1970.

LORIMER, JAMES. *A Citizen's Guide to City Politics.* Toronto: James, Lewis and Samuel, 1972.

MASLOVE, ALLAN M. *The Pattern of Taxation in Canada.* Ottawa: Economic Council of Canada, 1972.

MASSON, JACK K. and JAMES D. ANDERSON, eds. *Emerging Party Politics in Urban Canada.* Toronto: McClelland and Stewart, 1972.

Municipal World, a monthly published in St. Thomas, Ontario. (Reports regularly on PMLC.)

Ontario Economic Council. *Government Reform in Ontario.* Toronto: Queen's Printer, 1970.

——. *Municipal Reform: A Proposal for the Future.* Toronto: Queen's Printer, 1971.

PLUNKETT, THOMAS J. *The Financial Structure and the Decision-Making Process of Canadian Municipal Government.* Ottawa: CMHC, 1972.

RICHARDSON, BOYCE. *The Future of Canadian Cities.* Toronto: New Press, 1972.

II
NORMAN PEARSON

Regional Government and Development

I T IS not generally realized that the traditional system of local government in Ontario originated before Confederation. Under Lord Elgin, the Baldwin-Lafontaine ministry brought responsible representative government to what is now Ontario in 1848–49, and rapidly passed the basic Municipal Act which remained essentially the local governments' system until the end of the Second World War. The very success of that original system worked to prevent comprehensive review.

During that period there were some dramatic changes. From being in direct contact with the government of what was effectively an unitary state (albeit colonial), local government was transformed in 1867 when the British North America Act produced a federal state, in which a new province, Ontario, like all the others could point to the constitution which designated local government institutions as "creatures of the Province" without entrenched rights. The older municipal corporations could point in vain to their charters which ante-dated the province, while enjoying the illusion of a "local autonomy" which was in practice more due to problems of communication and regional diversity than to any basic right to that state.

In addition, Ontario very rapidly expanded. In 1876 it extended to Keewatin; in 1880 it moved west to Kenora; in 1889 it expanded north to James Bay, and in 1912 to Patricia, to a total of 412,000 square miles. This expansion raised the question of what system of local government was to be applied in this "New Ontario." In "Old Ontario" the Baldwin system worked well. This was a system in which the rural municipalities (police villages, townships, villages and towns) were part of the county system, and the urban municipalities (cities and certain separated towns) were excluded from the counties. Thus there was a two-tier system in the rural areas, and a one-tier system in the urban centres. Originally there were certain population levels at which a hamlet in a township could move as it grew to the status of a police village (run by elected trustees) and then to become a village, or eventually a town. The systems interlocked by sending the two senior elected representatives (reeve and deputy-reeve) to county council.

This system was not extended to northern Ontario. For the annexations, the Province of Ontario inherited a number of "districts." Essentially these were areas of colonization in which the dominion government had laid out townships, which in due course became settled and achieved elected councils. Under the federal aegis, the district was essentially an embryonic province. When Ontario expanded, it maintained the same system. Thus the north had no county system, and as townships, villages, towns and cities emerged, they had no elected county system, but only provincial districts which were run by the civil service, and served to decentralize the provincial bureaucracy.

This produced two kinds of local government: the old Baldwin system in the original Ontario south of Muskoka, and the new district system without counties, in northern Ontario.

From the first census (1871) Ontario was and has remained the most populous province. The province passed through a series of changes in rapid succession. Between 1850 and 1880 it became a strong agricultural area with a few urban centres. There was a knitting together of the hitherto separate regions by an elaborate and efficient network of railways. In the period 1878–1900 there was the exploitation of northern minerals, and the beginnings of rapid urbanization, which proceeded in the period 1900–1920 with an increasing interest in conservation, a Planning Act (1918), and a remarkable network of electric railways, industrialization, and the exploitation of water power (Ontario Hydro Electric Power Commission). During the 1920s there was a rapid development of automobiles and the road system, as well as a further burst of exploiting and developing natural resources. The decade of the 1930s was dominated by the world-wide economic depression and the financial collapse of the old municipal structure. The war years saw the beginnings of the rapid expansion of "welfare state" politics and the great growth of provincial government, together with the increasing fragmentation and erosion of local government. The postwar years were emphatically directed to economic growth, increasing degrees of affluence, and the advent of massive urban and metropolitan impact on the whole of Ontario. Recent years (from 1960 onwards) have been much affected by the overwhelming strength of provinces relative to local institutions, the growth of economic nationalism, and the new conservation movement with its interest in ecology and environment.

It is against this background that the concern for regional government and regional development can be viewed, for it gives the linkages between these efforts and problems of regional planning and of the reorganization of federal and provincial governments.

A measure of the change is that in 1788 Ontario had four regions and twelve local governments; in 1845 nineteen regions and about three hundred and thirty local governments; in 1920 more than nine hundred local governments; and by 1965 there were at least ten provincial government departments with regional administrative operations (ranging from ten regions used by the then Department of Economics and Development to about forty-six used by the then Department of Energy and Resources Management).

By the 1950s Ontario had reached the position of having a manufacturing output greater than the rest of Canada combined, with about 80 per cent of the provincial population concentrated in the southern 15 per cent of the total area. Preeminent in that region was the dominance of the Toronto metropolis. But this economic development, at a level of population then approaching six million, had been achieved at the cost of regional disparity. Although a disadvantaged region in Ontario is generally prosperous by Canadian standards, eastern Ontario notably lagged behind the rest of Ontario, and the non-urbanized region of Georgian Bay also did not reap many of the benefits of growth. Northern Ontario (360,000 square miles) reached a relatively static state and then slowly began to show signs of losing population. Growth was increasingly concentrated in the axis of the old Grand Trunk Railway, the Ontario section of the Chicago–Quebec City corridor of communications which is increasingly urbanized, and is now one of the world's largest industrial areas.

In this section of the province the problem was one of responding to unprecedented change. Local governments prior to 1930 had generally provided services ahead of development. Over-extended in the depression, and dependent on the property tax base, they collapsed financially, and after a period when a great many had been run by the province, they were not capable of extending services quickly. Similarly, their generally antiquated management systems and physical boundaries no longer corresponded to the realities of community life. Over the period 1849–1949 no real attempt had been made to integrate new functions into the municipal structure, and in addition, Ontario retained the historic division of local government into two independent branches, educational and municipal, characteristic of pre-industrial societies. New functions such as public utilities, and those inter-connecting municipal services needed to link obsolete entities of dwindling local autonomy, were established as independent commissions. Others, such as those for health, suburban roads, parks, libraries, cemeteries, airports and planning, were established as separate boards and agencies, often inter-municipal in nature. In the worst examples, there was one unit of local government for every seventy-five people; councils became obsessed with trivia and unable to set policy; and coordination was virtually impossible. In this situation, property taxation was increasingly incapable of sustaining local government, which then became dependent on grants and aid from the province. The illusion of local autonomy persisted, but the reality was evident in every phase of municipal life.

In the 1950s municipal government was able to commit independently only 5 to 10 per cent of the total funds locally spent. Municipal planning was subject to detailed provincial approval, and municipalities were increasingly directed financially by the province. Most local governments tried to improve their tax base by locating supposedly lucrative land uses such as commerce, industry or even apartments, without much regard to planning principles, in an attempt to improve their assessment base. Scarcely surprising was the resultant revolt of taxpayers who increasingly exercised their right of appeal to the provincial supervisory body, the Ontario Municipal Board (OMB), thus further decreasing local autonomy. While a detailed study of the Ontario Municipal Board is beyond our present scope, it has immense power. Indeed the Court of Appeal defined it as "the hidden seat on the Cabinet." The board, for example, showed no hesitation in extinguishing local governments, such as the town of Merritton in the Niagara Peninsula, on these grounds, awarding its territory to the adjacent municipalities of St. Catharines and Thorold.

It was increasingly evident that there was a great need for municipal reorganization, for an overhaul of the machinery of provincial government, for some more comprehensive regional planning, and for measures which would aid development in the non-metropolitan regions. As valuable resources such as the tender fruit soils of the Niagara Peninsula, the scenic qualities of the Niagara Escarpment, the water of the Great Lakes, or access to the shorelines, were increasingly eroded or polluted, these needs became the focus of public dissatisfaction.

It must be noted that there had been attempts to meet these needs. The 1918 legislation on housing and planning was swept away in the euphoria preceding the great crash of 1929. The attempts to create metropolitan government in Toronto in 1931 in the Henry ministry failed. During the depression and the war the planning opportunities were neglected as the profession crumbled because of public hostility to planning. The Hepburn government's amalgamation of small municipalities in Windsor and the creation of a Department of Municipal Affairs met with hot resistance. Municipalities abused the power given to urban areas to control fringe development, and were unable to make joint planning areas work.

Small wonder, then, that there was an actual breakdown of municipal services in the Toronto suburbs. In 1953 the City of Toronto's belated attempt to annex the suburbs and to politically unify the area was thwarted by the province's creation of the municipality of Metropolitan Toronto. In essence this was an up-dated county, a federation of thirteen core municipalities given planning powers over a further thirteen fringe municipalities. This was the first modern "regional government" in North America. But while it was copied in Manitoba, which then later saw Metropolitan Winnipeg go on via progressive functional integration to the unicity or essentially one-tier system, Metropolitan Toronto made a few halting steps along that path and then stopped. In 1966 the Goldenberg Commission's recommendations resulted in the educational function being moved to the Metropolitan level, and there was a reduction in the number of municipalities to six (five "boroughs" and the City of Toronto). The planning function was never able to produce an adopted statutory plan, and considerations of assessment led to a highly restrictive form of fringe area planning, quite unable to cope with the pressures of metropolis becoming conurbation.

Subsequent research has shown that this crisis might well have been the catalyst to drive industry to seek independent non-metropolitan locations. The political reorganization of Metropolitan Toronto under Chairman F. G. Gardiner as a "bulldozer" agency, providing services, increased once again the comparative advantage of the metropolitan core and inhibited regional development elsewhere in the province, where the crisis conditions continued to build up to the housing shortages of the 1970s. In addition, the intervention of the OMB and the active provincial highway and public transit developments enabled the core metropolis to achieve a poly-nucleated form, with many active sub-cores and large-scale urbanization by private developers (Don Mills, Flemingdon Park and the unique suburban apartment concentration).

But this very success worsened the regional development problem. The outlying urban centres and small rural towns declined. The main development facilities tended to further concentrate development in the Grand Trunk Corridor. The impact of the urban, industrial, agricultural and metropolitan revolutions, and changes in transport, economic structure and culture, as Ontario moved from an agricultural–small town orientation to an international-metropolitan existence, produced intense concern, especially in the northern and eastern areas, about the patterns being followed.

It is worth noting that during wartime, the federal and provincial governments had produced, both for wartime economic planning and for use in postwar reconstruction, a 68-region system covering the whole of Canada. These federal-provincial regions (ten in Ontario) were used in the initial steps in the regional development program, since the Progressive Conservative government had in 1943 helped to develop the scheme. When the postwar period showed no great need for reconstruction, the ten large regions were used for statistical purposes.

In the next decade (1943–53) the government was also exploring the need for some units which might serve as an answer to the outmoded municipal system. Pleva, a noted geographer, had examined the functional structure of Ontario and noted the existence of about seventy "local regions" which might be suitable for what were then called "area municipalities." In addition he had played a fundamental role in three other areas: the creation of joint planning areas (combining real communities into functional entities); the establishment of river basin agencies called Conservation Authorities; and the setting-up of what came to be known as the Ontario Water Resources Commission, following the path of Sir Adam Beck's Hydro Electric Commission, to do large-scale regional servicing, and hopefully to create a "grid" of provincial services.

These ideas (new forms of local government and area planning, the conservation agencies, and the grid of provincial services run by an autonomous authority) were remarkable conceptual advances. They were not, however, implemented fast enough, or on a large enough scale, to solve the problems of regional development, to create effective regional planning, or to solve the problems of municipal governments. The pressure for regional reforms steadily increased. To meet the increasing concern expressed in conferences of such bodies as the various citizen and industrial associations, the municipal organizations, and the independent environmental associations such as the Conservation Council of Ontario, the Progressive Conservative government moved to establish Regional Development Associations in the ten economic regions. At first, it was widely expected that these would become like some "Geneva of the municipalities" whereby large-scale regional planning could be accomplished. The incentive of provincial aid, and the evidence that these would be sounding-boards for regional needs, gradually led to the various associations taking on independent forms and characteristics reflecting local and regional concerns. During their lifetime (1953–73) they were able to do much useful work. Although they had to overcome the initial criticism that they were really enlarged industrial development commissions, they provided a forum in which citizens, local governments and agencies, industry, commerce, agriculture, and universities could study matters and make reports.

While this step headed off the drive for any real regional planning, the proliferation of welfare state functions at the provincial level created the need for either a set of common regions (like the ten) or a set of independent regions (one for each agency). In practice, the 1955–65 period saw each department creating its own set of what might be called "provincial service regions," to enable the province to deal with sub-provincial matters, on a scale greater than that of the area municipal entities identified by Pleva and others.

There is much confusion in the public mind; it is generally assumed that one network of regions will serve all purposes. This is not necessarily so. For large-scale economic planning and for the delivery of senior government services to groups of local areas, some pattern of federal-provincial and sub-provincial scale regions is needed. These will be large in both extent and population, and few in number (five to ten). For better local government at the next scale down, there is a need for enlarged area governments which can replace the outmoded existing structure (making seventy or a hundred good-sized units out of nine hundred municipal governments). *Regional development* is the process of trying to give each region a fair share of the process of growth and change. *Regional planning* is a process of systematically guiding the spatial destiny of an area with common characteristics, and in the Ontario context has been used to describe both the provincial process of "large-region" planning and the "small-region" planning of an area of local municipalities corresponding to a real community of interest fragmented by unreal boundaries. *Regional government* has many meanings, but in Ontario it has become quite specifically identified with local government reform.

The advent of various kinds of regions under various kinds of legislation seemed like launching a number of experiments without any particularly clear path, to see which one would "take." After initial success, the metropolitan government concept simply raised the evident inadequacies of municipal government on the grand scale, plus the inherent problem that once Toronto's federation reached two million (1964) and was clearly headed for about eight million in the next century, if it ever did begin to plan, then Ontario would either be run by Metropolitan Toronto or by the province, but not both.

Similarly, conservation authorities made great strides but faltered on the broad land-use powers in their enabling legislation, and eventually got diverted into settling for diluting pollution by constructing dams, and then into providing urban recreational lands where municipalities failed to provide parks. The Planning Act regions, joint planning boards, showed a disturbing tendency to fall apart when they tried to implement any plans, and the planning function became obsessed with controls and trivia, just like the municipalities which they advised.

Not surprisingly, the result was to accentuate centralized provincial control. Ontario in the decade 1955–65 witnessed the spectacle of separate bureaucracies at war in the body politic. First, the grand coordinating Department of Planning and Development was dismantled. Conservation authorities were shuffled from department to department so that their on-going drive suffered. Then the interested citizen could see the Department of Economics and Development (or its current equivalent) promoting regional development, apparently at odds with the Department of Municipal Affairs. While the one department launched its ten regional development associations into the first stages of economic inventory and planning, the other cajoled its laggard municipalities into ever more grandiose regional studies (such as the monumental Metropolitan and Toronto Area Regional Transportation Study, the Waterloo-Wellington Study, the Oshawa Area Planning and Development Study). These seemed oddly at variance with each other.

During this period geographers and planners such as Carol, Krueger and Gertler, were documenting the changes and exploring both the "economic region" concept and the "urban-centred region" idea, while Beecroft, Mayo and others were developing the "regional government" theme. These became the intellectual bases for later changes.

Meanwhile, the actual pattern of development was being set by the OMB, by the municipal struggles for tax-base, and by the shortages of services, to the point where agencies like the Ontario Water Resources Commission would launch gigantic regional servicing schemes (like the South Peel Water and Sewer scheme, the London pipeline from Lake Huron, and the Central York Servicing scheme) far ahead of actual planning, simply to prevent further crises.

It was the municipal tax problem which emerged most fiercely, via two strands: firstly, the need to reorganize local government structures, responded to by the creation of Local Government Review Commissions (Ontario Department of Municipal Affairs), and secondly, the efficient use of tax revenue (the Ontario Committee on Taxation, and its consequence, the Smith Report). The outdated municipal structure and the increasing complexity of centralizing matters which should be locally handled, and the drain on the provincial treasury, lay at the root of both measures. Many changes were postponed pending the results of the Smith Report. Essentially, it pointed to both the need to reorganize the provincial government to get better policy direction and coordination, and a more coherent pattern of provincial service regions, as well as to the need to reorganize local government, the concept of regional government essentially being an up-dating of the old county system and the drastic rationalization of the lower-tier municipalities.

It is now clear, in retrospect, that Ontario could have moved to unite the educational and municipal branches of local government into one system using the same units. It is important to realize that while all this was going on, the educational branch of local government was reorganized to a near-county basis. While education as such is beyond our present scope, it should be noted that it represents a significant lost opportunity.

The Progressive Conservative government then launched the ambitious Design for Development, which followed a zig-zag path in the succeeding years. The first document (1966), entitled "Design for Development," under the Robarts government was in fact a proposal for breaking through the encrustations of the out-moded municipal structure, a bold attempt to achieve development, and head off the already-evident incipient housing problems. As we follow its strange course, it should be realized that this first intent was subsequently totally frustrated. This reorientation appears to be due to the advent of great bureaucratic strength able to manipulate virtually impotent local governments and to convert a scheme for decentralizing power and loosening up rigidities in control back into a scheme for increasing centralization, tighter controls and an even more lengthy decision-making process. The prospect of ministers not apparently in control of policy, and of a civil service collectively oblivious to reality, can be laid to the failure to decide on a concept of what local government should be. This failure to drive intensively to a complete once-for-all revision of Baldwin's original Municipal Act and all its massive piecemeal unrelated amendments, in accordance with some policy concept of what local government should be in a metropolitan-urban age, explains the erratic course of Design for Development.

The failure to grasp that nettle has frustrated the whole scheme, as the subsequent evolution of Design for Development reveals.

The statement entitled "Design for Development" emerged in 1966 after a series of reports, including the International Conference on Regional Development and Economic Change, held in Toronto in 1965 under the auspices of the Ontario Department of Economics and Development; the Select Committee on the Municipal Act and Related Acts; the coordinated views of the Regional Development Associations, via their agency, the Ontario Regional Development Council; and a report by Krueger, Horton and Pearson of the Geography and Planning Department, University of Waterloo, prepared for the Ontario Economic Council. These were quoted by Premier Robarts in making the statement to the Legislature.

It placed the provincial government very clearly in the business of planning provincial development, in a role the Premier's statement described as "complementary to the private sector in helping to create an atmosphere for growth and development." (By 1974 the government had virtually reached the position of seeking to replace private development, at least in urban affairs, via the Ontario Housing Corporation, which became in a few years the world's largest landlord, and via such proposed agencies as the Ontario Land Development Corporation. This was a signal reversal of the roles as originally forecast, symptomatic of some kind of statist revolution.)

The original document, "Design for Development" (1966), stated "when development occurs in any part of the province, it shall take place as a result of good regional planning," in a context of "the best possible environment for the people," and seeking to "encourage economic growth and development throughout the province." Stressing coordination at the provincial level and "face-to-face" relationships between the province and its municipalities, it spoke of having "any regional undertaking by the government . . . in the hands of a central authority which can cut across both departmental lines and county on municipal boundaries in meeting and solving regional problems."

The program forecast regional plans, the selection and stimulation of growth centres, and particular regional economic specialization, using the program as an "umbrella" for guiding the "smoothing-out" of conspicuous regional differences. To remedy problems of coordination, a cabinet committee chaired by the Premier was set up, together with a senior departmental advisory committee "to examine and submit regional development plans to the Cabinet Committee" and to coordinate the ten regional advisory boards of the senior civil servants in each region. Part of the exercise was to seek common administrative regions for all departments, and to launch research for a regional planning program initiated at the provincial level.

The structures of regional development associations, regional tourist councils and county ARDA committees (the latter dealing with federal-provincial programs under the Agricultural Rehabilitation and Development Act), were modified. First, the Regional Development Associations were renamed regional development councils and made, increasingly, arms of the province rather than autonomous local associations, with supporting grants payable upon approval of the annual program of each council.

This was intended as "the beginning of a comprehensive approach to regional development planning." Later, three further dimensions were added: 1, federal liaison via an inter-governmental secretariat in the Department of Treasury and Economics, mainly working with ARDA and the federal Department of Regional Economic Expansion; 2, two extra committees for provincial liaison, both chaired by Regional Development Branch of the Department of Treasury and Economics, and essentially to stop the contrary efforts of the economic and municipal planning divisions of the civil service; one dealt with central and southwest Ontario, and mainly the Toronto-Centred Region, the other was the northern and eastern committee, dealing with the non-metropolitan sector of the province; 3, for sub-provincial liaison, the beginnings were made on the path which later appeared in Phase Two of Design for Development. (These "phases" emerged later. While in retrospect we can call the 1966 statement "Phase One," it was never identified as such.)

Here it must be noted that the whole notion of a general comprehensive strategy for the whole of Ontario, a provincial plan, as had been advocated for many years by such bodies as the Conservation Council of Ontario and a number of experts in the field, was glossed over, perhaps because of the difficulties of federal-provincial cooperation in such an undertaking. But perhaps this was also due to the acceptance of the concept of the "urban-centred region" philosophy, and the idea inherent in it, that since Toronto was so dominant, to plan it would be effectively to set the destinies of the other regions in any case. No machinery yet exists for matching together the various regional plans, but in the period 1966–74 no statutory regional plans emerged. This is also a vital consideration. Rather than go the route of changing the Municipal Act and the Planning Act and devising a set of strategic statutory regional plans which could be dealt with comprehensively by the Legislature, the Progressive Conservative government, in the Robarts and the subsequent Davis ministries, chose to go a piecemeal route, in the sense that the "grand design" was deemed to be too complex to bring to the House at one time. Rather, it was to be brought forward in bits. It is small wonder that the Liberal opposition and the New Democratic Party were not able to make much impact either on the Design for Development or on its later phases. They had no alternative comprehensive plan, and they were unable to find out the plan being followed.

In this context, the non-statutory route of planning could only further erode the effectiveness of both central ministerial policy and local autonomy. For the first time in Ontario, citizens could discern that the civil service had moved into a bureaucratic phase in which elected people seemed increasingly to be manipulated by public servants, who were increasingly remote from the real public needs and concerns. For this, we should not blame the civil service, but rather the elected people who let policy slip from their grasp.

A whole package of policies under the general umbrella of Design for Development were swiftly implemented. It is only in looking back that we can discern any trends. A notable achievement was the monumental *Economic Atlas of Ontario* (Dean and Matthews, 1969). A renowned regional geographer, Richard S. Thoman from Queen's University, was appointed Director of Regional Development in 1967, and subsequently launched an intensive process of research and coordination aimed at implementing the 1966 program.

In this period the independent local government review commissions were working and eventually reported. The main ones were: (1) Niagara (Mayo); (2) Ottawa-Carleton (Jones); (3) Lakehead (Hardy); (4) York (Jones); (5) Muskoka (Paterson); (6) Sudbury (Kennedy); (7) Waterloo (Fyfe); (8) Peel-Halton (Plunkett); (9) Brant (Smith); (10) Hamilton-Wentworth (Steele); (11) Haldimand-Norfolk (Richardson); and the Metropolitan Toronto review (Goldenberg). There were also administrative reviews of the Timmins-Porcupine, Durham-Ontario County areas, and later simply the encouragement of local government reviews by cooperating groups of municipalities in areas such as Essex, Lambton, Oxford, Middlesex, Grey-Bruce, and other unreconstructed areas.

In essence the process was a gradual change from the launching of independent review commissions to internal civil service recommendations and then to locally guided consultant studies. The review documents were generally perceptive and much more concerned with fundamental issues than the white papers or eventual legislation which emerged. It appears that at some point the decision was made to launch again a number of separate experiments. No two regional governments are alike.

For example, in Haldimand-Norfolk the planning function, including the control over land severances and building and plumbing permits, is lifted directly to the regional level, thereby making strategic regional planning at the level of the regional municipality much more difficult, and giving the lower-tier only very limited responsibilities. In Timmins-Porcupine a vast northern area is combined in one unitary municipality with all functions directly exercised by council, except that there is an independent library board! In the Lakehead and in Timmins, the pattern is one of unitary control and amalgamation. The Lakehead, for example, combined the former cities of Port Arthur and Fort William, leaving local inhabitants the option of choosing the name. All the rest are two-tier systems, with local lower-tier municipalities amalgamated to form fewer units, and the upper-tier having varying patterns of regional responsibility. In retrospect, it looks suspiciously like a modified county system. Fyfe, Plunkett, Goldenberg, Hardy and Kennedy all pointed to the need for a more fundamental revision of the system, particularly to cure tax-base problems, but their insights were not accepted.

Nevertheless, the Robarts administration sought "to make local government as strong and meaningful as possible," and grant structures were modified to favour the new regional municipalities which emerged. First, there came the Regional Municipalities of Niagara (twenty-six local municipalities reduced to twelve), Ottawa-Carleton, and Sudbury, and the new cities of Thunder Bay (Lakehead) and Timmins (Timmins-Porcupine).

One essential issue was avoided; unification of the municipal and educational branches of local government. As noted earlier, in this period the education branch of local government was drastically reorganized. In 1965 the existing 3,267 locally elected school boards were reduced to 1,673. In 1969 these were once again reduced to 235. Only a few of these conformed to the new regional municipal system which was emerging. In essence, this new system frustrated hopes for social planning. Understandably, in view of the political history of educational autonomy, the Progressive Conservative government was not ready to make the educational function one directly part of municipal regional government. This problem remains. We are still locked in to nineteenth-century concepts of two branches of local government.

The research activities of the Regional Development Branch were leading to statements about emerging regional plans at the provincial level. In 1968 the then Premier Robarts and the Hon. W. Darcy McKeough produced (November 28, 1968, and December 2, 1968) in the Legislature "Design for Development, Phase Two." This noted that a number of regional programs were being reviewed: the Master Tourist Plan (by the Department of Tourism and Information), the recommendations of the Goals Plan of the Metropolitan Toronto and Region Transportation Study (MTARTS), and a special study of the Niagara Escarpment. The regional development councils were to produce strategy plans for 1968–72, and three regional strategies were to be launched: a special ARDA development program for northwest Ontario; the Central Ontario Region, based on MTARTS; and a pilot approach to regional planning in midwest Ontario. Further, an extensive study of the Oshawa Area Planning and Development Systems (OAPADS) was launched and similar studies proposed for the other urbanized parts of southern Ontario.

The objective then was to knit together the strands of regional economic development and local government reorganization, bearing in mind the Beckett Report (the Select Committee on the Municipal Act and Related Acts), the Smith Report (Taxation) and the White Report (Select Committee on Taxation). A special Inter-Departmental Committee on Northern Ontario was created. Regional government was to be advanced rapidly in Niagara, Ottawa-Carleton (the first real regional government, operative January 1, 1969), and on all sides of Metropolitan Toronto, as well as in Lakehead, Muskoka, Sudbury. The minimum level for a lower-tier municipality was set at 8,000 to 10,000, at a time when 90 per cent of Ontario municipalities were below this figure. All proposed annexations or amalgamations initiated by municipalities were, under Section 25A of the Municipal Act, referred to the minister for study. This was, in effect, a moratorium on municipally initiated change. The minimum regional municipalities population was set at 150,000 to 200,000 and the education regions were to be generally coterminous with the new regional municipalities.

The MTARTS report of 1962 dealt with the main commuter field of Toronto. In 1968 the reports with their suggested planning strategies, called goals plans, were published. No final version was proposed. Instead "the Government will publish a development plan for each of the areas covered by Ontario's ten Regional Development Councils, and in addition, a single, comprehensive provincial plan, according to Richard Thoman, Director of the Regional Development Branch of the Treasury." (Toronto *Globe and Mail*, March 7, 1969)

This plan has never appeared, and neither have the ten regional plans. On March 7, 1969, the ten advisory plans of the regional development councils (the strategy plans for 1968–72 requested in Phase Two of Design for Development) were tabled in the Legislature. The Central Ontario Council, for example, rejected all four current government plans. The Mid-West Council forecast rural decline. The North-East Council pointed to lack of job choices and the need for an industrial location policy. The Georgian Bay Council pointed to the widest gap in prosperity. These plans were short-lived. In 1972 the councils were abolished. Later so were the ten economic regions, to be replaced by five administrative regions.

The next phases moved with great speed. First, in 1970 the province defined the preferred growth strategy for Toronto in a report called "Design for Development: The Toronto-Centred Region." This set out three basic zones: conurbation and parkway belt; agriculturally oriented commuter area; and rural area with reinforced centres. It also recommended a reorientation of Toronto growth eastwards. This became policy. (The joint federal-provincial location of the new airport at Pickering then thwarted OAPADS which was suspended.) It is important to note that this was not a statutory plan; it contradicted approved official plans under the Planning Act, it was not capable of being implemented other than by "umbrella" control of provincial finances, or by subsequent piecemeal measures.

At this point it is worth reviewing the various major policy statements which attempted to rationalize the shifts in direction in Design for Development:

1) The original policy statement, "Design for Development" (1966), was a bold sketch for inter-departmental coordination in a rudimentary framework of provincial planning on a regional scale. It was oriented to achieving economic growth and development, and to the use of financial incentives to guide new industry to under-developed regions. We could call this document "Phase One" but it was not envisaged as such.

2) The second major policy statement, "Design for Development, Phase Two" (1968), was a shift to tie together regional development and regional government and to link that idea to the theme that provincial regional planning needs revised local government. As much as anything, this was caused by the rivalries between the various economic ministries and those dealing with local government. These opposing bureaucracies launched a plethora of contra-dictory studies, and were all eventually swallowed up in the massive Ministry of the Treasury, Economics and Intergovernmental Affairs by 1972.

3) The advent of the Toronto-Centred Region Concept (1970) was the shift to structuring development (and to curb the power of the Toronto federation, as in the killing of the Spadina expressway). This may be called an "interventionalist" strategy. It also avoided the problem posed by the MTARTS (Metropolitan Toronto and Region Transportation Study, 1962–1970) group, which was designing a physical plan for the metropolis and southwest Ontario to fill the void resulting from municipal plans.

4) Since the task of doing major regional plans proved to be much more complex than had at first been imagined, the provincial bureaucracy then moved to set target populations for the various municipal entities without actually designing the housing areas. So many changes were made to the original Toronto-Centred Region concept and to the strategy plans that some status reports were issued to rationalize these further shifts. Other regions were given lower priority. The status reports (August 1971) on the Toronto and Northwest Ontario regions were treating those as priority areas.

5) By April 1972, even though the regional development councils had been abolished, there was virtual completion by the provincial bureaucracy of what were called Phase One Reports for all ten economic regions. (The ten regions still remained as provincial planning entities in what was now a highly centralized operation.) These were simply discussion documents for alternative growth strategies, heavily oriented to a few selected "growth centres."

6) This was then succeeded by a further statement, "Design for Development, Phase Three," published by Premier Davis in April 1972. Once again there was a shift in course. Phase Three purported to deal with provincial-municipal fiscal reform and was an attempt to knit together that prong of attack with provincial regional planning and development, and regional government. Regional development was now simply equated with regional planning.

The next steps were the Parkway Belt legislation in the Mississauga conurbation (the Hamilton-Toronto-Oshawa urban belt), confiscating private use rights; the setting of population targets for 2000 A.D. to be imposed on all municipalities in the Toronto-Centred Region; the steering of funds to change official plans; task forces to build new or expanded cities in Barrie, Port Hope, Cobourg and in Pickering (Cedarwood); studies by the new Management Board (the main coordinating body derived from the reorganization of the Ontario government itself) for means to decentralize government services to five new regions, each urban-centred (Toronto, Ottawa, London, Sudbury, Thunder Bay); the creation of the Niagara Escarpment Commission; the location of a new city in Haldimand-Norfolk to be developed by a new Ontario Land Corporation; new legislation on land speculation; a new regional advisory system with five committees to represent industry, universities, the public, and local governments; a schedule by 1975 for local government reform for all southern Ontario; the end of the regional government provincially imposed system; and the idea that the province will build ten new cities in southern Ontario.

Regional municipalities were rapidly put in place in York, Durham, Hamilton-Wentworth, Waterloo, and new advisory boards (one in each of the five provincial regions) set up. Once this was done, with regional government covering all the urban areas, steps were taken to decentralize some provincial operations to the five selected centres (Toronto, London, Ottawa, Sudbury and Thunder Bay).

Not the least of the changes was the new Ontario Planning and Development Act, 1973, which gives broad powers to the minister, pays no real attention to private land rights or the real problem of compensation and betterment, and sets up a means by which arbitrary planning areas can be designated, as well as a planning process so fraught with public participation that the tight urban control process is further strengthened and decision-making extended by about a further five years. The functions which had been separately exercised by the Departments of Economics and Development and Municipal Affairs were first, in the government reorganization, concentrated into one Ministry of Treasury, Economics and Intergovernmental Affairs. With the onset of the inevitable housing and development crisis resulting from the reversal of the original Design for Development came the shift of the housing and planning functions to a new Ministry of Housing. Ontario also used two agencies for industrial development (Ontario Development Corporation and Northern Ontario Development Corporation) increasingly within the total context. Rural local government still remains unreconstructed.

Ontario still has not found a satisfactory method for provincial planning and, despite many drastic and dramatic changes, it has yet to put municipal government on a workable base. Had the Progressive Conservative government revised the Municipal Act, resolved the tax-base problems of, say, seventy to a hundred new regional municipalities, and then delegated to them the essential functions for implementing broader segments of an overall provincial planning strategy, it would have freed itself for doing federal-provincial joint regional planning in the five to ten larger economic planning regions. Had it established an industrial location policy setting up planned industrial estates and providing serviced land, instead of just using financial incentives, and had it used a public-private partnership to create new towns and cities, and to expand existing ones, it would have achieved more durable patterns. The process has been like a poker game in which the depressed regions, the metropolis, and the local municipalities were allowed to win all the chips, but on cashing them in, found them worthless. The province is now even more highly centralized than before.

Ontario has in the period 1954–74 passed through a revolution. Socially, the province has moved very substantially towards state socialism, and away from the concept of local autonomy and the significance of private property to a confiscatory form of planning. Housing and urban development have been increasingly controlled and directed. When the Design for Development process began, it typically took about two years to gain the necessary approvals to begin development. By 1974, a period of five or six years was not unusual. During this period Ontario became dominated by urbanization, by the fact of metropolis, and began to experience the problems of post-industrial society. Large questions still remain in the agricultural areas and in the non-metropolitan regions, substantially the same as at the outset of these government programs. A strong centralized bureaucracy has emerged. Local government has been significantly weakened in the guise of reform. Policy is dominated by technocrats, so that an allegedly private enterprise conservative government has moved significantly to statist, socialist and directive economic, social and political systems.

Whether the result is what anyone wanted is an open question. The prospect of the future is the need to go back to first principles, and it will not be an easy task in this new setting. Should there be an economic depression, however, the present structure is unlikely to survive, for it still contains the same weaknesses as at the outset.

Regional government and development will likely stay on Ontario's agenda for the next generation or more. The real tasks of regional planning, regional development and regional government, like the real purpose of Design for Development, have yet to be fulfilled.

SELECTED BIBLIOGRAPHY

BECKETT, H. *Select Committee of the Ontario Legislature on the Municipal Act.* Toronto: Queen's Printer, 1965.

BREWIS, T. H. *Regional Economic Policies in Canada.* Toronto: Macmillan of Canada, 1969.

CAROL, H. *Development Regions in Southern Ontario based on City-Centred Regions.* Ontario Geographer 4, 1969, pp. 13–29.

DEAN, W. G. (ed.) *Economic Atlas of Ontario.* Toronto: University of Toronto Press, 1969.

FIELD, N. C., and KERR, D. P. *Geographical Aspects of Growth in the Metropolitan Toronto Region.* Toronto: Regional Development Branch, Ontario Dept. of Treasury and Economics, 1968.

FRANK, R. H. *A Pilot Study on Regional Labour Income in Ontario. Ontario Economic Review*: 2:7, 1964, pp. 3–12.

GERTLER, L. O. *Regional Planning in Canada.* Montreal: Harvest House, 1973.

GOLANT, S., and BOURNE, L. S. *Growth Characteristics of the Ontario-Quebec Urban System.* Toronto: Centre for Urban and Community Studies, University of Toronto, 1968.

Government of Ontario. *Design for Development.* Toronto, 1966.

———. *Design for Development, Phase Two.* Toronto, 1968.

———. *Design for Development: North-Western Ontario Regions, Phase Two, Policy Recommendations.* Toronto, 1970.

———. *Design for Development: A Policy Statement on the North-Western Ontario Region.* Toronto, 1971.

———. *Design for Development: The Toronto-Centred Region.* Toronto, 1970.

———. *Design for Development: A Status Report on the Toronto-Centred Region.* Toronto, 1971.

———. *The Niagara Escarpment Study.* Toronto, 1969.

———. *Design for Development, Phase Three.* Toronto, 1972.

———. *Design for Development: The Niagara Escarpment.* Toronto, 1973.

———. *Design for Development: The Parkway Belt.* Toronto, 1973.

HILLS, C. A.; LOVE, D. V., and LACATE, D. S. *Developing a Better Environment: Ecological Land-Use Planning in Ontario.* Toronto: Ontario Economic Council, 1970.

HODGE, G. *Theory and Reality of Industrial Location in the Toronto Region.* Toronto: University of Toronto, 1970.

KRUEGER, R., et al. (eds.) *Regional and Resource Planning in Canada,* second edition. Toronto: Holt, Rinehart and Winston, 1970.

THOMAN, R. *Design for Development in Ontario: The Initiation of a Regional Planning Program.* Toronto, 1971.

12
A.K. MC DOUGALL & M.W. WESTMACOTT

Ontario in
Canadian Federation

THE PROVINCE of Ontario was created in 1867 by the British North America Act, a statute of the imperial Parliament, which outlined the federal structure for Canada. It established two levels of government beyond the municipality and defined the jurisdiction of each. In addition, the power to tax and thus raise revenue was defined so as to give the central government in Ottawa not only the main planning and development powers but also an overriding power to finance its programs. The provincial governments, on the other hand, were given a general power over matters of a local and private nature. In addition, social and cultural powers were assigned to provincial governments so that differences in population and heritage would not require continuous recognition in the functions of the central government. Thus the provinces were relegated local and social problems, while the central government developed and defended the country.

Federation had two major effects on politics in Ontario. First, it created two levels of government beyond the municipality. This required the political resources to run both levels. Secondly, it divided the financial resources between the two levels of government. This meant that neither the provincial nor the federal government was isolated when it was planning its activities. Instead, the activities of each level of government had an impact on the same community and should the demands of either become burdensome, they would have an effect on the actions of the other. At Confederation, this problem was not significant in Ontario.

From 1867 to 1872, political resources were common and a separate provincial political entity did not appear until the Costigan Act of 1872 precluded members of provincial legislatures from sitting in the House of Commons. Political leaders such as John Sandfield Macdonald, Edward Blake and Alexander Mackenzie were leaders in both the federal House of Commons and the Legislature of the Province of Ontario. During these early years the courts also were confirming the predominance of the federal Legislature. In 1871, however, the situation changed. The threat of a North American war was subsiding with the conclusion of the Treaty of Washington between Great Britain and the United States; the Fenian movement was effectively thwarted from its border excursions by the U.S. border patrol which arrested the raiders as they crossed into Manitoba; and the provinces were vocal in their criticism of the financial arrangements under Confederation.

The removal of external threat, combined with internal politics, made the creation of two independent political entities reasonable, if not necessary. It had a profound impact in Ontario. The provincial premier and leader of the coalition of groups which eventually became known as the Liberal party, Edward Blake, chose to retain his federal seat and leave the provincial Legislature; so did his lieutenant, Alexander Mackenzie. These two men were to lead the federal government after Sir John A. Macdonald was defeated by the Pacific Scandal. Before they could leave, however, they had to find a leader for the Ontario party. Oliver Mowat, a Father of Confederation, who had retired to the Bench, was persuaded to take the job. Mowat was a long-time acquaintance of Sir John A. Macdonald, but he believed in a strong and equal partnership between the central and provincial governments. When he assumed office in 1872, Mowat used provincial power over the administration of justice to pursue Ontario's claims to the northwestern portion of what is now Ontario. In addition, he challenged Macdonald over federal power to disallow provincial legislation and over the inadequacy of the federal-provincial transfer payments defined in the BNA Act. His and the other provincial premiers' struggle to establish a sovereign provincial authority led to interprovincial co-operation. Their efforts eventually resulted in a meeting of provincial reform premiers in 1887 to define a new status for provincial governments within the federal system. Their actions were supported by contemporary decisions of the Judicial Committee of the Privy Council which favoured the provinces at the expense of a paramount federal government.

When Laurier became Prime Minister in 1896 and the Liberal party finally filled the void left by the Conservative party after Macdonald's death, the provincial leadership provided the nucleus of his cabinet. The opposition of many provincial premiers to the central government was thus transferred to the federal scene. Mowat himself entered Laurier's cabinet as Minister of Justice. The new government illustrated the importance of provincial experience and support as a basis for strengthening the federal parliamentary opposition for government.

In Ontario the process also has worked the other way. Federal members of Parliament have become leaders of the provincial party. The most outstanding illustration of this process is Mitch Hepburn. First elected to the House of Commons in 1926, Hepburn remained a backbencher much against his own assessment of his capacity until 1930 when he decided to enter the contest for the leadership of the Liberal party of Ontario. The provincial Liberal party was in disarray; Hepburn offered a new approach to politics, especially to prohibition, and he was elected. During the next four years he remained a federal Liberal backbencher and ran affairs in Toronto from Ottawa. Finally, in 1934 he ran and was elected to the Ontario Legislature.

The 1934 provincial election saw a change of government and Hepburn became Premier. Relations between the Liberal prime minister of Canada, Mackenzie King, and the Liberal provincial premier, Mitch Hepburn, remained superficially good, but friction quickly developed between the provincial and federal party organizers over the dispensing of political favours. This friction became serious after the 1935 election when Hepburn attempted to get Mackenzie King to place one of his supporters in the federal cabinet. King, of course, saw himself as leader of the federal Liberal party and refused to appear to bend at the direction of a provincial premier. This incident highlighted a fundamental source of conflict between the Liberal party of Ontario and the Liberal party of Canada— the personality and demand for paramountcy of each leader within their common segment of the party. The result was a contest between King and Hepburn over the control of the Liberal party machine in their home province of Ontario. The conflict, aggravated by differing priorities of the two levels of government in policy areas such as hydro, predictably led to serious struggles between the federal and provincial factions for control of offices within the Liberal party of Ontario. The Hepburn faction was eventually successful. At the public level, it led to increasingly strong anti-Mackenzie King outbursts by Hepburn and finally in January 1940 to an all-party coalition within the provincial Legislature to challenge King's war policies.

Hepburn's drive to maintain control of his party combined with his political success in provincial elections to remove the Ontario Liberal party from the federal domain. King responded by calling a federal general election to justify his war policy. His success drove many Hepburn Liberals from the party and Ontario's reaction led to the rise of the Conservative party under George Drew, a man who supported Hepburn's stand against King.

It is interesting that Hepburn's reaction to King coincided with unprecedented government involvement in welfare and fiscal policy. The problems posed by the depression exceeded the competence of any one government. The federal government responded by appointing a royal commission to rationalize government fiscal and welfare responsibility so that similar crises could be met within the federal system.[1] By 1938 Hepburn had turned outside of Ontario for support in his battle with King. He found an ally in Maurice Duplessis, the Premier of Quebec, and between them they formed an alliance to protect provincial rights. The royal commission received little support from Quebec and less from Hepburn. The findings of the commission were shelved, but the commitments arising from the depression and then the Second World War demanded some sort of intergovernmental cooperation, since financial resources were no longer great enough to permit the two levels of government to tap the resources of the same community independently.

The political resources within Ontario were divided, however. The provincial rights stand of Hepburn and Drew challenged federal plans and countered federal political ploys at the provincial level. A divided provincial-federal political system thus was confronted with the necessity for an increasingly integrated fiscal system. The dispute centred on the definition of government priorities. Ontario focused on the needs of the province, but accepted its position as a patron of the poorer areas of the country. Canada focused on the overall needs of the country and not

1 The Royal Commission on Dominion Provincial Relations (known as the Rowell-Sirois Commission, after its co-chairmen) was appointed in August 1937 and the report was presented to the government in May 1940. For a detailed examination of terms of reference of the commission, see D. V. Smiley, ed., *The Rowell-Sirois Report Book I* (Toronto: McClelland and Stewart, 1963), pp. 1–6.

those of its most economically viable unit. The result was a continuing struggle between Toronto and Ottawa over who was best capable of governing the area which is Ontario. Fiscal resources provided a focus for the dispute and specific policy issues added intermittent flashes to the smouldering fire. If a federal program corresponded to Ontario's plans, it was exploited. If one was not so significant, it was ignored. The problem was to provide a fiscal base for both the federal and provincial governments without destroying the source of that revenue—the population and the corporate structure.

Since 1945 Ottawa and Toronto have met at federal-provincial conferences and at meetings of ministers and public servants, in an attempt to establish mutually acceptable long-term goals and priorities. These negotiations have centred on two main areas: the role of the provinces and federal government in the development of economic policy, and the division of the power to raise revenue by direct taxation.[2] These areas are significant enough to trace each in turn.

ECONOMIC PLANNING

The role of the provinces and the federal government in the development of economic policy has been a subject of continuing controversy between Ottawa and the Government of Ontario. Ontario has consistently argued that intergovernmental machinery should be established to ensure that the provinces have a regularized and significant say in policy development. The conflict between the two governments on this issue can be illustrated by reference both to the response of the Government of Ontario to the federal government at the Federal-Provincial Conferences on Reconstruction convened in 1945 and 1946 and to the policy position adopted by Ontario at a federal-provincial conference on inflation in 1971.

In August 1945 a federal-provincial conference was convened to discuss the post-war development of the Canadian economy. The federal government put forward a series of

2 For an analysis of some of the issues of conflict between the federal government and the Government of Ontario, see Joe Martin, *The Role and Place of Ontario in Confederation: The Evolution of Policy in Contemporary Ontario*, Series No. 4 (Ontario Economic Council, 1974).

proposals dealing with the division of tax revenue between the two levels of government, social security and public investment policy. These programs were presented to the provinces as a package and collectively they became known as the "Green Book Proposals." In particular, the federal government recommended that the provinces give up their right to levy personal and corporate income taxes as well as succession duties. In return, the provinces were to receive a per capita grant from the federal treasury. A number of shared-cost programs dealing with old age pensions, health insurance, public health and hospital insurance were also included as part of the package. Finally, the federal government offered financial assistance to those provinces and municipalities who would plan their investment programs in accordance with federal objectives. Only investment projects approved by the federal government would be eligible for federal assistance.

The reaction of the Government of Ontario to the federal proposals was swift and very predictable. Premier Drew rejected the proposals on the grounds that they would seriously limit the autonomy of the provinces. In a series of specific counter-proposals, Ontario proposed the establishment of two federal-provincial structures specifically designed to give the provinces a larger role in the development of economic policy than was envisaged in the federal proposals. Premier Drew recommended the establishment of a Dominion-Provincial Coordinating Committee composed of the Prime Minister and the provincial premiers. The committee was designed to act as a "continuing channel of information between all governments of Canada" and to assume overall responsibility for the development of economic policy. The committee was to be assisted in its work by a Dominion-Provincial Economic Board. The board, comprised of technical representatives from the federal and provincial governments would assemble information pertaining to taxation and investment policies of both the federal and the provincial governments.

Twenty-five years later, Premier William Davis advanced a similar proposal when he urged the establishment of a continuing federal-provincial committee to develop and coordinate economic policy. Implicit in the Premier's proposal was the belief that both levels of government should jointly participate in the development of national economic policy.

In both instances the proposals put forward by Ontario were rejected by the federal government, although it was willing to acknowledge the need for more intensive and more regularized consultations between the two levels of government. The federal authorities, in essence, have refused to accept the proposition that both levels of government should participate jointly in the development of economic policy for the entire nation. The dispute between Ottawa and Queen's Park continues, centring on such explosive policy issues as unemployment and inflation.

THE DIVISION OF REVENUE FROM DIRECT TAXATION

The Government of Ontario, in a similar manner, has consistently argued the case for a greater degree of fiscal autonomy for the provinces and has strongly resisted any attempts by the federal government to control an ever-increasing share of revenue from direct taxation. Conversely, the federal government has resisted Ontario's demands for greater fiscal decentralization and has taken the position that it must have access to a significant portion of the revenue from direct taxation to regulate the level of economic activity and to redistribute income within the federal sysem. This ongoing controversy between Ottawa and Toronto can be illustrated by an examination of the events surrounding the negotiation of the tax rental and the tax-sharing arrangements.

During the Second World War all nine provinces enacted legislation relinquishing their right to levy corporation and income taxes as well as succession duties. In return, the provinces were to be compensated by the payment of an unconditional subsidy from the federal treasury. Despite the fact that the War Time Tax Agreements were to be a "temporary" measure, Ottawa proposed in 1945 that these agreements be renegotiated for a further five-year period. The federal proposal came as no great surprise because the continuance of the tax rental agreements was clearly in the interests of the federal government. In Ottawa's view, tax rental would standardize tax rates, stabilize provincial income and ensure that the provinces (particularly the have-not provinces) would have the fiscal capacity to develop programs within their jurisdiction. In J. A. Maxwell's view, "no great perspicacity was required ... to foresee that the forces that made for the federal occupancy during the war would be spent after the war, that taxpayers might wish to retain the luxury of one law and one return, and that those provincial governments which received more by way of subsidies than from provincial collections might prefer to continue the agreements."[3]

The policy objectives of the federal government and the Government of Ontario were clearly in conflict. On the one hand, the federal government was pursuing a policy that would inevitably lead to fiscal centralization and ensure federal dominance in the postwar development of the Canadian economy. Furthermore, the federal government was determined to stabilize provincial revenues and redistribute income from the have to the have-not provinces. The thrust of these policy proposals was not in the best interests of Ontario and the response of the Government of Ontario was negative. While Queen's Park was prepared to accept a common income and corporation tax base, Premier Drew observed that in his view both levels of government should continue to levy taxes in these two fields. It was the Premier's view that "from Confederation onwards a tacit understanding existed to the effect that direct taxation should be reserved for the provinces." In addition, Ontario urged the federal government to vacate the following fields of direct taxation: succession duties, gasoline, amusement, race track pari-mutuel, security transfers and electricity.

The Government of Quebec supported Ontario's position and both governments refused to participate in the 1947–52 Tax Rental Agreements. With the expiration of the War Time Agreements in 1947, Ontario and Quebec levied a 7 per cent corporation tax. In 1950 Ontario enacted legislation authorizing the collection of a provincial income tax equal to 5 per cent of the federal tax. While the legislation was never proclaimed, the Government of Ontario has continued to use the threat of a provincial income tax as a bargaining point in discussions with the federal govern-

3 See J. A. Maxwell, *Recent Developments in Dominion-Provincial Fiscal Relations in Canada* (New York: National Bureau of Economic Research), p. 13.

ment over the division of direct taxation revenue between the two governments.

After prolonged negotiations, Ontario agreed to participate in the Tax Rental Agreement which was to last from 1952 to 1957. Under the terms of the agreement, payments from the federal government were to be based on the "potential tax capacity" of the province to raise revenue at stipulated rates of taxation. This option, known as the "tax yield option," was specifically developed for the Province of Ontario.[4] The negotiation of this option was significant in that the federal government explicitly recognized differences in the fiscal capacity of the provinces and the need to distinguish between the tax rental and the fiscal capacity aspects of the tax rental agreements.

The Tax Rental Agreements of 1957–62 were a logical extension of the 1952 agreement. For the first time the tax rental and the fiscal capacity aspects of the agreement were separated into two distinct parts. Under the terms of the agreement, participating provinces would receive 10 per cent of personal income tax collected in the province, 9 per cent of tax revenues paid by corporations and 50 per cent of the succession duties raised by the federal government in the province. The size of the rental payments paid to the provinces varied not in accordance with provincial population or gross national product but in accordance with the level of economic activity in each of the participating provinces. This type of arrangement had certain distinct advantages for the Province of Ontario. Ontario could participate in the tax rental agreements with the assurance that the amount of revenue returned to the province by the federal government would be directly related to the level of economic activity in the province. Ontario agreed to participate in that portion of the agreement relating to income tax.

Since 1962 Ontario has agreed to share the field of personal income tax with the federal government. In recent times the principle of tax-sharing has not been an issue between Ottawa and Toronto. Rather, discussions between

4 See Rodney Grey, "Conditional Grants in Aid," *Proceedings*, Canadian Institute of Public Administration, 1953, p. 353, and R. M. Burns, "Recent Developments in Federal-Provincial Fiscal Arrangements in Canada," *National Tax Journal*, September 1962, pp. 228–229.

the two governments have centred on Ontario's repeated demand that the federal government vacate an increasingly larger portion of the direct tax field. The most recent proposal, in May 1973, put forward by Ontario was that the federal government withdraw from all shared-cost programs in the fields of health and welfare and post-secondary education. The province then would assume full responsibility for the programs and in return would receive an additional thirty-three points of personal income tax. When added to the twenty-eight tax points that the provinces currently receive under the terms of the 1972 Tax-Sharing Agreement, this would give the provincial government control of over 60 per cent of the revenue raised from personal income tax. The federal government has refused to accept Ontario's proposals, arguing that it would significantly weaken Ottawa's ability to regulate the economy and redistribute income from the have to the have-not provinces. The conflict over the division of direct taxation revenue rests on the differing focus of the two levels of government; and although both realize that income should be redistributed, neither is willing to relinquish its perception of the paramountcy of its own long-term needs and responsibility.

ON THE POLITICAL FRONT

As federal-provincial fiscal relations unfolded, the relations between federal and provincial political resources remained significant. The federal Liberal party, although not pleased with a Progressive Conservative government in Ontario, was frightened of a provincial Liberal leader of the strength of Hepburn. Such a man would be a challenge to the federal Liberal party machine and thus might reduce Liberal influence in the province. Conversely, the established Conservative party in Ontario provided a source of leadership recruitment for the federal Progressive Conservative party.

Federal-provincial rhetoric over the allocation of resources between Ontario and the federal government is simplified if competing organizations and parties are in office. The problem of similar parties was witnessed with the rise and fall of Diefenbaker between 1957 and 1963.

Premier Leslie Frost was an overt supporter of Diefenbaker on the campaign trail. When Diefenbaker won in 1958, however, he spoke for the federal government and, although cooperation was evident in the renegotiation of federal-provincial fiscal relations in 1958, the latent problem of differing priorities remained. In 1961 a leadership convention was held for the Progressive Conservative party in Ontario. John P. Robarts became leader and assumed a more businesslike approach to government. He continued to support the federal Progressive Conservative leader but with a consolidated Ontario organization devoted to the development of Ontario. The result has been criticism of the Ontario effort by Diefenbaker as he attempted to explain his defeat by Lester Pearson in 1963.

With Pearson, the Liberal party returned to power in Ottawa and party loyalty was no longer challenged by federal-provincial differences. The result was increased flexibility for Prime Minister Robarts of Ontario. Both Pearson and Robarts were having problems within their own jurisdictions. The federal Liberals were rocked by scandals. Robarts was preoccupied with public concern over alleged government meddling with police services and then with public outcry over proposed investigatory powers for the Ontario Police Commission. At the intergovernmental level, Pearson was confronted with an active separatist movement in Quebec. Premier Lesage was modernizing Quebec and attempting to lead the volatile province without losing the support of the cultural majority. He pressed his claims at the federal-provincial conferences in 1963, and then at a conference in Quebec City in March 1964. Pearson, the diplomat, encountered Quebec's demands and responded by moderating his proposed Canada Pension Plan to reflect Quebec's desire for autonomy and by establishing a Tax Structure Committee to provide a data base from which both sides could negotiate subsequent fiscal relations. Pearson's action modified federal-provincial relations and provided a chance for provincial intiative. Mr. Robarts, still rebounding from issues in his home province, seized the opportunity. The similarity of the fiscal aspects of the demands of Quebec and Ontario for more provincial autonomy combined with the lack of federal initiative to permit the creation of a new interprovincial alliance against the predominance of the federal government.

On January 5, 1965, the Ontario government established an Advisory Committee on Confederation to explore, define, and suggest ways to ameliorate the position of Ontario in Confederation. The committee reviewed contemporary constitutional issues, and their work provided the basis for a new provincial assault on the federal position. Then, in January 1967, Robarts announced that Ontario would host a conference of provincial premiers in Toronto to assess the relationship between the federal and provincial governments in Canada, and the place of French Canada in Canadian society. Ottawa was not pleased with Ontario's initiative, but they sent observers to the meeting. This meeting, the Confederation of Tomorrow Conference, offered an opportunity for the provinces to coordinate their attack on federal power and the BNA Act. It also offered Quebec a chance to press for its cultural and financial demands within a broader "decentralization" alliance rather than on its own. Ontario's initiative, under the leadership of a Conservative premier, permitted an alternate constellation of power outside of the House of Commons to challenge the federal government in the name of provincial rights. Unlike the 1887 experience, however, the coalition which challenged Pearson did not succeed him. Instead, a new Liberal leader, Pierre Elliott Trudeau, who personified federalist reaction to the more extreme separatists, followed Pearson as Prime Minister.

Internal political relations, if less sensational, are still important in both the Liberal and Conservative parties. Federal Liberal leaders actively supported Robert Nixon in the Ontario Liberal party's 1974 leadership convention against the more aggressive federal backbencher, Norman Cafik. In a similar fashion, Toronto-based Tories actively supported Michael Meighen as national Conservative party president against a potential Ontario rival, Don Matthews, thus eradicating any potential challenge to Premier Davis' predominance in the province. Such conflict supports the predominance of the rival political dynasties in Toronto and Ottawa.

In the last decade this struggle has assumed an added dimension. With increased professionalization, government has become more complex. The Robarts ministry responded by using its resources to build an expert, urban-based government capable of harnessing the resources offered by expertise. Government bureaucracy grew and after 1963 included a central coordinating structure capable of bringing modern expertise in fiscal and policy areas to the bargaining table with the federal government. The result is an increasingly complex relationship between Toronto and Ottawa with experts ranged on opposite sides of the table refuting each other's findings, as they struggle for scarce fiscal resources and for minor alterations to intergovernmental agreements which will permit one or the other to realize their priorities within the general wording of the agreement.

Recently the federal government has attempted to avoid this conflict by using its superior revenue-creating power to construct and deliver programs directly to the public. Their attempt to by-pass the provincial government has accentuated the inconsistency of national and provincial goals at the community level. This inconsistency, combined with intergovernmental competition over political paramountcy in the province, has taken federal-provincial negotiations into the public forum. Political rhetoric has become more obvious since 1971, and the expert has been harnessed to construct and interpret indicators which prove that either Toronto or Ottawa is responsible for current fiscal problems or for accentuating or prolonging social problems. This struggle, in many ways, is a struggle between the political resources of two parties, both of which rely on the support of the electorate. The complexity of the modern federal-provincial structure has made it increasingly difficult to allocate responsibility. The technical nature of the negotiations has combined with the dogmatic flavour of political rhetoric to make the condition chronic.

The relationship between the Government of Ontario and the Government of Canada is one of competition for control of the political resources of the population. Each feels solely competent to govern in the name of the good of its jurisdiction. Neither party in power will tolerate the creation of a rival which may eclipse its paramountcy and destroy its mission. Federal-provincial relations in Ontario are marked by confrontation at the political level, increasing integration at the fiscal level, and confusion and competition at the community level.

SELECTED BIBLIOGRAPHY

DUPRE, J. S., *et al. Federalism and Policy Development.* Toronto: University of Toronto Press, 1973.

MC KENTY, NEIL. *Mitch Hepburn.* Toronto: McClelland and Stewart, 1967.

MOORE, A. M., J. H. PERRY, and D. I. BEACH. *The Financing of Canadian Federation.* Toronto: Canadian Tax Foundation, 1966.

SIMEON, R. *Federal-Provincial Diplomacy.* Toronto: University of Toronto Press, 1972.

SMILEY, D. V. *Canada in Question: Federalism in the Seventies.* Toronto: McGraw-Hill, 1972.

———. *Constitutional Adaptation and Canadian Federalism Since 1945.* Ottawa: Queen's Printer, 1970.

TRUDEAU, P. E. *Federal-Provincial Grants and the Spending Power of Parliament.* Ottawa: Queen's Printer, 1969.

PART THREE

POLITICS

13
JOHN WILSON

The Ontario
Political Culture

A N IMAGE born of a century of experience cannot be expected to disappear overnight. It is not surprising, therefore, that our understanding of the most essential characteristics of the Canadian political system is still dominated by the contrast between the two founding cultures. Indeed, the difference between French and English Canada is so great, it is said, that where questions of fundamental political values are concerned the variation in political experience which is acknowledged to exist among the English-speaking provinces can be dismissed as virtually irrelevant. In short, if Canada has more than one political culture in the eyes of most modern observers the distinction between Quebec and the rest of the country is the only one which should be made.

There could hardly be a more striking illustration of the extent to which such a judgment overstates the case than the almost universal tendency of social scientists to assign to English Canada as a whole a pattern of beliefs and values which most historians would recognize as properly belonging only to Ontario.[1] But even at the level of political behaviour there is some ground for supposing that the diversity which is found *within* English Canada may reflect differences in attitudes and orientations to the political system every bit as profound as the broader contrast between Quebec and the rest of the country.[2] Moreover, and this merely reinforces the point, the evolution of the federation—particularly in the years since the end of the Second World War—has left each of the provinces (and not merely

---

1 See, for example, S. M. Lipset, "Revolution and Counter-Revolution —the United States and Canada," in *The Revolutionary Theme in Contemporary America*, ed. T. R. Ford (Lexington, Ky., 1967), pp. 21–64; S. M. Lipset, "Value Differences, Absolute or Relative: The English-Speaking Democracies," ch. 7 of his *The First New Nation: The United States in Historical and Comparative Perspective* (London, 1964); Gad Horowitz, "Conservatism, Liberalism, and Socialism in Canada: An Interpretation," ch. 1 of his *Canadian Labour in Politics* (Toronto, 1968); and S. D. Clark, "Canada and the American Value System," in his *The Developing Canadian Community*, 2nd ed. (Toronto, 1968).

2 An exploration of this possibility can be found in my "The Canadian Political Cultures: Towards a Redefinition of the Nature of the Canadian Political System," *Canadian Journal of Political Science*, vol. 7, no. 3 (Sept. 1974), pp. 438–483.

Quebec) master in its own house to the point where substantial variation in the economic and social life chances
of Canadians can easily occur from coast to coast.

It may be granted, of course, that such differences do not,
by themselves, constitute the evidence which would be
required to establish the existence of distinct political
cultures within English Canada. For the moment, therefore,
it will be sufficient to observe that political life in Western
Canada is manifestly different from political life in the
Atlantic provinces, and neither bears much resemblance to
Ontario.

THE DISTINCTIVENESS OF ONTARIO POLITICS

There are many reasons for supposing that Ontario may be
a province quite unlike the others. Not the least of these
are the relatively advanced state of her economic development and the fact that despite the often considerable
electoral success of the CCF (and later the NDP) since 1945
neither of the two original parties has shown much sign of
disappearing.[3] It is a pattern of party competition which is,
on the face of things, not only different from that of
Western Europe (where the rise of the social democratic
party has nearly always been accompanied by the decline
of the liberal centre party) but also quite unlike the experience of most other parts of English Canada where the
CCF/NDP has become a significant force.

In the context of these broader considerations, however,
what distinguishes Ontario from the rest of Canada is less
the strength of the traditional parties in the face of a
challenge from the left than the fact that it has been the
Conservatives who have dominated the province's politics
almost without interruption throughout the modern period.
In the years since the end of the First World War their
record far outstrips that of their counterparts in every
other part of Canada as well as at the federal level. They
have been in office at Queen's Park for forty-four of the
fifty-seven years since 1918, exactly twice as long as their
closest Tory competitor—in Nova Scotia—in the same

3 For a detailed account of the development of the Ontario party
  system see John Wilson and David Hoffman, "Ontario: A Three-
  Party System in Transition," in *Canadian Provincial Politics*, ed.
  Martin Robin (Scarborough, 1972), pp. 198–239.

period.[4] The Ontario Conservatives have, in fact, spent more time in office in the modern period than any other party in Canada, at any level. When these facts are combined with our knowledge of the nature of regional economic development in Canada, Ontario begins to look a good deal more like Great Britain (at least during the transitional phase in the development of the British party system) and rather less like any other part of Canada or the United States. For in Ontario, as almost nowhere else in North America, the Conservatives appear to have been the successful party of the right during and after the transition to an industrial society.

But there is another dimension to the success of the Ontario Tories in the modern period which suggests that the province may be unique. The most remarkable feature of their record, of course, is the fact that they have been *continuously* in office since 1943. By itself that is not a particularly outstanding accomplishment; although there is no other example of a really long-serving Conservative administration in Canadian history, there are several cases where one party has remained in power without interruption for a longer period of time than the thirty-two consecutive years of Tory rule which we have had in Ontario. But in every one of these cases—the Liberals in Ontario (1871–1905), in Nova Scotia (1882–1925), and in Quebec (1897–1936), and Social Credit in Alberta (1935–1971)—the government appears to have been dominated by one man, and was defeated at the polls within a short time of that man's vacating the office of premier. In fact, in every single case of a long-serving provincial administration in the modern period *outside* of Ontario almost identical circumstances have prevailed; the most obvious examples are the Liberals (under Angus L. Macdonald) in Nova Scotia, the Union Nationale (under Maurice Duplessis) in Quebec, and the CCF (under T. C. Douglas) in Saskatchewan. It seems likely, as well, that the lack of an obvious alternative within their own party had a part to play in the defeat of the Smallwood government in Newfoundland in 1971 and the

4 Even regarding the Union Nationale as the formal conservative party in Quebec makes little difference to the record. It has held office for only twenty-three of the fifty-seven years since the end of the First World War.

Bennett government in British Columbia in 1972. In other words, the customary pattern in cases of one-party dominance at the provincial level in Canada is for the government's extended life to depend upon the particular ability of a single individual who cannot be replaced when the time comes. Only in modern Ontario has there been a government capable both of changing its leaders and staying in office on a continuous basis.

There can hardly be any doubt that the Ontario Conservative party has, by any measurement, an extraordinary record of achievement. It is easy to observe, of course, that that record has been very substantially buttressed in the years since 1943 by the constant struggle for second place between the two opposition parties, or that in the period after the collapse of the Ross government in 1905 Tory dominance was virtually assured by the progressive decay of the Liberal party's organization in the province. But while these conditions have unquestionably affected the direction of modern Ontario politics, relying upon them exclusively as an explanation of the Conservative party's success (as many observers do) overlooks the extent to which the Tories have more or less consistently reflected the mood of the people of the province, and by doing so have themselves contributed heavily to their ability to stay in office.

It is not, in other words, simply the electoral record of the Conservative party—striking as that may be in comparison with other provinces—which distinguishes Ontario politics. The fact that the Ontario electorate has nearly always preferred the Conservative party throughout the modern period of industrial development suggests that the dominant political values of the province may be fundamentally different from those of the rest of English Canada.

THE IMPORTANCE OF COMPETENT GOVERNMENT

Different rates of party success, or variations between different political systems in the immediate circumstances of economic and political life, do not by any means prove the existence of different political cultures. But if it is granted for the moment that the very important political differences which clearly do exist between Ontario and the rest of the country at least point to the possibility that the province has a distinct political culture of its own, there is one way in which the proposition may be tested, so to speak, even without the thorough analysis of contemporary political attitudes which would be required to establish the case beyond any reasonable doubt.[5]

Governments do not, as a general rule, change hands by accident. No doubt there are a number of factors—such as the maldistribution of constituency boundaries—which may be decisive in a very close contest, but it remains the case, as David Hoffman has observed, that "elections are not so much won by oppositions as lost by governments." If its leaders do not make proper use of the tremendous manipulative powers which office in a parliamentary system provides, a government can easily engineer its own defeat.

Not infrequently, however, there is more to it than mere technical incompetence. It may also be the case that the government's ability to administer the political system as a whole has come generally into question. It seems probable, therefore, that the occasion of a government defeat can be a time when the electorate is expressing, by its condemnation of those in office, a judgment about the way in which government should be carried on within the system. If this is so, it would not be surprising if a careful study of the circumstances surrounding government defeats revealed something rather more fundamental about the dominant political values of that system. In short, the occasion of a change in government which has been brought about by the electorate may be one of the few times in a developed liberal democratic state when the particular dimensions of its political culture come into public view.

There are several reasons for believing that this is especially true in the case of Ontario. The most obvious, of course, is the fact that changes in government in the

---

5 Hardly any attention at all has been paid to these questions in the Ontario context. A number of studies at the constituency level have touched on the problem but by far the most thorough inquiry into the structure of political attitudes in the province was carried out in 1968 in a survey conducted by David Hoffman and Fred Schindeler. For an analysis of some aspects of their data see Fred Schindeler, "Perceptions of Federal-Provincial Relations in Ontario," paper presented to the annual meeting of the Canadian Political Science Association, Montreal, 1972.

province have been a comparatively rare occurrence in the hundred-odd years since Confederation. If the defeat of Sandfield Macdonald's administration in 1871 is ignored (on the ground that it was due less to a change in popular opinion than to mismanagement of the legislature after the election), the party in power at Queen's Park has changed only five times since 1867 (in 1905, 1919, 1923, 1934, and 1943), less than any other province with a history of party competition during the same period.

Of greater significance, however, is the extent of the shift in popular support which has usually accompanied these changes. More often than not only a small change in partisan loyalties will be sufficient to dislodge a government in a competitive party system, and where the franchise is restricted the number of people involved may constitute a very small proportion of the population. Even when it is recognized that in the modern period such changes have frequently occurred within a broader atmosphere of doubt about the government's capacity to administer the system (which may well be the most decisive influence when power is about to change hands)[6] the number of people who actually change their vote is normally too small to serve as a basis for generalizations about the political values of the system as a whole. It is therefore important to notice not only that each government defeat in Ontario has occurred since the achievement of manhood suffrage—four of them since the establishment of full political democracy in 1917[7]—but that in all but one of them very substantial shifts in popular support took place which were considerably in excess of the degree of change customarily associated with a general election in the province.

6 The loss of a few supporters to the opposition is rarely what defeats a government. If its ability to govern has come generally into question, dissatisfaction may be expressed in many other ways. Significant numbers of normal government supporters may choose, for example, to abstain rather than vote for another party, or it may become extraordinarily difficult to find suitable candidates, or the needed workers in the constituencies. These, as well as other factors, such as the attitude of the media, all have a bearing on any party's success in an election. When a government is defeated, therefore, many more people than merely those who switched parties may be said to have contributed to the outcome.
7 Full manhood suffrage was achieved in Ontario in 1888. The

Table I, which gives the results of all Ontario elections since Confederation with the votes cast for each party shown as a percentage of the total registered electorate in each constituency in which there was a contest (which allows us to observe in the aggregate the movement to and from abstention), shows that at least a fifth of the electorate changed its behaviour in the four cases of government defeats which have occurred since the end of the First World War. Moreover, it seems clear that the comparatively small net change associated with the defeat of the Liberals in 1905 is a result of the fact that the shifts required to remove them had gradually taken place over the previous decade.[8] In other words, all but one of the five government defeats in Ontario's history have occurred within a framework in which the whole adult electorate was involved, and all of them have taken place apparently as a result of a deliberate choice by an unusually large number of people. Clearly these occasions have been more than the routine transfer of power from one party to another which is supposed to be the hallmark of a healthy democratic polity.

The fact that power has changed hands so infrequently at Queen's Park lends support to the idea that those values which have been assigned to the whole of English Canada—

Franchise Act of 1917 extended the vote to all adult women. The voting age was lowered to 18 prior to the 1971 election.

8 Of the remaining twenty-four occasions on which the electorate had an opportunity to pass judgment on a government's record only six show a net change of more than 10 per cent. Two of these (1871 and 1929) appear to have been instances of random changes in the rate of abstention not particularly directed at any party. Two more (1926 and 1945) seem to have been directly connected with the government defeat which immediately preceded them, in the sense that they involved a moderately heavy movement from the abstention column to the incumbent government as a kind of belated confirmation of the earlier result; that is to say, in 1923 and 1943 a substantial number of people appear to have used the technique of not voting as a kind of halfway house on their way to a change in party allegiance. Something broadly similar seems also to have happened in 1894 and 1898 where the change is evidently due almost exclusively to the rather abrupt entry (the exodus was just as quick) of the Patrons of Industry and the Protestant Protective Association into Ontario politics. If the intervening elections are ignored, the net change from 1890 to 1905 is 13 per cent of the registered electorate, based apparently almost exclusively on a shift from abstention to the Conservatives.

Percentage of the Registered Electorate Supporting One of the Parties, or Abstaining, in Ontario General Elections Since Confederation

Year	Abstentions %	change	Conservatives %	change	Liberals %	change	Other Major Party %	change	Others %	change	Net Change†
1867	26	+10	37	−8	36	−3			1	+1	11
1871	36	−3	29	+2	33	−1			2	+2	4
1875	33	+3	31	−1	32	−1			4	−1	3
1879	36	−2	30	+1	31	+1			3	none	2
1883	34	+3	31	−1	32	−2			3	none	3
1886	37	+4	30	−3	30	−1			3	none	4
1890	41	−9	27	−3	29	−1			3	+13	13
1894	32	−5	24	+11	28	+6			16	−12	17
1898	27	+2	35	none	34	none			4	−2	2
1902	29	+1	35	+3	34	−3			2	−1	4
1905	30	+4	38	−2	31	−5		+2	1	+1	7
1908	34	+9	36	−2	26	−3	2[a]	none	2	−1	7
1911	43	+9	32	−4	22	−4	2[a]	none	1	−1	9
1914	35	−8	35	+3	25	+3	1[a]	−1	4	+3	9

Year											
1919	29	+21	23	+2	19	−8	24[b]	−11	5	−4	23
1923	50	−14	25	+11	11	+3	13[b]	−5	1	+5	19
1926	36	+8	36	−4	14	+4	8[c]	−5	6	−3	12
1929	44	−17	32	−3	18	+19	3[c]	+2	3	−1	21
1934	27	+2	29	−1	37	−1	5[d]	−1	2	+1	3
1937	29	+13	28	−7	36	−18	4[d]	+14	3	−2	27
1943	42	−13	21	+11	18	+3	18[d]	−2	1	+1	15
1945	29	+3	32	−4	21	−1	16[d]	+2	2	none	5
1948	32	+4	28	+3	20	none	18[d]	−6	2	−1	7
1951	36	+4	31	−2	20	none	12[d]	−2	1	none	4
1955	40	+1	29	−2	20	+2	10[d]	none	1	−1	3
1959	41	−4	27	+4	22	none	10[d]	none	*	none	4
1963	37	−3	31	−3	22	−1	10[e]	+7	*	none	4
1967	34	−7	28	+5	21	−1	17[e]	+3	*	none	7
1971	27	−7	33	+5	20	−1	20[e]	+3	*	none	8

*Less than half of one per cent.

39

†Total percentage point change divided by two.

[a] All Labour and socialist candidates.

[b] UFO and ILP candidates.

[c] All Labour, farmer, and progressive candidates.

[d] CCF candidates only.

[e] NDP candidates only.

"ascriptive," "elitist," "hierarchical," "stable," "cautious" and "restrained"[9]—belong in fact only to Ontario. And it is easy to see the province's reluctance to engage in change for the sake of change as a natural extension into the twentieth century of that conservatism which distinguished pre-Confederation politics in Upper Canada.[10] But while there is no doubt that substantial traces of the earlier tradition can be found in modern Ontario politics, such a judgment is too simple to be left as it stands. For the passage of time has woven subtle variations into the fabric of that original conservatism to create a contemporary political culture in the province quite distinct from that of other parts of Canada, such as the Atlantic provinces, where more traditional political attitudes prevail.

Nothing illustrates this more clearly than the history of government defeats in Ontario. To be sure, each of them has been marked to some degree by what I have called technical incompetence on the part of the government. Poor party organization, for example, appears to have had a bearing on the outcome in every case except the election of 1934. In 1905 the Liberals were simply not equipped to fight an election properly at the constituency level, a consequence of Mowat's preference for appealing to the people on his record, which had forced them to adopt other methods of ensuring their success. The death of their principal provincial organizer just before the beginning of the 1919 campaign severely weakened the Conservatives in that election.[11] The UFO, of course, never pretended to have a developed central organization for election purposes, but in 1923 they were further hampered by the rigid insistence of the farm organization's executive that there should be no interference with the autonomy of local UFO clubs.[12] And the fact that Mitchell Hepburn had never taken the trouble

9 Lipset, *The First New Nation*, pp. 250–268, *passim*.
10 For commentary on the roots of the Ontario political culture, see S. F. Wise, "Upper Canada and the Conservative Tradition," in *Profiles of a Province* (Toronto, 1967), pp. 20–33. See also his "Conservatism and Political Development: The Canadian Case," *The South Atlantic Quarterly*, vol. 69, no. 2 (Spring 1970), pp. 226–243.
11 Peter Oliver, "Sir William Hearst and the Collapse of the Ontario Conservative Party," *Canadian Historical Review*, vol. 53, no. 1 (March 1972), pp. 46–47.
12 David Hoffman, "Intra-Party Democracy: A Case Study," *Canadian*

to restore the Liberal party's machinery in the constituencies had a telling effect on the result of the 1943 campaign.

Unimaginative handling of major issues of the day—another way in which governments can fail to use their resources to their fullest extent—has also had a prominent role to play in each of the five defeats. The Ross government's irresolute response to the demand for prohibition at the turn of the century;[13] the Conservatives' peculiar solution to the same problem before and during the 1919 election;[14] the UFO's inability to explain the cost of social legislation to an economy-minded farm population and Drury's conflict with Sir Adam Beck throughout the life of the UFO-Labor government;[15] hydro contracts with the Quebec "power barons" for which the Conservatives had to accept responsibility in 1934, to say nothing of their difficulties with the question of financial support for the province's separate school system; and the legacy of Hepburn's bitter feuds with the CIO and Mackenzie King; in every case its treatment of these issues must have created for the government that laboured with them an image of ineptitude which could not have failed to contribute to its defeat. And for sheer bad judgment directly affecting the result of an election it would be difficult to match Hearst's decision

---

Journal of Economics and Political Science, vol. 27, no. 2 (May 1961), pp. 232–233.

13 Ross had at one time been a strong supporter of prohibition but when he was forced to deal with the question after the 1901 decision of the Judicial Committee of the Privy Council he backed away. His solution to the dilemma was a referendum in which a two-thirds majority was required to establish prohibition. When it was held, in December of 1902, the worst happened (from the point of view of settling the matter)—prohibition was approved by a substantial margin but by slightly less than the required two-thirds majority. For the details see W. S. Wallace, "Political History, 1867–1912," in *Canada and its Provinces,* ed. Adam Shortt and Arthur G. Doughty (Toronto, 1914), XVII, pp. 181–182.

14 The Ontario Temperance Act was passed in 1916, but the government postponed a referendum on the question until after the war. It was actually held on the same day as the 1919 election but instead of requiring a simple "yes" or "no" to the continuation of the Act four questions of varying degrees of hostility to the maintenance of prohibition were asked, each of which had to be answered to have the ballot count. See Oliver, p.44.

15 R. A. Farquharson, "The Rise and Fall of the United Farmers of Ontario," *Saturday Night,* June 21, 1952.

to hold the temperance referendum on polling day in 1919 or Drury's sudden dissolution of the Legislature in 1923 in the midst of debate on a bill specifically designed to save his government.[16]

But it is unlikely that this kind of technical incompetence alone was the decisive factor in any of the changes which have taken place in the province. Few Ontario administrations have escaped criticism for their handling of such issues as the public financing of separate schools or the liquor question yet most of them have come out of it unscathed. Equally, weak party organization, or questionable political judgment, while perhaps more significant, could hardly have brought down a government in the absence of any compelling reason for its removal.

There is, however, another element which in combination with demonstrated technical incompetence might ordinarily be expected to constitute a sufficiently imposing indictment against a government to be the cause of its destruction. One of the most intriguing aspects of Ontario political history is the extent to which charges of corruption, in one form or another, seem always to have been associated with the defeat of a government. No doubt in some cases the opposition's claims amounted to little more than ritual observance of the established rules for political debate, but in others they were a good deal more serious.

The outstanding example is, of course, to be found in the collapse of the Liberal party in 1905. Contemporary observers agreed that the principal cause of the massive Tory victory (in terms of seats) was the appalling level of electoral corruption which the government had permitted— and frequently encouraged—after the general election of 1902 had left the parties at almost equal strength at Queen's Park. "In successive bye-elections," wrote Sir John Willison, "there was organized personation, violation of the sanctity of ballot boxes, intimidation, coercion and direct purchase of voters."[17] A widespread suspicion that the

16 The bill would have established an alternative voting system in the province, which Drury believed would have enabled Liberals to support the UFO as a second choice. He later admitted that his decision to call an election was taken in a moment of anger. See E. C. Drury, *Farmer Premier* (Toronto, 1966), pp. 150–155.

17 Sir John Willison, *Reminiscences: Political and Personal* (Toronto, 1919), p. 321. See also Wallace, "Political History," pp. 182–183.

government would stop at nothing to preserve itself in office was merely intensified by allegations that it had tried to buy the support of a Conservative member of the Legislature.[18] Although this attack does not appear to have led to a particularly strong shift in partisan support across the province as a whole in 1905, the judgment of more recent writers suggests that it had a significant impact on the most important part of the traditional Liberal vote—the farm community—enabling the Conservatives to make substantial constituency gains.[19]

Charges of corruption of less dramatic proportion were also prominent at the time of the defeat of the Hearst and Drury governments. In 1919 the already weakened image of the Conservative administration was further damaged by the claim that Howard Ferguson had used his power as the minister responsible for lands, forests and mines to raise money for the party's campaign fund. And although the Home Bank scandal did not surface until after the 1923 election it is generally agreed that the UFO suffered in rural Ontario from dark hints about its purity, kindled by opposition tales of "that last awful night" at Queen's Park.[20]

On the remaining two occasions, the immorality of the

---

18 See Charles W. Humphries, "The Gamey Affair," *Ontario History*, vol. 59, no. 2 (June 1967), pp. 101–109.

19 Wilson and Hoffman, p. 208. It is likely that a more detailed analysis of the 1902 and 1905 elections, using aggregate data by township, would establish this point beyond doubt. The increase in the relative strength of the urban population, where Conservative support was concentrated in the late nineteenth century, coupled with the decline in their vote which began to occur in the 1890s, ought to have defeated the Liberals before 1905. But judicious attention to the redistribution of constituency boundaries kept them in office. In 1890, to take only one example of the effect of this practice, Toronto had a population equal to that of the counties of Bruce, Grey, and Huron combined, but had only a third of the seats. In short, as has already been suggested, many of the voters who might have left the Liberal party to defeat it in 1905 had already gone over to the opposition by then (in both 1898 and 1902 the Tories won more votes than the Grits) and only a small further shift was required to do the job.

20 J. L. Harrington, "The Drury Debacle," *Canadian Forum*, October 1948. The phrase was coined by the UFO Secretary, J. J. Morrison, to describe a wild party which had taken place in a cabinet minister's office while the Legislature was debating the government's proposal to introduce the alternative vote. For Drury's account of the circumstances see *Farmer Premier*, pp. 154–155.

premier himself appears to have been an important issue. While Hepburn and his principal lieutenants battered the Conservatives endlessly in 1934 with largely unsubstantiated charges of corruption on nearly every front, the government's position had already been severely undermined by Henry's admission to the Legislature the previous year that he owned $25,000 worth of bonds in a company which his administration had saved from bankruptcy. And in the 1943 campaign, despite the fact that Hepburn had resigned from the premiership in the fall of 1942, and had been dismissed as Provincial Treasurer five months later, the Liberals could not escape responsibility for the eccentricities of his leadership—among which were the sordid stories of loose living in the former premier's suite in the King Edward Hotel, while the business of governing the province was left to senior civil servants.[21] The record is an imposing one; but there is more to it than that.

THE ONTARIO POLITICAL CULTURE

It would be very surprising, of course, if a government which had not demonstrated a capacity to manage the system effectively—and which was at the same time thought to be guilty of the kind of corruption which has from time to time appeared in Ontario—was found acceptable in any modern democratic polity. The fact that every government which has been defeated in the province has had these faults is therefore less striking than the evidence which suggests that they are not, by themselves, particularly important in Ontario. There have been numerous occasions (most noticeably since 1945) when administrations which were open to attack on both counts not only survived an election but actually increased their majorities. The most obvious examples are the highways scandal which dominated the election of 1955, the involvement of cabinet ministers in the allegedly improper purchase of Northern Ontario Natural Gas stock which was an issue in 1959, and the charges of corruption in dealing with organized crime which the opposition made against the government in 1963.

21 Philip Sykes, "Ontario's 28 Tory Years," *Toronto Daily Star*, September 22, 1971. See also Jack Cahill, "The Tory Years," *Toronto Daily Star*, February 14, 1968, and McKenty, *Mitch Hepburn* (Toronto, 1967), pp. 182–183 and 244.

And there could hardly be a better example of questionable political judgment than the Robarts government's introduction in 1964 of the notorious "police state" bill.

If an examination of the circumstances surrounding government defeats is going to lead us to a clearer understanding of the nature of the Ontario political culture, then, something more fundamental than simply rejection of technical incompetence on the one hand, and corruption on the other, must lie at the root of it. That is not to say that these things are irrelevant to Ontario politics, but rather that the political culture is composed of a set of values and beliefs which are *not* violated merely by some degree of technical incompetence or even a great deal of corruption, but which *are* violated by other inadequacies on the part of government in the context of which the presence of technical incompetence and corruption simply add to the degree of condemnation.

What is being suggested is that each occasion of a government's defeat in Ontario history has been marked by circumstances which have not occurred at any other time, and that the isolation of these unique circumstances will tell us something of substance about the nature of the province's political culture. To be sure of the analysis, therefore, it would be necessary to conduct a detailed examination not just of those elections in which a government was defeated, but of all elections and of the alternatives which were available in those cases in which the government survived. For if it is true that in dismissing a government the Ontario people are saying something about the character of their dominant political values, it must also be true that in retaining a government—and therefore by implication rejecting an alternative government—they are saying the same thing.

It is not intended to undertake an exhaustive inquiry of this kind in what follows, but merely to indicate the kinds of things it might reveal. It seems to me likely, however, that such an analysis would confirm that two requirements have been absolutely crucial to the successful conduct of government in Ontario in the years since Confederation. It would show, moreover, that while both of them have been very much in doubt at the time of each government defeat, neither of them was seriously in question at any other time. By extension, therefore, they lead to a description of the

Ontario political culture simply because they reflect the existence of a specific set of values and beliefs which Ontario governments have violated at their peril.

The two requirements are comparatively easily derived from even the most cursory examination of Ontario political history, and since they may appear at first glance to be little short of truisms it is perhaps worth recalling that the argument so far suggests that they are *not* undermined by either technical incompetence on the part of government or the existence of corruption in the political system. The first requirement, to put it in its shortest form, is that to be acceptable a government must be able to provide adequate leadership; the second is that it must have a capacity for maintaining an equitable balance between the principal interests of the province.

On the face of things it might be expected that the two requirements stated in this way would be so intimately connected one could not exist without the other. In practice, however, the demand for adequate leadership appears to have meant nothing more than a capacity to manage the affairs of the province in a businesslike way. And it is exactly this aspect of the question which has been in doubt on each of the five occasions when a government has been defeated.

From time to time, of course, what I have earlier called unimaginative handling of major issues is due to circumstances which are the evidence of an incapacity to govern. By 1905, therefore, the fact that the Ross government's solution to the problem of prohibition had satisfied no one was probably less important than the divisions over the question within the Liberal party which had caused the dilemma in the first place. Moreover, the position of the premier himself had been increasingly called into question after the inconclusive result of the 1902 election. Ross was known to have proposed a coalition government to Whitney —easily characterized as a cowardly device for keeping his government in office. At the same time a number of prominent Liberals had called on him to resign. When these facts are added to the allegations of electoral corruption— which in this context can be seen less as a sign of immorality than an admission that the government had lost its administrative nerve—it is not difficult to see why there might have been some doubt about the capacity of the

Liberals to run the province. A divided party and an indecisive leader are hardly the hallmarks of a sound administration.

Almost identical circumstances appear to have been present in 1919. Virtually the whole of Hearst's premiership (he had replaced Sir James Whitney some four months after the 1914 election) was marked by administrative and tactical blunders—his equivocation over the extension of the franchise to women and his extraordinarily clumsy treatment of the temperance question are only the most outstanding—which by 1919 must have created a massive sense of the government's inability to manage Ontario's affairs in every part of the province. Such a feeling must surely also have been fostered by the constant rumours that leading cabinet ministers were on the verge of forcing his resignation as early as 1916 and the openly expressed conviction of many Conservatives on the eve of the 1919 election that the government was not doing its job.

In 1923 and 1934 the image of a government incapable of providing sound leadership is, perhaps, less clear, but the internal struggle in the UFO between those who wished to make it a genuine "people's party" and those who wished to restrict it to the role of representing the farm population—the so-called "broadening-out" controversy—and Drury's evident inability to stand up to J. J. Morrison must have intensified the impression that the farmers were not fit to govern. And while each charge of maladministration levelled against the Conservatives in 1934 cannot be precisely documented, it is nonetheless the case that Hepburn was able to make them stick in the minds of the voters—evidence, perhaps, that a sense of the government's inadequacy on this count existed throughout Ontario.

However that may be, there cannot be much doubt that the issue of the Liberals' capacity to manage the affairs of the province was the decisive factor in the 1943 defeat. During his first term as premier Hepburn appears not to have had much difficulty, but after 1937 the growing evidence of the government's deterioration must have been plain for all to see. Indeed, it went beyond merely the failure of Hepburn himself (if a united party is one of the prerequisites of sound leadership his struggle with Mackenzie King and the resignation of such able ministers as Croll and Roebuck, to take only two examples, cannot have been of much help) to the brief record in office of his successors. Conant, who had been endorsed as premier by the caucus, could not muster enough support even to stay in the race at the leadership convention. And as if there were not already sufficient evidence of indecision, the new leader, Harry Nixon, actually endorsed Hepburn's candidacy as an independent Liberal in the 1943 election.[22]

It hardly seems necessary to demonstrate the importance of leadership in Ontario politics by contrasting this sorry record with that of the governments which have been successful, and yet the comparison is instructive. Whether one thinks of Mowat—in whose cautious management of the province's affairs we can see the beginning of the tradition—or of Whitney or of Ferguson or, indeed, of the record of Conservative administrations since 1943, the evidence is all in the same direction. No doubt an examination of the other side of the coin—the alternatives which were rejected each time these governments were returned to office—would make the point as well.[23]

The second of the two dominant themes of Ontario politics—the requirement that to be acceptable a government must have the capacity to maintain an equitable balance between the principal interests of the province—is less easy to isolate. In part this is because it is not always clear whether it is the character of the government itself which is at issue or whether (as a consequence, perhaps, of its ineptitude) the appearance of new forces in the society has temporarily upset that balance. Nonetheless, on each occasion of a government defeat it seems quite clear that an important sector of Ontario society was thought not to be receiving its just due, while at other times nothing even remotely resembling this condition appears to have been the case.

The principal interests in the province have not, of course, always been the same. Indeed, one of the most prominent characteristics of those Ontario governments

22 McKenty, *Mitch Hepburn*, pp. 265–267.
23 In this context it may be observed that the Liberal record since 1943 cannot have been of much help in their attempt to reconstruct their image. There have been no less than eight changes in the party's leadership since that time, although Farquhar Oliver served on three different occasions.

which have managed, over the years, to retain the confidence of the electorate has been their ability to recognize that important social and economic changes have taken place and to react to them in a positive manner. And in 1905 it was a failure to do exactly this which seems to have contributed to the defeat of the Liberals.

The coalition between farmers in the countryside and manufacturers in the towns which Mowat had developed in the later years of the nineteenth century had been sufficiently broad in character to serve as a basis for stable government. But by the turn of the century the progress of urbanization had wrought a substantial change in the structure of Ontario society, and had created an entirely new set of demands upon government which, as long as they remained unanswered, constituted exactly the kind of imbalance between the interests which was potentially explosive. Yet the Liberals, tied to their earlier perceptions, made no attempt to meet those demands. It is difficult not to accept Charles Humphries' judgment that "they were penalized for their insensitivity."[24]

By contrast, Whitney's new government moved immediately to recognize the changes which had taken place. Such important measures as the establishment of the Ontario Hydro-Electric Power Commission and the passage of the Workmen's Compensation Act provided, apparently, for at least a temporary restoration of the balance. But by 1919 the full impact of industrialization had begun to have an effect, and without the knowing touch of Whitney to guide them, the Conservatives lost their bearing. Yet it is clear that a new kind of imbalance had developed between those who were thought to be benefitting from the system and those who were not—this time represented by both the frustration of the farmers, brought on by the decline of rural society, and the anger of the burgeoning working class in the towns. In the context of the argument it is perhaps worth observing that the sense of the imbalance ran so deep that the representatives of these two groups were actually able to work together in the Legislature for a time.

24 "The Sources of Ontario 'Progressive' Conservatism, 1900–1914," *Historical Papers Presented at the Annual Meeting of the Canadian Historical Association, Ottawa, 1967*, p. 119.

But the experiment failed. The UFO-Labor government was said to be a class government, wholly oriented to the welfare of only one sector of Ontario society, and so it was dismissed. Ferguson, on the other hand, went out of his way to court virtually every significant interest in the province, with the result that his government was rewarded handsomely in 1926.

The Depression produced yet another kind of imbalance (although of course a much more extreme one) and if its cause cannot be laid entirely at the door of the provincial government there is not much doubt that the contrasts it created were skilfully exploited by Hepburn in 1934. The Liberals were, he said, "in it for the little man," and in every corner of Ontario his call was heeded.

But Mitch Hepburn never really understood the complexity of modern industrial society. And because of his insensitivity (represented, for example, by the struggle to keep the CIO out of Ontario) the principal conflict of the modern age—between labour and capital—was allowed to get out of hand. Even the most superficial examination of the results of the 1943 election shows how much the CCF owed its success to the inability of the Liberal party to meet the second requirement for successful government in Ontario. And by extension, although a much more detailed account of the period would be required to establish the point, it may be said that the Conservative party has managed to preserve its position in the province since that time simply by ensuring that no sector of Ontario society could ever realistically claim to have been left out of the reckoning.

It may be argued, of course, that the two requirements which appear to characterize the kinds of demands which the Ontario people make of government are really only variations on a single theme: the desire for stability. Yet each of them reflects a different, and perhaps conflicting, set of values. On the one hand the demand for sound leadership, especially in the form in which it has appeared at the time of government defeats, suggests a rather *conservative* cast of mind, oriented only to the maintenance of order. The idea that a balance must be maintained between the interests, however, points in a different direction, to the rather more *progressive* notions of fair play and equal treatment for all. Thus if the structure of the analysis is correct, that is to say, if it is accepted that in their behaviour at the time of a government defeat the people of Ontario can be said to be expressing their view of the proper ends of government, there is only one way to describe the Ontario political culture. It is, we may say, a "progressive-conservative" political culture.

In one sense, of course, all advanced industrial societies may be described in this way. People who are well off are always motivated both by a desire to preserve what they have and an inclination to improve the quality of life in the system. In fact, the second demand, which is probably the essential prerequisite of any movement for social reform, rarely appears except in good times. The protest which develops in times of economic and social crisis is nearly always short-lived, if for no other reason than that the situation which gives rise to it is generally short-lived. The demand for permanent social reform, on the other hand, seems precisely to be born of the natural human inclination to consider the quality of one's life only *after* one's basic material needs are being met. But, simply because of the prosperity which that condition represents, the demand for change is always made in a conservative way.

In Ontario, however, it appears that these very general observations can only be made within the framework of a rather special set of circumstances which may, on reflection, allow us to claim that the province's political culture is unique. It has been suggested by S. J. R. Noel that even the most modern manifestations of political values in any polity which originated as a colony can be traced to the way in which its early settlers sought to tame their surroundings, and in particular to the characteristics of the principal natural resources on which they depended for their livelihood. In the case of Ontario, according to Noel, the principal values of the nineteenth century arose from the exploitation of agricultural land which, because it was a non-renewable resource, generated a deep sense of the need to manage its use with care. These attitudes thus came to dominate the expectations which people had for the role of government, with the result that an administration such as Sir Oliver Mowat's, which practised careful and economical management of the province's affairs, was virtually assured of repeated electoral success simply because it was reflecting the most fundamental values of the people.[25]

But such a conception corresponds almost exactly to what the earlier analysis has suggested has been expected of governments in Ontario in this century as well as the last. Careful and economical management of the province's affairs is nothing more than cautious government. It does not reject change where change is needed; rather it merely seeks to introduce that change always within the framework of protecting the interests of at least the major sectors of the society.

Cast in this way it is not difficult to see why leadership itself should have been so important in Ontario over the years, or why indecisive leadership on the one hand, or leadership which either could not or would not maintain an equitable balance between the interests on the other, has always been rejected. It is easy to see, as well, what the foundation for political success has been. Sir Oliver Mowat's record in office, it has been said, was "a model of conservative reform."[26] Whitney, wrote Sir John Willison, "thought he was a Tory, which he was not; he was stern in word and compassionate in action."[27] Ferguson did not try to undo the new measures in social welfare which had been introduced by the UFO; instead he sought to build on them. Even Hepburn, in his earlier years, showed signs of the kind of understanding which is required of successful Ontario leaders: for example, in his insistence on the compulsory pasteurization of milk.[28] And since the end of the Second World War it has been the Conservative party's capacity to give precisely this same kind of leadership based on cautious reform, rather than simply the fragmentation of the opposition, which has guaranteed its hold on the reins of power. Whether one takes Drew's commitment to the changes necessary to foster Ontario's indus-

25 S. J. R. Noel, "Nature and Political Values: The Ontario Experience," unpublished lecture delivered at the University of Waterloo, November 22, 1972.
26 Wallace, "Political History," p. 177. See also Willison, Reminiscences, p. 101; and Margaret Evans, "Oliver Mowat: Nineteenth-Century Ontario Liberal," in Oliver Mowat's Ontario, ed. Donald Swainson (Toronto, 1972), p. 51.
27 Willison, Reminiscences, p. 330. See also Wallace, "Political History," p. 185.
28 McKenty, Mitch Hepburn, pp. 175–177.

trial development, or Frost's introduction of public hospital insurance, or Robarts' recognition of the importance of biculturalism, in every case there is the unmistakable trace of that ability to respond to the circumstances of the time which has been the hallmark of the legacy of Sir Oliver Mowat.

The conclusion seems inescapable. The dominant values of Ontario politics are, after all, unique, because they arise from something which is peculiar to Ontario, the special circumstances in which the province began its life. We are, in short, a red tory province.

14
DON SCOTT

Northern
Alienation

ALIENATION is the word that recurs most frequently in any discussion of northern Ontario—that part of the province lying north of a line running roughly from Sault Ste. Marie to Mattawa. It isn't just the rhetoric of disaffected politicians: it reflects a deep, if diversified, feeling by most citizens of the north that they are being short-changed.

This sense of alienation has several sources: geographic, economic, social and cultural. In fact, the diversity is so great that within a group alienated by geographic remoteness, there can exist a smaller group alienated socially, and within it, another alienated sub-group. A case in point is the town of Gogama, located on the CNR mainline north of Capreol.

In Gogama, as is obvious to most visitors, there is a social grouping which revolves around the provincial government administrative complex. The railroad provides a fairly clear line of demarcation between that part of town where the provincial government employees live in well-built and maintained homes, and the rest of the town which is characterized by polluted wells, smelly sump-water in ditches, gravel roads and a jerry-built quality of housing.

But alienated from the town on both sides of the tracks —culturally, economically and socially—is a small Indian reservation seventeen miles out in the bush. When a move was initiated in 1966 by the Indians to move their village closer to Gogama, the residents of the town united in opposition to it.

Despite the complexity of such a labyrinth of influences, it is possible to isolate the major factors which create this alienation.

GEOGRAPHIC

Northern Ontario is quite distinct from the southern part of the province. Essentially the area is the forest, rock, lake, swamp and muskeg of the Precambrian shield. Here and there are clay belts, such as that of the Sudbury Basin or in the Cochrane area, running from Hearst through to Matheson. In the northwest, there are intrusions of the western prairie.

These geographic conditions dictate to a great extent the nature of the lines of communication. The first routes were the rivers and lakes used by Champlain and the voyageurs. The latter travelled from Montreal, by the Ottawa and Mattawa Rivers, Lake Nipissing and the French River, to the north shore of Georgian Bay, and on to Lake Superior and Western Canada. English fur traders moved less vigorously south and west from Hudson Bay.

This river route was succeeded by, and for a while integrated into, the two principal rail lines. The railroad was conceived as a way to link the prairie wheat fields and the colony of British Columbia with eastern Canada. Northern Ontario, like the Rockies, was viewed more as a challenge to the engineers than as a resource area; but it soon became evident that its minerals would provide an unexpected economic bonus. (In fact, it was during the construction of the CPR through the Sudbury Basin that a surveyor named Salter recognized the rusty hue of the nickel-iron ore.) In addition to the main lines, various feeder rail routes were planned, and some actually built.

Roads were slow to follow. Highway 69, linking Sudbury with the south, was trail-blazed by German prisoners of war between 1942 and 1945. Highway 144, from Sudbury north to Timmins, was not opened until 1969. The last link in the Trans-Canada Highway bumped its way from the Lakehead to the Manitoba border for years after transcontinental standards had been achieved elsewhere. Every area of the north has its pet road or bridge project, and every provincial election produces its flurry of surveying and brushing crews.

The airplane has been the most flexible and dynamic element in the communications network. Float and ski-equipped planes have been able to use the countless lakes which dot the terrain. Many mines, tourist resorts and government stations have been developed and maintained by air travel.

Finally, the role of lake steamers should be noted. They carried bulk produce to and from Sault Ste. Marie to the north. Early in the century some communities were entirely dependent on lake traffic, but this has largely been changed by roads that have pushed in from the nearest highway. Steamship traffic is now restricted chiefly to carrying freight and has little role in linking communities in a social sense.

This network of rail, road, air and steamship routes comprises thousands of miles. However, these routes do little to establish a sense of community or to reduce the feeling of isolation. There are two possible explanations. First, the majority of communities are served by only one mode of transportation; there are only a handful of cities where all four intersect. Dependence upon only one of the four increases the awareness of isolation, and hence of alienation. In many cases, this is more than just a psychological response. In one instance, for example, there was an Indian reservation served only by air, where the federal government had refused to provide mail service. As a consequence, Eaton's catalogue was not available as a competitor to the Hudson's Bay store. The Indians were at the mercy of a single company for clothes, traps, drugs, food staples, and all the other merchandised necessities of life.

Secondly, the transportation routes do little to ease the sense of alienation because there are no suburban zones around most of the communities. There is no easing out of one community into another; on leaving the outskirts of a community, the traveller is quickly enveloped in the bush. The next community appears as suddenly as the last one disappeared, so the isolation is accentuated.

Sheer distance adds a qualitative difference; there is an added remoteness to the alienation of the northwest. Sudbury is a tank of gasoline and four hours from Toronto; Thunder Bay is two days by car, five tanks of gas and a twenty dollar motel.

ECONOMIC

If geography provides the physical basis for northern alienation, the economy of the region usually reinforces it. Most industries are primary and extractive. Psychologically, this is damaging because the products of labour are always seen in terms of going somewhere else. Nickel ore from Falconbridge is going to Norway; iron ore from Atikokan to Cleveland; uranium from Elliot Lake to Japan. Furthermore, extractive industries are known to be transitory: when the ore body is exhausted, the company will go. Although this is less true today when larger ore bodies with lower yields are scheduled for extraction over a longer

period of time, the mining town complex still lingers.[1]
There are enough ghost towns to keep the spectre alive—
Geraldton being a classic example.

In addition, extractive industries are usually foreign-
owned, adding to the sense of alienation. The senior management operates from New York or Cleveland. Middle
management resides in the area for a few years, then
returns to home base. Often the industry provides the
municipal services, including the police force; provincial
and federal levels of government may be little in evidence.
With rivers being polluted and the sky filled with sulphur
fumes, too often there is no one to halt the desecration.
The economy of large portions of northern Ontario is
essentially colonial in nature.[2]

To many northern residents, southern Ontario is almost
as foreign as New York or Ohio. Indeed, some northerners
have a grudging respect for the company which gets things
done, while the provincial and federal governments issue
pious statements about environmental preservation, but
do little to regulate the industry effectively. The Toronto-
Centred Region Plan has done much to bolster this impression. Despite all the promises about developing industries at the resource sites of the north, the Plan frankly
asserts that "the Toronto-Centred Region probably can
increase its economic role in processing resources which
currently originate in northern Ontario."

Discriminatory freight rates serve to compound the
economic problems. That stretch of central Canada from
Lévis, Quebec, to Armstrong, in northern Ontario, has the
highest freight rates in the country. Moreover, favourable
rates are granted for the export of raw materials, while the
rates are high for manufactured goods shipped in. Factors
such as this contribute to the income squeeze experienced
by the people of the north; annual incomes are below, while
their cost of living is above, the provincial average.

1 This concept is dealt with more fully by Ira Robinson in his essay
"Planned and Unplanned Patterns in Resource Towns," in Leonard
Marsh, ed., *Communities in Canada, Selected Sources* (Toronto:
McClelland and Stewart, 1970), pp. 76–83.
2 The "colonial" nature of the extractive industries of the north can
be compared with similar industrial patterns described in Salvador
Allende, *Chile's Road to Socialism* (Harmondsworth, Middlesex:
Penguin, 1973), pp. 125–133; or Kari Levitt, *Silent Surrender* (To-
ronto: Macmillan, 1970).

Tourism is another industry that tends to strengthen the alienation of the north. On a typical summer weekend there are 800,000 residents in northern Ontario with 275,000 vacationers from outside the region. Although vacationers are welcomed, partly because of an innate sense of hospitality, and partly because they spend money, several things are irksome. Generally the visitors drive better cars and tow powerful motor-boats or impressive house-trailers. Frequently they have bought or leased the choicest lakefront lands. Many hire Indians as "guides," but in addition to guiding, they are expected to carry the luggage, cook the meals and clean the camp-site for a few dollars a day.

There is a final consideration, related to company or government towns dotting the northland, which has an inextricable mix of economic and social implications. Too often they are set apart, and provide a sharp contrast with conditions in the surrounding communities. Typical is the federal government's Falconbridge Air Station. Located a few miles from Skead, Hanmer and other settlements, it has all the earmarks of a base for alien military occupation. In contrast to the native homes in the area, the base provides finished homes on paved streets and landscaped lots. There are playgrounds, a swimming pool and other recreational features. The whole settlement is surrounded with an eight-foot link fence. The Canadian Forces are more conscious of their public image and in recent years have opened more of the facilities to the neighbours, but the "nabob" impression dies slowly.

Likewise with the company towns; their paved streets, neat lawns (often company cut) and recreational areas stand in marked contrast to the gravel roads, unfinished tar-papered homes and wrecks of old cars which characterize the neighbourhoods a few miles away. If the company town has street names, often they derive from the management personnel; if the streets are numbered, First Avenue is invariably the street for middle management. Small points, but psychologically important.

SOCIAL AND CULTURAL

The social patterns created by this dichotomy are very complex. Resentment is created in neighbouring towns which do not enjoy the company benefit, even though some of the employees may live in them. While residents in the company town itself derive some sense of community and comfort from the physical amenities provided, the paternalism engenders unrest which festers over the years, and is often reflected in voting patterns favouring an anti-establishment party like the NDP.

The 1971 provincial election produced interesting examples in the riding of Nickel Belt. While the NDP won the INCO company towns of Lively and Levack, it lost the towns of Chelmsford and Chapleau, independent communities which are far behind the manicured company towns in such amenities as sewers, water treatment plants and recreational facilities.

There are, of course, communities which fall between the two extremes. Typical of these is the town of Capreol which has been fortunate in the number of persons willing to serve the community. As a result, it boasts paved streets, water and sewage treatment facilities, an arena and a recreational area. It also has a well-regulated growth program. The municipality bought several neighbouring farms some years ago and has pursued a policy of controlled expansion. Only when one sub-division is 90 per cent developed does the municipality open another, complete with services. The lots are sold on an individual basis, and speculation in land is practically impossible.[3]

The continuum from the completely company town to the dog-patch areas in unorganized townships provides a full range of conditions, but other factors contribute to the social alienation. One of these is the English-French duality. Some towns are regarded as "French," and others as "English." In the cities, some neighbourhoods are French and others English. These divisions may well contribute to the preservation of identity by other ethnic groups to a greater extent than exists in southern cities. If one is neither French nor English, social identity must be achieved by being Italian or Ukrainian or Finnish. Hence, many northern Ontario cities have well-delineated pockets of ethnic population. Generally these pockets are centred around the "Caruso Club" or the "National Ukrainian Federation Hall." The area of each city which is marked off from these ethnic pockets is "snob hill," populated by

3 Although geared to the younger reader, R. P. Baine, *The Sudbury Region* (Toronto: Holt-Rinehart & Winston, 1969), gives a good picture of selected towns in the north.

wealthier people who enjoy a sense of having risen above the ethnic life of the rest of the city. It is money which qualifies for admittance to the elite area where ethnic distinctions are seldom in evidence.

The smaller communities which are either French or English reflect even more sharply MacLennan's "Two Solitudes." This is especially true of the French villages in northeastern Ontario, from Mattawa and North Bay through to the District of Cochrane. Here there is a stronger identification because of the existence of Quebec-based CBC television. The advent of French-language secondary schools has heightened the consciousness of the francophone community; and in some instances opposition to their development by Boards of Education dominated by English-speaking members has unwittingly intensified it further.

If the northeast is inclined to identify with Quebec, for much the same reasons the northwest is inclined to identify with the prairie region. For example, Kenora is socially much more a part of Manitoba than Ontario. Winnipeg newspapers and Winnipeg-based CBC programming blanket most of the area west of the Lakehead. In addition, the tendency for people in Red Lake, Dryden, Kenora and Fort Frances to drive to Winnipeg for shopping, specialized medical services and other needs consolidates a western rather than a Toronto orientation.

In this situation part of the northern alienation can be seen writ large. The alienation of the French-language population (especially among the young) in the northeast has essentially the same well-springs as the separatist movement in Quebec. The alienation of the northwest is essentially the alienation of western Canada as a whole. Ironically, the area in between is largely occupied by the Indians who feel alienated from both.

In fact, the alienation of the Indian has aroused the least concern from either the federal government or Queen's Park. This may be due, in part, to the fact that a large percentage of the Indians are so alienated that they don't bother to vote. In Kenora there are enough alienated English-speaking voters who have switched from the Liberal-Labour to the NDP, and thereby have elected a Conservative with no more than the traditional Conservative vote. In Nickel Belt during the 1971 general election there

were enough French voters alienated by government policies to switch their vote from the Liberals to the NDP, and
thereby defeat the Conservative. But in both areas, where
the Indian vote could be decisive, it is seldom exercised in
a united and purposeful way.

The social alienation generates a cultural alienation. This
is particularly true of the younger French-Canadian population, but it is also felt to a degree by the population as a
whole. The north is the victim of serious cultural depriva-
tion. This is evident despite the occasional cultural activities which centre in ethnic groups, or are routed through
the hinterland from Toronto. Such events are often exciting
and important in themselves, but their fleeting presence
serves further to emphasize the normal cultural lack. The
scarcity of cultural activities is underlined again by the
fact that, if school children are to see anything of major
significance, they must be transported by bus some
hundreds, or even thousands, of miles, to Ottawa or Toronto and back. This is particularly true of Toronto, with
the provincially subsidized Science Centre, Ontario Place,
Royal Ontario Museum and Art Gallery. A visit to them
may be a lifetime experience for northern school children,
serving once again as a reminder of the cultural barrenness
of their home area.

Another factor in this cultural alienation is the virtual
monopoly of northern daily newspapers in the Thomson
chain. There is a standing joke in the north that Ontario
was subjected to two blights at the same time: the Thomson newspaper system and the Dutch elm disease. The
newspapers are generally conservative in policy. The strong
point (or at least the principal selling feature) of the
newspapers is their local news and the abundance of pictures of Chamber of Commerce executives, local PC women's socials, and similar establishment groups. Cultural
activities normally get very short shrift. The Sudbury *Star*
is typical. Its orientation appears to be, first, making
money, and second, preserving the status quo. When Mary-
mount College approached the *Star* one year about running
pictures of the grade 13 graduating class, the *Star* agreed
for a price, so much per picture.

The record of other media is much the same, with some
recent improvements as more communities develop a
second or third TV or radio station.

In many communities public spirited groups struggle against the sense of cultural alienation. This is most evident in the various little theatre groups which are found in communities, often with limited population. In spite of being staffed on a voluntary basis, and with limited finances from subscribers and local business, many of these groups do remarkably good work. However, an appeal for live theatre has not been developed among the majority of the community; in most cases, it is still the preserve of the elite.

An exception was seen in some of the work of the late Weir Reid, of the Mine, Mill and Smelter Union, in Sudbury. Reid was able to generate a grass-roots level of interest in ballet, drama and other arts forms over a number of years. At one point he tried to recruit the folk-singer, Cedric Smith, to direct a "workers' theatre." His object was to produce plays of social criticism that would capture the sympathy of the miners of the area. These activities were interrupted by the struggle between Mine Mill and the United Steelworkers. His death in 1971 removed a vital cultural influence from the labour scene.

Generally speaking, the union movement has not exerted much influence on the cultural tone of northern communities. With the exception of the Mine Mill activities mentioned above, the level of union involvement in cultural affairs is usually limited to renting halls to local people for wedding receptions, political meetings and evening bingos. Otherwise, the union halls operate as beer parlours that have not yet developed the community atmosphere of an English pub. Now and then a union will put up the prize money for a public speaking contest or other activity, but generally the efforts are sporadic and not very effective. They tend to lack an overall sense of social purpose, and therefore, as with other social influences, emphasize rather than reduce the sense of alienation.

This lack of social purpose frequently leads to factional splits within the union, crippling its potential as a rallying point in the community. The average worker seems to feel remote not only from his municipality, but also from his union. The net result is the anomoly of a predominantly union town with a municipal council made up largely of professional and business interests, frequently without a single labour representative.

POLITICAL

While northern alienation is rooted in basic geographic, economic, social and cultural factors, its chief manifestation is political. Its most extreme expression is the periodic call for a breakaway from the province of Ontario—for a new province comprising the whole of northern Ontario, or northwest Ontario, or sometimes even northern Ontario joined with northern Quebec. While these calls, often backed by petitions and always providing grist for the media mills, recur frequently, they have so far never evoked widespread public support. But the sentiment which they reflect is persistent, and, like the current Scottish Nationalist movement in the United Kingdom, it could take on more serious political implications at any time the circumstances are propitious.

This political alienation is bolstered by a widespread public belief that the provincial government's programs for the north are piecemeal at best, and often based on outrageously thin analysis. Thus, the chuckles have yet to die down from such observations in *Design For Development: Northeastern Ontario Region* where, in identifying area problems, the study profoundly observed that "the hazards of drowning appear to merit attention only in those districts bordering large masses of water"!

Governments are always conscious of the under-currents of disaffection; and they make gestures, such as holding cabinet meetings in the north, or policies designed specifically to meet the most urgent northern needs, to seek to forestall serious political consequences. On the other hand, the opposition parties are constantly trying to capitalize on the disaffection by championing the northern cause. For over thirty years the Conservatives have striven, with moderate success, to maintain their government position, while the Liberals and NDP have vied for the alienated northern vote.

In the 28th Legislature (1967–71), for example, the 15 northern ridings split: Conservatives 6; Liberals 5; and NDP 4. In the 29th Legislature (1971–75), the Conservatives increased to 7, the NDP to 6, and the Liberals dropped to 2. In the 1943 election, which brought the current succession of Conservative governments into power, the CCF (predecessor of the NDP) virtually swept the north, winning all but two seats. Thus, the record indicates that, while political fortunes ebb and flow, the Conservatives tend to win approximately half, or less of the seats, with the NDP generally holding the edge as challenger.

But within these overall statistics, the north provides fascinating examples of voting patterns within each riding as the governing party loses the support of alienated groups, or they switch their support from one opposition party to another. Political success in the north is not built on moving a heterogeneous population toward a different political ideology; rather, it is a process of mobilizing a sufficient number of alienated groups to effect the election of a candidate. One or two cases provide an interesting test of this hypothesis.

In 1966, a by-election was held in the provincial riding of Kenora, which had a long history of voting Liberal-Labour. That hyphenated party had its beginning back in the thirties when the Liberals displayed an ideological versatility and endorsed a Labour candidate who went on to win the election. Over the years the tie of the Lib-Lab candidate to the Liberal party grew in significance; and the Labour aspect of the label tended to diminish until the Lib-Lab candidate was seen as essentially a Liberal candidate with a special concern for the rights of labour.

When the NDP decided to make a determined effort to win the seat, it recognized that two major groups would have to be won away from their traditional loyalties: the labour vote had to be persuaded to abandon the Liberals and the Indian vote to abandon the Conservatives.

The effort to break the link between the Liberal party and the labour movement was largely successful while the effort to win the Indian vote from the Conservatives was much less so. When the votes were counted, the NDP had risen from 2,187 to 4,376; the Lib-Lab had dropped from 6,774 to 4,452, while the Conservatives remained essentially the same, rising from 5,934 to 6,335. The Conservatives won by holding the traditional Tory vote. They won by virtually standing still while the alienated groups shifted around them!

Sudbury from 1943 to 1971 presented a different picture. In 1943 Robert Carlin, as the CCF candidate, won the support of labour, farm and the French-Canadian vote. The opposition to Carlin were the traditional supporters of the status quo who rallied around the banner of the Sudbury *Star*. In fact, on election night several thousand chanting supporters of Carlin marched on the *Star* office because they viewed it as the focal point of resistance to political change.

However, the political fortunes of Carlin and the CCF fell upon evil days. The various groups of the alienated who had come together in an anti-government coalition split badly. In the 1948 election, the Conservatives polled 8,892 votes while close behind was Carlin, as an independent CCF, with 8,613 votes, and the official CCF candidate with 5,821 votes. In short, the opposition polled 14,434 official and independent CCF votes and another 6,949 for the Liberals, but the Conservatives won the seat with 8,892.

It was more than twenty years before the same combination of labour-farm-ethnic votes returned NDP members in all three Sudbury Basin seats in 1971. In this instance the vote coalesced around Elie Martel, MPP for Sudbury East, who had been in the Legislature for only one term. Martel's general stance was a somewhat brash "damn the establishment," but it was underpinned with policy positions which resulted in basic voting shifts: the separate school issue won the support of the Catholic Church, and hence the French-Canadian vote; the tough challenge to INCO and Falconbridge won the Mine Mill workers away from the Liberals and, together with the traditional support of the Steelworkers, produced a more solid NDP labour vote; a strong stand on pollution control and an assault on "shyster" real estate operators, combined to win a large part of the middle-class vote in conservation groups and ratepayers associations. By 1971 the coalition of the forties had reassembled. The kaleidoscope of northern Ontario's alienated groups backed the NDP candidate, resulting in 15,522 votes in Sudbury East as against a combined 13,398 for the Conservatives and Liberals. The swing was massive enough to carry the two neighbouring Sudbury Basin seats.[4]

It must be conceded, however, that northern alienation

4 For further detail on the "group" influence on voting patterns, see Peter Regenstreif, "Group Perceptions and the Vote: Some Avenues of Opinion Formation in the 1962 Campaign," in John Meisel, ed., *Papers on the 1962 Election* (Toronto: University of Toronto Press, 1964), pp. 235–252.

does not produce a consistent anti-establishment vote; rather, it merely tends, or threatens, to do so. Thus, in the traditional way that disadvantaged areas usually tend to stick with the party in power, northern Ontario has regularly sent approximately half its MPP's to the Conservative side of the Legislature. To an even greater extent, federally it has elected Liberals, almost to the exclusion of the Conservatives—leaving the NDP with fluctuating fortunes as a challenger. As in the Maritimes and rural Quebec, the northern voter, despite his alienation, often votes for the government for fear of being cut off from something.

It must also be acknowledged that northern Ontario has no monopoly on alienation; it is a characteristic of much of modern society. It can be found in the loneliness of the bigger southern cities, as well as in the isolation of the northern bush. But, as we have seen, there is an extra dimension—indeed, many dimensions—to the alienation of the north.

In 1967 Premier Robarts called Ontario the "golden hinge" of Confederation. If the analogy be accurate, then northern Ontario is the rusty linchpin. If Canada is to work, then northern Ontario, where all the alienations meet, must be made to work for it. It is here that eastern Canada meets the alienated west. It is here that English Canada meets alienated French Canada. It is here that the Indian suffers a silent alienation within sight of a standard of living far above his own. It is here that a colonial industrial system functions with an alienated work force.

It is ironic that, at a time when the Maritime provinces are talking union and the prairie provinces are exploring greater regional cooperation, northern Ontario should periodically be talking of separation. Intellectually, the case is strong that the solution lies in better government, not more government; but emotionally, something more than political rhetoric will be needed to counter the north's long-standing feeling of neglect.

15
FREDERICK J. FLETCHER

Between Two Stools:
News Coverage of
Provincial Politics
in Ontario

Provincial politics tends to fall between two stools. Ottawa is viewed as the most critical centre of political news and city hall is seen as the source of decisions which relate directly to the concerns of individuals. Both tend to get more attention from news media than Queen's Park.

MARK HARRISON, Toronto *Star*

Mr. Speaker, I read the *Globe and Mail*, and every other paper I can, religiously.

WILLIAM DAVIS, Premier of Ontario

THERE are few subjects which cause more shouting and arm-waving among politicians and political activists than the mass media. In Ontario, government supporters complain that the media take minor issues and try to make scandals of them. Liberal supporters criticize the media for not giving them the attention their position as official opposition calls for, while New Democratic Party sympathizers feel the media fail to realize that only they are raising really significant issues. Supporters of all the parties believe that provincial politics gets inadequate coverage.

This general concern about the mass media reflects their importance in the political process. They are important for the government, not only to publicize its virtues, but also to let the public know about new laws and programs. They are important to the opposition parties because they must use the media to communicate their criticisms of government policies and their alternative proposals to the electorate. Indeed, election campaigns as we know them would be impossible without the media, with their ability to reach large audiences quickly, cheaply and conveniently.

Since Ontario, with more than eight million people, is too large for its citizens to experience directly most politically relevant events, it is largely through the media that people learn about the crucial issues of government and politics. News reports make it possible for citizens to keep informed about government policies, to follow election campaigns and to monitor the activities of public officials. In fact, it has traditionally been assumed in our system that a watchful press and an alert public opinion are primary checks on arbitrary or corrupt governments. The media also provide a forum for citizen grievances and, on a day-to-day basis, communicate the shared ideas which make Ontario a socio-political community.

In performing these functions, the media are not simply neutral channels of information. They influence public perceptions through their selection and presentation of news. The federal government's Task Force on Government Information concluded that the mass media "occupy so central a role in modern society that they may rightly be considered the main gatekeepers of most public information . . ." (Vol. i, p. 20). The media are gatekeepers in the sense that key personnel in news organizations make important decisions every day regarding what events and conditions will be covered or investigated, what stories will be printed or broadcast and what prominence various items will be given. These decisions determine to a great extent what information will be available to the public about government policies, political issues and the political process in general. These gatekeepers close the gates on some issues or spokesmen and open them for others, on the basis of what they think is important, legitimate and of general interest.

However, news reports seem to have more influence on what issues we think about than on the opinions we hold. For example, Anthony Westell noted recently that inflation outranked unemployment in the Gallup poll as the most important issue facing Canada only *after* the media had shifted attention from unemployment to inflation. In the 1974 federal election, the polls showed that most Torontonians agreed with the media that inflation was the major issue but rejected the argument made in editorials in the city's three daily newspapers that the best hope for solution was to vote Progressive Conservative. The Liberals won twenty-one of twenty-six Metro area seats. Research shows that people select what they will pay attention to in the media, what they will believe and what they will remember, according to their pre-existing beliefs, expectations and experiences, screening out contrary information and arguments.

In this chapter, we will examine both the quantity and quality of news about provincial politics available to Ontario citizens. Among other things, we will see that more and better news is available in Toronto than elsewhere, that investigative reporting is less common than journalists like to believe, that important information about policy-making is often given less attention than more trivial aspects of politics and that election coverage provides a limited and distorted picture of campaigns. In our analysis, we will look at the political implications of these patterns of media behaviour and at some of the reasons for them.

The mass media system which serves Ontario citizens is a highly developed one, made up of some 49 daily newspapers, nearly 250 weeklies, some 28 television stations (in two major networks) and about 130 radio stations. These news outlets are linked by a variety of news services, the most important of which is the Canadian Press (CP), a cooperative newsgathering and distribution agency owned collectively by the country's daily newspapers. Broadcast News (BN), a division of CP, provides a basic news service for broadcasters. For all but the larger newspapers and broadcasting stations in big urban centres, CP and BN (including BN Voice which distributes taped reports and interviews) are the major sources of non-local news. BN relies heavily on CP for the material in its hourly news summary and CP in turn gets most of its copy from its larger member papers, supplemented by the work of its own small reporting staff. The system makes international, national and provincial news available to virtually all Ontarians.

The most influential gatekeepers of information on provincial government and politics are the members of the Legislature press gallery at Queen's Park. The gallery, made up of reporters with special responsibility for covering Queen's Park, is on a day-to-day basis the single most important instrument of political communication in the province. As Donald W. Beeney, media relations officer for the Premier, put it in an interview, "the press gallery is really the key contact point between the government and the public." The government clearly views the gallery as a major channel through which it can get information to the public on government policies and programs and, therefore, a crucial agency for the effective functioning of government. Since, as the Committee on Government Productivity (COGP) commented in its Report on Communications and Information Services, "information represent(s) a critical first step in the delivery of services . . .," the way in which gallery members report a new program may have considerable influence on its success or failure.

Perhaps more important, at least in terms of democratic theory, the gallery plays an essential role in the legislative process. The parliamentary ritual acquires its significance in large part from the public attention it gets, and this attention is conveyed almost entirely through the mass media, since few Ontarians attend the sessions or read Hansard. The incentive for opposition members to question ministers, criticize government policies, and make alternative proposals in a chamber where the governing party holds a clear majority lies more in the hope of accumulating public support for the next election than in changing policy in the short term. Thus, the gallery is a necessary part of the system through which the Legislature performs its central function of making the government accountable for its actions.

In general, gallery members are responsible for reporting on the Legislature, including committees, the cabinet, the civil service (with twenty-six ministries and more than 60,000 employees), and the many agencies, boards, commissions and task forces which are a part of the Ontario government. In addition, many members write features on leading political figures and/or columns analysing Ontario politics. As well, gallery reporters are usually expected to cover party conferences, leadership conventions and provincial elections.

The press gallery's status as an essential institution in the Ontario political system is recognized in a number of ways. Its members have the exclusive right to take notes in the Legislature (in their own gallery) and to examine copies of the budget and Throne speeches before they are read. The gallery is provided with about five thousand square feet of office space in the legislative building (worth about $40,000 per year in rent) and other services costing the government more than $35,000 annually, as well as free copies of many government publications. Reporters also have access to areas closed to the public, such as the Legislature lobbies, cafeteria and library. These privileges are extensions of the gallery's "traditional right of access to the legislative process in order to inform the public," as it is expressed in the gallery's draft brief to the Ontario Commission on the Legislature (Camp Commission).

As of June, 1974, the gallery had forty active members

(that is, reporters with offices at the Legislature), representing twenty-seven news organizations, and sixteen
associate members, representing fourteen organizations.
The latter appear only for major stories. Only nine of the
forty-nine dailies have staff writers among the active members but some twenty Thomson dailies are served by a
three-member bureau. More than a third of Ontario's
dailies, with a total circulation of nearly 300,000, have no
reporters at Queen's Park, presumably relying excusively
on CP coverage. Among these are such substantial dailies
as the Kitchener-Waterloo *Record* (circulation, 56,524) and
the St. Catharines *Standard* (36,662). Except for some Toronto stations, few broadcast outlets have reporters in the
gallery but there are a number of services which provide
taped reports for subscribers across the province. Most
bureaus are one-person operations, but the Toronto *Star*
has five gallery reporters, the CBC four, CP three (plus a BN
staffer) along with the *Globe*, Toronto *Sun* and the Thomson group. The gallery has an executive to manage the office
and lounge space, but few rules. Membership is open to any
representative of a recognized news organization and there
is no code of conduct. As one member remarked in an
interview: "Each individual is hired and fired and paid by
his own outlet and individuals are responsible to their
[employers] and not to each other."

Although it is difficult to trace the influence of a reporter's background in his work, since most professionals
work hard to keep their personal views from intruding
excessively into their copy, certain patterns in the gallery
membership may be significant. Some editors think a
university degree is an asset for gallery members but few
actually have one, though most have attended a college or
university briefly. However, most members had considerable reporting experience before being assigned to Queen's
Park (at least six years), usually involving a variety of
assignments and at least some experience of political reporting. In more personal terms, the typical gallery reporter is male (there were three women in June 1974),
about thirty-five, of British origin, born and educated in
Ontario, with a lower middle-class family background. Few
of the members have ever held a job outside of journalism.

Several implications of this profile may be suggested.

First, the middle-class background (and current status, at an average salary of about $15,000 per year) probably reinforces the middle-class bias of most Canadian media. Second, the underrepresentation of women and persons of non-British origin may make the gallery insufficiently aware of the problems and aspirations of these groups. The fact that there are no representatives of the ethnic press may underline this tendency. Lack of experience in non-journalist occupations may reduce the capacity of the gallery to grasp the full implications of certain policies.

The output of the gallery also seems to suffer from the rapid turnover of its personnel. With the exception of a half dozen "veterans," the average member has been at Queen's Park less than two years. Between June 1973 and June 1974, fourteen reporters were replaced. Yet several reporters commented in interviews that experience is important in mastering the procedures of the Legislature and the complicated structure of the civil service, as well as in acquiring the contacts necessary to obtain access to needed information. Others noted that because policies often develop over long periods, new reporters lack the background to understand events and, therefore, to explain them. Yet many organizations prefer to transfer reporters after two years to avoid the strains involved if a reporter becomes attracted to one of the parties or gets caught up in the insular world of the politicians and loses his reader-oriented perspective. It would seem that the losses involved in this policy exceed the gains.

There is also controversy over the degree to which recruits to the gallery should be specialists in political reporting. Some reporters take the view that covering politics is much like any other assignment and that specialized knowledge can best be acquired on the job. One radio reporter commented that "it's better not to be too interested in politics [because] a degree of detachment is useful." However true this may be, greater use of specialists might increase the depth and perspective in Queen's Park reporting. With a few exceptions, expert analysis of provincial politics is generally lacking.

Probably the most important factor influencing the quality and content of Queen's Park coverage, however, is the customary work pattern of gallery members. Although work ways differ somewhat, as, for example, between print and broadcast people, there are common patterns. As the gallery's submission to the Camp Commission notes,

The Legislature's question period is, naturally, the part of its sittings which is most intensely covered. It is the most interesting, most dramatic in personal and political terms, very productive of news (including the government statements which precede it) and clearly defined in time.

This period, between two and three P.M. every sitting day, is the key event for the gallery. Often, as many as 80 per cent of the stories filed from the gallery will be based on this single hour in the legislative schedule. It is, as one radio man put it, the "blood and guts" of the job. Another commented that his basic job is to "try to bring the question period to the people through tape." Since the sessions are not broadcast and taping is not permitted in the chamber, there is often a scramble for interviews as a dozen or more broadcasters (and as many more newspaper reporters) crowd around key figures in the Legislature lobbies. Broadcasters are seeking to have announcements, questions and comments repeated (and expanded) for taping while print reporters are seeking further details and clarifications.

The most fundamental work pattern in the gallery is this emphasis on the question period. Debates are much less closely covered. After the question period, reporters generally return to their offices to write and send in their stories. They do, however, follow the debates on the public address system piped into their offices, returning to the chamber if anything develops which they deem newsworthy. They also look in when major figures are speaking and generally have advance warning of particularly significant speeches. Most gallery members also cover the regular Wednesday morning cabinet meetings, waiting outside the meeting room for announcements and to catch ministers for statements on current issues. They also attend news conferences called by government or opposition spokesmen and, especially, the Premier's regular news conferences at which reporters may raise any issue. The latter are held at regular intervals and are chaired by a member of the gallery executive. Reporters must also sift through the flood of releases, speeches and reports which they receive every day from government departments and agencies, the opposition parties and pressure groups, as well as covering committee meetings and following up stories by talking with ministers, other MPP's or civil servants.

The most limited coverage is that provided by broadcast reporters. For example, they are interested almost exclusively in the utterances of politicians, since they feel a need to get voices (and faces for television) on tape and to be able to identify the speakers. Thus, they concentrate on authoritative spokesmen: the Premier, the ministers and, less often, the leaders of the opposition parties. Sometimes a particularly well-known or colourful MPP, such as Dr. Morton Shulman (NDP – High Park), will be interviewed. Virtually all of their stories grow out of the question period and government announcements. While newspaper reporters stress these sources, they also make more use of government reports and other documents and of contacts within the civil service.

Another important aspect of the gallery's work pattern is the matter of deadlines. The gallery's brief to the Camp Commission puts it clearly,

> Almost any time of day, someone here is on deadline. For afternoon papers it is all morning and up to and including question period. For morning papers it is late afternoon and everything through the evening. For radio reporters, it is every hour. This means that morning committee meetings, question period and afternoon and evening debates are always being covered by someone on deadline.

The schedule of a radio reporter provides an extreme example. Arriving at Queen's Park about 9:15 A.M., having already checked the newspapers for leads, he goes through the releases on his desk and prepares one "cut" or story (40 to 60 seconds) before noon, usually on something left over from the previous day, and another for the 2 P.M. news, usually from releases. The question period, with taped comments collected in the lobbies, provides cuts for the 4, 5 and 6 P.M. newscasts. Before going home, between 6 and 8 P.M. he prepares several tapes for evening newscasts and one or two for the next morning. Many stories involve interviews. For other reporters, life is less hectic, but time pressures still make it difficult for most to seek out background materials or to examine announcements sceptically. These deadline pressures are exacerbated by the fact that most bureaus consist of a single reporter, without filing or research assistance.

Between sessions, the pace slackens and newspaper reporters get a chance to do feature stories on ministers or agencies, to look into issues which arose during the session, and to do more investigation of policies and their implementation. However, many broadcast people are given other assignments and come to Queen's Park only for the cabinet meetings, meetings of important committees and news conferences.

Within the gallery, the CP bureau is expected to provide a comprehensive basic news coverage of the provincial government, leaving other bureaus free to pursue stories of special interest to their editors. The bureau turns out twelve to fifteen stories a day (4,000 to 5,000 words), well over 150,000 words per session, with full coverage of question period, important debates, all major government releases and reports, committee meetings and public speeches by government and opposition leaders. In addition, the bureau chief writes background reports and a weekly interpretive column. The bureau also responds to frequent requests from member papers for stories of local interest. Because it serves broadcast outlets as well as newspapers, it must work quickly. Major stories are usually filed within an hour. As a result of the pressure to provide comprehensive coverage of routine events quickly, CP stories are brief (rarely exceeding 500 words) and, because CP serves many masters, usually general and bland. The bureau lacks the staff to dig deeper (even having to call in help from the Toronto office to cover committee meetings), though reporters would like to.

The output of the gallery is also influenced by the fact that some bureaus are more influential than others. Although the *Star* bureau is larger, the *Globe* is more influential, partly because it gives more emphasis to provincial politics, partly because it is read at the beginning of the work day, and partly perhaps because of its traditional ties with Tory governments. The *Globe* influences what other agencies cover and how they do it, including CP, whose editors have been known to transmit *Globe* stories in preference to those filed by their own reporters. The *Globe*'s influence extends to the legislators who often draw on it for their question period thrusts (and rebuttals).

Globe reporters are more often the recipients of news leaks and exclusive interviews and find it easier to get interviews on request than other bureaus. Whatever the *Globe* prints will be picked up by the *Star*, CP and other agencies, so the *Globe* is often seen as a convenient point of access to the media system. The *Star*, with its large staff and circulation (500,000) is also influential.

The most obvious problem area which emerges from this examination of the gallery's work patterns is the stress on the Legislature at the expense of the policy-making and implementation processes in the cabinet and civil service. While this has the advantage of helping to sustain the influence of the Legislature, it has the disadvantage of emphasizing what are often ritual conflicts at the expense of more genuine issues. Policy issues are often not reported until the point of decision has passed and only the legislative ritual remains. Ideally, the gallery should be reporting on the options being considered (and possible factors in the decision) long before the cabinet finally settles on a policy. But a shift in emphasis from Legislature to civil service is made difficult by gallery working conditions: tight deadlines, small staffs and little help, as well as demands from editors, audiences and publicity-seeking politicians for stress on the trivialities of politics rather than on less dramatic aspects of policy-making.

Access to information is also a major problem. The Ontario oath of office requires the public servant to swear that "except as I may be legally required, I will not disclose or give to any person any information or document that comes to my knowledge or possession by reason of my being a civil servant." The COGP Report on Government Information points out that the amount of information required by statute to be revealed is small and comments that most officials tend to provide only minimal information unless otherwise instructed. The report suggests greater use of white and green papers, with wide distribution, published far enough in advance of decision to permit public response to policy alternatives. Reporters commented that policy-related information can be obtained by reporters with good contacts and time to pursue a story, a circumstance, however, which is all too rare.

Even the gallery's basic job of covering the Legislature suffers from the government's habit of holding many bills till the end of the session. The Assembly generally convenes in late winter or early spring, recesses about the end of June for the summer, reconvenes in the fall and prorogues before Christmas, sitting for about six months in all. In the spring session of 1973, which was typical, twenty-six of the eighty-seven bills dealt with in the fourteen-week session (30 per cent) went through all stages except first reading in the last week (nine on the last day). This pattern makes it difficult for the gallery to explain and analyse legislation. The reporters lack not only time for analysis but also the assistance of opposition criticisms upon which they must often rely for help in understanding the significance and possible weaknesses of government legislation.

The gallery is, not surprisingly, subjected to constant efforts by both government and opposition to influence its work. These are not, as a rule, sinister attempts at news management but rather simply efforts to publicize a program, issue or point of view. Pressure groups also see the gallery as a target. It is very easy, according to a former gallery member, always to be reacting, "to be led around by the nose simply by the amount of material thrown at you." For example, spokesmen often use questionable statistics to support their arguments. Recently, one minister announced a large increase in certain benefits, a headline-grabbing announcement, but a close reading of the new policy showed that the increase applied to relatively few people, a fact which some reporters caught while others did not.

Within the gallery, there is disagreement regarding the degree to which reporters should be sceptical. Some organizations, led by the *Globe*, felt that the large majority gained by the Conservatives in 1971 left the gallery with a responsibility to supplement the weakened opposition. Despite its traditional Tory ties, the *Globe* has kept a close eye on the government since, employing special investigative reporters as well as gallery members to look into potential scandals. This feeling began to fade after the 1973 by-elections when reporters felt that the opposition parties had begun to reassert themselves. But some reporters still argue that gallery members should spend more time seeking out inefficiency, injustice and waste in government, looking critically at new policies and exposing contradictions or difficulties in government programs. Others, however, feel that these tasks should be left to opposition MPP's and that reporters should be neutral channels of information, reporting government statements, opposition criticisms and government rebuttals. Fortunately, there are important news organizations which do not share this passive view.

Before actually reaching the public, the stories produced by gallery members must be passed by other gatekeepers, who limit the amount of news about provincial politics made available to citizens. On a quantitative basis, there is evidence to support Mark Harrison's observation, quoted above, that news about provincial politics tends to fall between stools. An extensive study of daily newspaper content by Donald Gordon a few years ago found that news about provincial government and politics in Ontario daily newspapers made up less than 10 per cent of all news and less than 20 per cent of the political news. News from Ottawa was given four times as much space, as was news of crime and legal matters. In several other provinces, especially Quebec, provincial politics got considerably more attention (Manzer, p. 116). Coverage of provincial politics has significantly increased since Professor Gordon's study but it is still fairly low on the news priority list for many outlets. News of the provincial scene tends to be overwhelmed by international, national and local news, despite the growing importance of the provincial governments as policy-makers in the federal system.

The Toronto *Star*'s position is probably typical. The *Star*'s editors take the view that national news is of overriding importance and must be thoroughly covered as a matter of public duty. On the other hand, community affairs get high priority on the theory that political news on the local level is most likely to relate closely to the individual. As a result, the *Star* maintains a staff of eleven in Ottawa, assigns six or seven reporters to city hall, and has only five at Queen's Park. Space tends to be allocated proportionately. In the *Star*'s case, with its vast resources and large news hole, provincial politics is still given reasonably thorough coverage. The same philosophy at less affluent news organizations, however, means that provincial politics is often given short shrift.

News of provincial politics is also distributed unevenly. Citizens outside Metro Toronto and a few other major centres receive both less news of Queen's Park and poorer quality coverage. For example, many newspapers and broadcasting outlets outside Toronto gave only minimal attention to such items as the various conflict of interest charges and mini-scandals which surrounded the Davis government in the 1971–74 period. A good example is the case of the inquiry into Ontario Hydro held in the summer of 1973, which reporters at Queen's Park regard as one of the major political stories of recent years. A province-wide survey of voters published in the Toronto *Star* (September 22, 1973) showed that Metro voters were much more likely to have heard of the case than were those outside Metro. A sample of voters was asked: "Have you heard or read anything about charges of political favouritism being involved in the awarding of a contract to build a new head office for Ontario Hydro to a close friend of Ontario Premier William Davis?" While 80 per cent of voters in Metro answered yes, only 53 per cent of those living outside Metro did so.

Many smaller newspapers carry only the brief and general CP bulletins from Queen's Park. Many radio and television stations carry the national news and then cut to local items, ignoring Queen's Park altogether, except for items of overwhelming importance or significant local interest. The large, urban stations usually subscribe to several news services, including special coverage of Queen's Park, but a majority of stations fall into the "rip and read" category, employing one or two news readers who do nothing but rip the BN hourly summary out of the teletype and read it on the air (perhaps supplemented by excerpts from a local newspaper or, for television, some local visual footage).

A particular problem for the opposition parties is that their activities in the Legislature often get little attention outside Toronto, especially in ridings held by Conservative MPP's. Some of the smaller outlets have a tendency to rely heavily for news of Queen's Park on government-supplied releases (including sound and video tapes) or on riding reports put out by incumbent MPP's. For the opposition parties, if penetrating questions, constructive criticisms and alternative policy proposals in the chamber are not getting through to the public, there is an incentive to turn to other strategies. The Liberal party, for example, has decided to use tours around the province to carry its mes-

sage. Robert Nixon and other leading caucus members are
to make regular visits to media centres in regions outside
Toronto to appear on open line radio shows and television
talk shows and to give newspaper interviews. The Conservatives use policy announcements, grant awards and
ceremonial openings of public facilities to do the same.
While this does bring politics to the people, it may detract
from the importance of the Legislature.

One aspect of the problem of uneven news distribution
is the fact that news from Queen's Park must compete with
other news for attention. The problem is especially acute
in northern Ontario. In a recent interview, John Rhodes,
former mayor of Sault Ste. Marie and now Ontario Minister
of Transport and Communications, told reporter Bob Carr
that "Ontario is the most poorly served by the CBC . . . in
broadcasting Ontario matters. In the Northwest most of
the feed comes from Winnipeg. But the people of the Northwest are part of Ontario and should be serviced by programming and information that is coming out of Ontario,
not out of Manitoba." In addition, the 27 per cent of the
population of northern and eastern Ontario that is French-
speaking probably attends as much to news from Quebec
City as from Queen's Park. In southern Ontario, provincial
news must compete for attention with the flood of messages from the United States, especially on television.

The major consequences of this pattern are that the common images which create a sense of community are not
evenly distributed throughout the province and that the
store of information about the government of Ontario and
its policies is not equally available everywhere. In addition,
the dominance of the Toronto-based media in the system
tends both to crowd out information on conditions elsewhere and to impose on the news a Toronto-centred view
of Ontario's major problems.

During election campaigns, the media step up their
coverage of provincial politics. In the process, they make
the campaign visible and, through their selection of news,
help to shape the images of candidates, define campaign
issues and influence the tone of the election. In our system,
the media are expected to provide sufficient unbiased information to permit citizens to make a reasoned voting
decision. In recent years, the newspapers have joined radio
and television in avoiding overt political bias in their news

coverage, though it still creeps in. (Bias is often claimed by political observers but it is hard to prove. It is always possible that one candidate will receive more attention than another simply because editors perceive that candidate or party as doing or saying more interesting or newsworthy things than his competitors.) The fact that the NDP rarely receives editorial endorsements probably reflects the pro-business bias of the media, which does show up in news selection from time to time.

In a study of campaign coverage in the Toronto media during the 1971 provincial election, Stephen Clarkson noted three trends: a tendency for the media to pay more attention to the governing party than to the others; heavy stress on the party leaders at the expense of other candidates; and a tendency to limit the capacity of the parties to communicate their platforms to the electorate by stressing only a few major issues.

There was a clear pro-incumbent bias in all of the media in terms of attention paid to parties. This was most pronounced in the broadcast media, which gave Conservative spokesmen about twice as much air time as the two opposition parties combined. Even when news related to government was removed, the Conservative total still exceeded that of the other two parties. With one exception, the two opposition parties received approximately equal attention. The pattern in the newspapers was similar but differences were much less pronounced.

The dominance of the party leaders was evident in all media, but again most evident in the broadcast media. On all stations, the items reporting on the leader outnumbered those dealing with other party activities or candidates, in some cases by a substantial margin. The coverage gave the impression that the election primarily involved a choice among leaders rather than among platforms or party "teams." The efforts of the NDP to project a team image failed to make a major impression on media coverage. On one station, leader Stephen Lewis was the only NDP candidate mentioned. Apparently responding to media practices, the parties have increasingly been planning their campaigns around their leaders.

In terms of issues, the media tend to simplify party platforms greatly. For example, 52 per cent of the news items in all media referring to Liberal party policy dealt with one major issue, economic and cultural nationalism, although there were a total of 293 issues in the official platform. The leader, Robert Nixon, also stressed this issue, but not to the same degree. The television stations especially gave little attention to issues, making fewer than half as many references to the Liberal position on issues as did radio. Not surprisingly, since they have much greater news capacity, the newspapers provided the most extensive issue coverage. Liberal positions on all but one or two major issues were poorly communicated and Professor Clarkson concludes that

. . . the mass media reinforce the natural tendency of parties to give high priority during a campaign to a limited number of issues rather than attempt to cover the whole . . . of their party programme. Equally the media reinforce the tendency already evident in pre-electronic politics to give primacy to the leaders in election campaigns ("Policy and the Media," p. 37).

In general, then, the news organizations simplify election campaigns by focusing attention on a few major issues and, more especially, on party leaders. While this process may make things easier for voters, it can obscure the importance of the supporting cast and of some potentially important issues. In addition, by stressing the state of the campaign at the expense of policy positions (as did all the outlets monitored for Professor Clarkson's study) the media reinforce the image of the campaign as a sort of political beauty contest among leaders (and their families).

We have seen that such factors as the work patterns of the press gallery, the structure and operation of the mass media system and the selection of campaign news all influence the kind and amount of political information available to Ontario citizens. And we have seen that the flow of news places limits on the capacity of citizens to take part in the policy process, to make informed voting decisions and, in some parts of the province, simply to understand and feel a part of the provincial political process. These are the indirect effects of media behaviour. But what about the direct impact of the media?

Although research shows that the media cannot really swing elections any more (though they can affect them indirectly), the influence of the press on public policy can

be more direct, primarily because the politicians themselves and the leaders of important pressure groups pay
attention to it. The media have their greatest impact
through the reaction of elites to the exposure of embarrassing facts or conditions resulting from investigative
journalism. In Ontario, much of this is done by specialists
working for some of the major outlets who supplement the
work of gallery reporters.

A good example of the impact of investigative journalism is the Workmen's Compensation Board (wcb) case
reported in chapter 6. In that chapter Jonathan Manthorpe notes that the publication in the *Globe* of a series
of articles containing sensational charges regarding the
wcb led to a major reassessment of the board. A committee of members of the Legislature found a good many
problems at the wcb and the investigation ultimately led
to the resignation of the board's chairman and significant reforms in its operations. Although there had been
demonstrations against the board previously, many believe that the *Globe* articles were an essential catalyst in
getting government action. But it was not only fear of
publicity that triggered the legislative investigation. It
appears that pressure from a large corporation charged
in the series with unethical conduct also played a role, as
did the fact that many MPP's (of all parties) had already
been antagonized by the board. The press's role here was
one of "creating a crisis" by focusing attention on the
situation and getting things moving.

The impact on the public of the wcb case and the various
conflict of interest cases uncovered by reporters since
1971 is unclear. The *Star* survey quoted above showed a
13 per cent drop in Conservative popularity from the 1971
election in Metro, where the Hydro hearings were most
widely publicized, as compared to only a 4 per cent drop
outside Metro, where they got less attention. But such
effects are often transitory and could be caused by other
factors. What is clear is that the government reacted by
reorganizing the wcb and by tightening conflict of interest
regulations. The press can reasonably take credit for these
reforms.

In this survey of news coverage of provincial politics in
Ontario, we have found that the pool of information available to Ontario citizens is relatively small, unevenly

distributed and derived mainly from coverage of the Legislature, with emphasis on the question period. We have also seen that gallery members often lack the time and access to information necessary for probing analyses of government programs and policy options. These patterns have the effect of limiting the capacity of citizens to influence public policy and sometimes of reducing the effectiveness of government programs because citizens who might benefit from them never hear about them. The influence of the Legislature is reduced by inadequate coverage (especially of debates) and the uneven distribution of information helps to exacerbate problems such as northern alienation.

The analysis also highlights the fact that the media severely limit the amount and complexity of information that candidates can communicate to the public. They simplify election campaigns by focussing on a few issues and by emphasizing leaders, thus limiting the bases upon which voters can judge. In addition, they tend to pay more attention to government leaders than to opposition spokesmen, giving incumbent officials a (perhaps inevitable) built-in advantage in the never-ending contest for public attention.

By way of conclusion, let us explore briefly some of the reasons for these patterns. Why is news of provincial politics neglected? Why is hard-nosed investigative reporting rare? Why is news so narrowly defined? A major factor accounting for all of these patterns is the profit-making orientation of most news outlets, many of which are "big business," especially the corporations which own groups of newspapers and/or radio and television stations. Primarily in the business of selling audiences to advertisers, many outlets see little reason to spend the money necessary to improve coverage of provincial politics, especially the broadcast media whose main function is entertainment. A good many syndicated features (such as advice columns) can be purchased for the cost of maintaining one reporter at Queen's Park. Similarly, investigative reporting is rare in part because it is expensive. It requires the commitment of reporters for long periods to projects which may produce nothing publishable. Often, experts must be hired and there is always the threat of libel suits. In short, it is too expensive for most editorial budgets, which must often be stretched simply to cover the costs of routine newsgathering. This position is supported by a deep-seated conviction among editors (supported in part by audience surveys) that people are most interested in local news, followed by international and national news, with news of provincial affairs trailing.

The shortage of hard-hitting investigative reporting can also be traced in part to a general reluctance in many news outlets to deal with controversial subjects. In their quest for large audiences to sell to advertisers, many organizations are reluctant to offend any major segment of their communities affluent enough to buy advertised products. It is fact, as Jerry Goodis, the well-known Toronto advertising man, pointed out to the Davey Committee, which accounts as much as anything else for the middle-class orientation of the media (and for their neglect of marginal audiences). It is also true that the major media organizations are themselves well-established parts of our present economic and political system and have no desire to undermine it (though they may seek to reform it). Publishers are generally pillars of the business community and tend to identify its interests with the public interest.

Reporters and editors are often more venturesome than their publishers but they are often inhibited by the existence within their newsrooms of a subtle set of norms which discourages some kinds of reporting and encourages others. There is, in fact, little deliberate suppression of news by publishers, but, as the Davey Committee observed,

> More often it is a result of a certain atmosphere—an atmosphere in which boat rocking is definitely not encouraged—and of news editors trying to read the boss's mind. This leads to journalistic sins (of omission mostly) that result from lassitude, sloppiness, and too chummy a relationship with the local power structure (Vol. I, p. 87).

The result often is that reporters stick to reporting what others have said and done (such as in question period) and avoid sceptical reporting or analysis, which is more risky.

In short, many of the defects of what is on the whole a relatively good media system are inherent in the organization of the system itself. It is clear that the profit orientation leads news outlets to gather news where it is cheapest and to stress dramatic and audience-attracting items at the expense of more significant news. It also leads to meagre editorial budgets which make quality journalism difficult. Perhaps the best antidote for these ills is an aware and critical audience.

APPENDIX

*Organizations Represented in the
Ontario Legislative Press Gallery*

ACTIVE MEMBERS

Wire Services
The Canadian Press

Newspaper Groups
Thomson Newspapers

Daily Newspapers
Globe and Mail (Toronto); *The Star* (Toronto); *The Sun* (Toronto); *Le Droit* (Ottawa); *The Citizen* (Ottawa); *The Journal* (Ottawa); *The Montreal Star*; *The Free Press* (London); *The Spectator* (Hamilton); *The Star* (Windsor).

Radio-Television News Services
News Radio (CKEY); Contemporary News (CHUM); Standard News (CFRB); Broadcast News; Independent News Group; Global Television; CFTO TV (CTV); CBC TV (CBLT); CBC Radio; CHIN Radio; CHCH TV (Hamilton).

ASSOCIATE MEMBERS

Time International; CITY-TV; *Financial Times*; Southam News; *The Canadian Register*; UPI; *Toronto Mirror*; *Northern Miner*; *Financial Post*; Daily Commercial News (The following organizations have an associate member in addition to their active member(s): CFRB; CTV; CFTO; CHUM; CBC Radio)

SELECTED BIBLIOGRAPHY

BLACK, EDWIN R. "Canadian Public Policy and the Mass Media," *Canadian Journal of Economics*, vol. I, no. 2 (May 1968), pp. 368–379.

Broadcaster, November 1973.

BRYDEN, KENNETH. "Structural Change in the Ontario Government." Unpublished paper presented to the 46th Annual Meeting of the Canadian Political Science Association, Toronto, June 6, 1974.

CLARKSON, STEPHEN. "Policy and the Media: Communicating the Liberal Platform in the 1971 Ontario Election

Campaign." Unpublished paper presented to the 46th Annual Meeting of the Canadian Political Science Association, Toronto, June 3, 1974.

————. "Unfair at Any Wavelength: Political Broadcasting During the Ontario Provincial Election (September–October 1971)." Report prepared for the Research Division, Canadian Radio and Television Commission. (Mimeo, no date).

Editor and Publisher International Yearbook, 1973.

GORDON, DONALD R. *Language, Logic, and the Mass Media.* Toronto: Holt, Rinehart and Winston of Canada Ltd., 1966.

Government of Canada. *To Know and Be Known.* Report of the Task Force on Government Information. Ottawa: Information Canada, 1969. 2 vols.

————. Special Senate Committee on Mass Media. *Report* (Davey Committee Report). Ottawa: Information Canada, 1970. 3 vols.

Government of Ontario Committee on Government Productivity. *Interim Report Number Seven: Report to the Executive Council of the Government of Ontario on Communications and Information Services.* June 1972.

KESTERTON, W. H. *A History of Journalism in Canada.* Toronto: McClelland and Stewart Ltd., 1967.

MANZER, RONALD. *Canada: A Socio-Political Report.* Toronto: McGraw-Hill Ryerson Ltd., 1974.

PEERS, FRANK. "Oh Say, Can You See," in Ian Lumsden (ed.), *Close the 49th Parallel, etc.* Toronto: University of Toronto Press, 1970, pp. 135–156.

PORTER, JOHN. *The Vertical Mosaic.* Toronto: University of Toronto Press, 1965, ch. XV.

SEYMOUR-URE, COLIN. *The Political Impact of the Mass Media.* London: Constable, 1974.

SINGER, BENJAMIN D. (ed.). *Communications in Canadian Society.* Toronto: Copp Clark, 1972.

WARNOCK, JOHN W. "All the News it Pays to Print," in Ian Lumsden (ed.), *Close the 49th Parallel, etc.* Toronto: University of Toronto Press, 1970, pp. 117–134.

WEBSTER, NORMAN. "Behind the Scenes, a New Edge to Robert Nixon." Toronto *Globe and Mail.* October 29, 1973, p. 7.

16
DAVID HOFFMAN

Interacting
with Government:
The General Public and
Interest Groups

I F THERE is no agreement on the single most striking difference between the Ontario of Confederation days and contemporary life in the province, of indisputable importance are the sheer growth in the number of people, the shift in their pattern of living from a rural to an urban environment and the far greater impact which the government has on the lives of everyone. These facts are fundamental for appreciating the character of relations between the government of Ontario and the people of the province.

Of course, not only the provincial government has increased its role in the economy and society generally; especially since World War Two, the federal government has developed a vast array of public policy instruments typical of the modern welfare state. But specialists in the study of the Canadian constitution and the political process are deeply impressed by the extent to which the initiative in the development of the role of the state has shifted to the provinces. They observe that a large and powerful provincial government like that in Ontario is capable of rivalling the federal government in the management of the level of economic activity through manipulation of a number of structural policies involving labour, natural resources, commercial activity and transportation. Even more significant has been the pre-eminence of the provinces in the leading trio of social services in the modern welfare state: education, health care and welfare. Less obvious—but with tremendous potential for extending the impact of government on society—have been recent developments reflecting a greater sensitivity to the precariousness of the environment and the complexity of urban living: provincial policies in resource and environmental planning. When it is considered that the provincial presence in many of these areas has come at the expense of responsibilities traditionally carried out at the local government level the new significance of the provincial administration is fully revealed.

And yet, strangely enough, it seems that the Ontario public is not fully aware of the degree to which the provincial government has asserted itself. With all levels of government doing more for people (some would say doing more *to* people) the average person is often confused over which level of government is responsible for a particular matter, and studies of public opinion have shown that

Ontarians share with other Canadians, but to a more marked degree, a tendency to underestimate the extent to which the government at Queen's Park and not the national government in Ottawa has a major impact on their lives. This fact may account for the relatively slight degree of interaction that occurs between the ordinary citizen and the provincial government. It is an idea that can be pursued later, but first it is necessary to go beyond generalizations about "the ordinary citizen" or "the general public" to recognize that modern Ontario is a complex, diverse society, and to put forward the proposition that relations with government will in all likelihood vary depending on knowledge of the political process, resources and access to holders of power in the system.

Perhaps it is useful to go back to the point from which we began and pick up the implications of the tremendous growth in the numbers and variety of people living in the province of Ontario since 1867. At Confederation there were roughly a million and a half people in Ontario, nearly all in the towns and countryside of southern Ontario. Today there are nearly eight million, spread over a much wider area but more concentrated too: Metropolitan Toronto, with more than two million people, has a larger population than the entire province had in 1871.

There is no way of knowing whether people felt more attached to the political process in those days; whether, for example, they had closer contacts with the Legislature through their members of the Legislative Assembly than is the case today. But there are reasons for deducing from the greater size and heterogeneity of contemporary Ontario that the trend has been in the direction of less rather than more interaction with the political process.

Take, for instance, the effect of increasing the number of people in a single constituency. In 1867, elections were decided in constituencies of not more than two to three thousand voters. Admittedly the suffrage was not extended to all adult residents of a given area, but for those who were permitted to vote, the scale of activity more resembled the democratic politics of classical Greece than the situation today when MPP's have to look after and appeal to as many as 100,000 electors in a single riding.

It would be a mistake to idealize the politics of the nineteenth century town or village; indeed, there are just enough reminders in present-day rural Ontario of the practice of direct bribery at election time to help us keep the matter in perspective. However, it must be conceded that in principle the smaller the scale of the political unit, the greater the potential for interaction with the political actors. We might hypothesize that interaction with politicians and a feeling of involvement in the political process would be lower among citizens living in large urban centres than for those living in small towns and rural villages.

The degree of ethnic homogeneity and commonality of language should also to be related to a sense of involvement and interaction with the political process. Without arguing for the moment whether the hypothesized relationship exists, we may consider the nature of the incontestably dramatic demographic changes which have occurred since 1867.

At Confederation Ontario's population was remarkably homogeneous from an ethnic and linguistic point of view: the vast majority were English, Scottish or Irish, with a sprinkling of French (relatively fewer than today) and some fairly sizable concentrations of Germans in the southwestern counties of the province. English was the mother tongue and/or language of normal use of all but about a tenth of the total population. As the numbers grew over the next decades, the ethnic mix began to change as well. Internal migration—the movement of French Canadians into the northern and eastern counties—and the shift away from the prominence of Great Britain as a source of immigrants first to central or eastern Europe then to southern Europe and more recently to Asia and the Caribbean, have greatly increased the ethnic variation of the province. The dynamic nature of the Ontario economy in the postwar period served as a magnet for still further migration both from other parts of Canada and from abroad. People came and they tended to stay; moreover, they attracted relatives to come and join them. As a result, in the period from 1951 to 1971 total net migration (the figure that is left after those who leave the province are deducted from those who come) counted for more than 40 per cent of Ontario's population increase in the period, with net international migration accounting for three quarters of this total.

While those of Anglo-Saxon origin are still the largest single group in the province, there is now a good deal more

cultural pluralism. Ontario has always had a fair proportion of people who were foreign born—for decades the
census figures hovered around 20 to 25 per cent—but postwar immigration added a substantial number of people
whose first language was neither of the official languages
of the country. Moreover, immigrants to the province have
not been evenly distributed across its cities, towns and
countryside. On the contrary, most immigrants have settled
in a few cities, mainly the Golden Horseshoe of southern
Ontario. Consequently, there are a number of constituencies in the Toronto-Hamilton area where the ethnic composition of the population is markedly different from the
provincial profile: places where Anglo-Saxons appear as a
distinct minority and where large numbers of people reside
whose language within the home is neither English nor
French. In many of these same constituencies considerable
numbers of people are such newcomers to the country that
they have not yet taken out citizenship and are therefore
not eligible to participate to the same extent as others in
the political process. The social composition of Spadina
riding in Toronto is very different from that of Leeds or
Stormont for that matter. One might expect the difference
to be reflected in the relationship between people and
government if only because, all things being equal, it takes
newcomers a while to become accustomed to the rules of
the political game and to acquire the knowledge and perhaps even the confidence to intervene in the political
process.

But before too much is made of ethnicity, nativity, or
even the language factor as inhibitions to political involvement or interaction with government, it would be as well to
take account of another social basis of difference within
Ontario society—differences of education, status and income—that could be significant.

To put the proposition in its most dramatic form, let us
compare two individuals in terms of their potential for
effective interaction in the political process in Ontario.
One, Voter A, is a well-to-do lawyer at a stage in his career
where he can now afford to take considerable time away
from the office if he wants to; he has always been interested
in politics, knows a fair amount about the system and
actually is a personal friend of three or four MPP's and a
couple of senior bureaucrats in the Ontario civil service.

He used to be active in the Ontario Bar Association and now devotes some of his spare time to working for the Canadian Civil Liberties Association.

The other, Voter B, is a helper in an automated car wash. Forced to leave school at fifteen, he has only completed elementary school. Having moved recently from Nova Scotia, he knows relatively few people in his OHC apartment building, has little time or money for books and magazines; in fact he often works nights for a little extra cash as a parking attendant. Far from being on a first-name basis with local or provincial politicians and senior bureaucrats, he is not all that certain even about their existence. He belongs to no club or association and his doctor is about the only high-status individual with whom he has anything approximating a personal relationship.

The proposition, simply put, is that, leaving aside the possibly offsetting effects of personality differences, the probabilities are greater that Voter A and people like him will be personally involved in the political process than Voter B and people like him. Or, to be more general than the extreme cases selected as illustration, the degree of political involvement will vary directly with level of education and social status.

It has now been suggested that a complex of factors have a bearing on whether people become involved in the political process in Ontario. Fortunately we can go beyond merely arguing about their reasonableness to seeing whether we can find empirical support for these propositions from surveys of public opinion in the province. The set of data does not exist which would allow us to check out all the notions that we have suggested; but there is enough to test the main thrust of the argument.[1]

1 The data used in this analysis are drawn from three studies in which the author was directly involved: (1) A national survey, with a large Ontario sub-sample, completed in 1969 for the Task Force on Government Information. The results have been published and appear in Raymond N. Morris, Ruth Morris, David Hoffman, Fred Schindeler, C. Michael Lanphier, *Attitudes Towards Government Information* (Toronto: Institute for Behavioural Research, 1969); (2) A study of social and political attitudes in Ontario; data collected with Fred Schindeler from 1598 respondents in Ontario in 1968; and (3) "The Public's Perceptions of the MPP in Ontario," a report from data collected from 1540 respondents for the Ontario Commission on the Legislature in January 1973.

276 / David Hoffman

One problem is that there is not much information about
the attitudes and behaviour of Ontario people with specific
reference to the provincial government. There have been
more studies of the general political attitudes of Ontario
residents, however, and we may start with these. From a
wide variety of questions put to a large sample of Ontario
citizens in 1968 it is possible to devise a rather complex
index, at one end of which is represented what might be
taken to be the "ideal citizen" (someone who is well informed about politics, has a highly developed sense of his
duty to participate in the political process and enjoys a
feeling of being personally effective in the political process), and at the other his complete opposite (someone
who is very badly informed about politics, feels almost no
responsibility to participate in the political process and,
not surprisingly perhaps, feels no sense of political
efficacy).

Most of the people of Ontario do not appear at either of
these extremes; the vast majority fall somewhere in the
middle, being fairly well informed, somewhat efficacious
and having a modest sense of responsibility to participate.
To look for an association with some of the social characteristics discussed earlier, however, the analysis will focus
on differences in the composition of the extreme groups,
and in particular on the makeup of the ideal citizen group.

Interestingly enough, in view of our speculation about
the effects of the size of community on one's disposition to
become involved in the political process, knowledge of
politics and attitudes towards involvement in it did not

TABLE I

*Index of Ideal Citizenship by Education of Respondent
(percentages)*

| | LEVEL OF EDUCATION | | | | |
	Less than 4 years	5 to 8 years	9 to 12 years	13 years	Some/completed university or equivalent
Low	6	11	5	1	1
Middle	92	83	84	82	62
High	2	6	12	20	37
N =	110	427	510	363	178

SOURCE: Hoffman and Schindeler, "Ontario Study"

appear to be affected by differences in residence. Nor were there differences between those who were born in Canada and those who were not. In fact, the use of a more complicated classification which compared on the one hand those who were born and raised in Ontario with three groups of immigrants, classified by period of immigration, failed to reveal any statistically significant differences.

The main differentiator was socio-economic status. The higher the respondent's level of education, family income and status of his occupation, the greater the tendency to appear in the "ideal citizen" classification. Using education to illustrate this correlation, Table I shows that within the most poorly educated group of Ontario citizens (those with less than four years of elementary school) only 2 per cent are classified as ideal citizens whereas 37 per cent of those who have had at least some university education fall in that category. Neither of these groups is very large in Ontario; however, the point is that the best educated form a proportion of the ideal citizen type far beyond their numbers in the society, and actually represent a third of all respondents in this category. It is worth noting, too, that a separate analysis showed that the language which the respondent uses in the home was also related to ideal citizenship, although not as strongly as in the case of educational differences. Nevertheless English speakers were proportionally three times as prominent among the ideal citizens as French speakers or those who spoke a language other than English most of the time at home.

One of the components of the index of ideal citizenship— political knowledge—can be used to compare Ontario residents with those of the other provinces. Interestingly, the results of a nation-wide public opinion survey showed that Ontario residents were below average in political knowledge, at least when it is measured by questions dealing with awareness of which level of government has jurisdiction over a number of policy areas. Even when allowance was made for the larger number of foreign born in Ontario (who might be thought to be less familiar with the situation) the Ontario figure remained below the national average. However, although nativity was not found to differentiate among respondents within Ontario, language used in the home did: those who speak English in the home were inclined to give more accurate responses to the questions than those who speak a language other than English. Obviously, access to information that comes out in the dominant language of the province is a useful ingredient of fuller involvement in and knowledge of the political process.

One further curiosity about the less informed respondents in the Ontario survey: it was they who were disposed to say that government is very effective, in contrast to the more knowledgeable who tended to look on government as only moderately effective or even ineffective. One possible explanation for this finding is that governments *are* ineffective and the better informed are simply more aware that this is so. More likely is the probability that the less informed (who are also less likely to discuss politics or participate in the political process) tend to believe the best about their government, regardless of the facts. It would be interesting to speculate further about these relatively few uninformed but basically charitable or approving citizens, but there is little to guide us. Perhaps it is better to move on from attitudes and extent of political knowledge to consider the degree to which political *behaviour* differs among some of the socio-economic and cultural groups we have identified.

First it must be admitted that data on actual political behaviour are not available; only respondents' *reports* of their behaviour exist and then only to a very limited degree as it relates specifically at the provincial level. Nevertheless, a general index of political activity (based on several questions about political involvement, ranging from the mere act of voting, which many Ontarians do, to contributing to a political party, which is characteristic of relatively few) can be useful in exploring some of the propositions put forward earlier. Canadians have been described as political spectators more than political participants and Ontarians are no exception to this generalization.[2] Most of the respondents appear at the low end of the scale of activity (in a nine-point scale the modal point is two!), and the "highly active" classification includes very few people receiving scores of eight or nine. There is, in other words, not a great deal of variation in political activity to be

2 Rick Van Loon, "Political Participation in Canada in the 1965 Election," *Canadian Journal of Political Science* III, no. 3 (September 1970), 376–399.

"accounted for" and it is perhaps for this reason that none of the associations is very strong. Nevertheless, we do find that of the demographic variables examined, the same ones which related well to the attitudes of ideal citizenship relate to the behaviour as well. In other words, lower levels of political activity are characteristic of the less well educated, those with lower income and lower status occupations. Among the most politically active, high status individuals with university educations appear beyond their numbers in the population as a whole.

The discussion thus far has centred on general orientations to the political process on the part of Ontario citizens, but it has not related these attitudes or behaviour specifically to politics in Ontario. To that task we now turn with the use of survey data on the Ontario public's perception of the MPP.

Although MPP's were accorded a fairly high status in the minds of the Ontario public as providers of an important service to society, it was also the case that in January 1973, well over a year after the Ontario general election, MPP's were not very well known by their constituents. Differences in level of knowledge, it emerged, were systematically related to socio-economic differences among the population. The validity of this generalization can best be shown through the use of a rough index of "knowledge of MPP's" which combines answers to both the name identification and party affiliation identification questions. Respondents can then be compared according to whether they knew both the name and the party (33 per cent of the sample) party or name (20 per cent) or neither (46 per cent). The latter percentage may seem shockingly high, for it indicates that nearly half the citizens of Ontario were ignorant of two fundamental facts about their provincial member, but it may not be entirely unexpected in view of the analysis thus far.

In contrast to the situation with respect to many other questions, the level of respondents' education was not related to knowledge of their MPP's. Age differences were more significant; the proportion of those who knew neither name nor party dropped from a high of 65 per cent among the youngest group (18–24 age group) to a low of 34 per cent among the 45–49 age group with a slight rise again (to about 38 per cent) among respondents over 45 years of

TABLE II

• *Knowledge of MPP by Size of Community and Length of Residence*
(percentage)

	SIZE OF COMMUNITY											
	Metro		100–500 m.		30–100 m.		10–30 m.		1–10 m.		rural	
	3 yrs. or less	more than 3	3 yrs. or less	more than 3	3 years or less	more than 3	3 yrs. or less	more than 3	3 yrs. or less	more than 3	3 yrs. or less	more than 3
Knew Name and Party	7	21	14	38	9	55	12	63	30	41	8	44
Knew Name or Party	21	23	12	17	34	13	48	12	16	30	21	24
Knew Neither Name nor Party	71	56	74	45	57	32	40	25	54	29	71	32
N =	110	362	71	269	19	181	7	59	22	116	41	235

SOURCE: Commission on the Legislature Study

age. Ignorance of the basic information about one's MPP was, therefore, nearly twice as great among the young as it was among the older respondents in Ontario.

However, the most striking differences in knowledge of the MPP appeared when answers were compared by the size of the community in which the respondent lived: at the one extreme were residents of towns of from 10,000 to 30,000 people in which 57 per cent knew both the name and party of their MPP and at the other were residents of Metro Toronto, where only 18 per cent could name both. Since other analysis showed that knowledge was related to whether or not the respondent was Canadian born or foreign born and also to the length of time a respondent had lived in the community and since both these variables tended to be related to the size of community (there being far more foreign born people with short residence in Metropolitan Toronto than in the smaller towns of Ontario), it was necessary to try to determine whether it was in fact city size or some other variable associated with differences in city size that appeared to account for the differences in knowledge of MPP. Table 2 shows that both size of community and length of time the respondent had lived in the community were associated with knowledge: that is to say, knowledge of MPP's was higher among both long-term and short-term residents in smaller communities, and in the rural areas of the province, but within each size of community, the longer-term residents were even more knowledgeable. In Metropolitan Toronto, ignorance of the MPP was very great among all respondents, but among those who had lived in Toronto for three years or less ignorance of both name and party was characteristic of no less than 71 per cent. The interpretation of the phenomenon is actually rather complex; among respondents with three or fewer years in the community there is not much difference in knowledge of the MPP, but knowledge increases among those who have lived in a community for more than three years as the size of the community decreases.

All of this goes to show that there are wide variations in the knowledge people in Ontario have of their MPP's: the table reveals that 63 per cent of the people who have lived in small towns for more than three years know both the name and party of their MPP. On the other hand, as we have seen, in Metropolitan Toronto only a small fraction of the population is that familiar with their MPP. Part of the difference in the knowledge of MPP's revealed between Metro and the smaller communities is the difference in the proportion of residents living there three years or less; part of the explanation may be related to the size and actual composition of the community. To some extent the observed differences may also be accounted for by the fact that party and candidate turnover may be greater in constituencies in larger population centres. It is therefore to be expected that urban respondents would find it more difficult to remember the MPP's name than would be the case in smaller towns and rural areas. Whatever the explanation, it seems reasonable to suggest that in constituencies where less than a fifth of the respondents could identify the name and party of their MPP, linkages between the citizens and the Legislature and consequently the government of the province seem tenuous indeed.

Some further clarification of the linkages between the general public and the political process through the MPP can be obtained by examining the extent of agreement and disagreement with the following statement put to a large sample of people in Ontario early in 1973: "I can get in touch with my MPP without much trouble anytime I want to." It must be admitted that this item is not altogether unambiguous, for an answer to it may be taken as a very general indicator of how available the MPP is, but it also may be taken as an indication of the disposition of the respondent to get in touch with his MPP. The largest proportion of the sample (30 per cent) strongly agreed with the notion that they can get in touch with their MPP anytime they want to. Presumably a strongly negative reaction would have indicated a considerable measure of perceived inaccessibility, a response given in fact by only 11 per cent of the sample. Also revealing, however, was the large number of respondents (23 per cent) who had no opinion on this statement, presumably because they had never tried to contact their MPP and therefore had no idea of how accessible he might be.

This fact raises the desirability of examining the degree to which MPP's are said to be contacted by the public. In order to try to obtain an estimate of the importance of the MPP, relative to MP's and municipal politicians, respondents were first asked if they had ever "tried to influence the political system." Those who said they had tried were then asked a second question: "To whom do you tend to go with your complaints and suggestions?" The coding of responses to the second question was sensitive to the issue of level of government approached.

Only a fifth of the sample said that they had ever tried to influence the political system; the second question was therefore asked of only a small proportion and these respondents divided almost evenly between stating that MPP's, MP's, and municipal politicians are sources of help with their complaints or suggestions. The fact that only 6 per cent of the sample stated that they regularly contacted their MPP's by letter or phone—precisely the same pro-

TABLE III

Attempt to Influence the Political System,
by Level of Education
(percentages)

	up to grade 10	grade 11–13	some/completed university
Yes	13	20	45
No	85	80	55
DK/NA	2	0	1
Totals	100	101	101
N =	646	538	309

SOURCE: Commission on the Legislature Study

TABLE IV

Experience of Contacting MPP by Letter or Phone,
by Education of Respondent
(percentages)

	up to grade 4	up to grade 8	up to grade 10	up to grade 13	some univer-sity	univer-sity degree
Regularly	6	3	4	4	6	11
Occasionally	8	21	23	26	33	43
Never	79	75	73	70	61	46
Totals	93*	99	100	100	100	100
N =	42	311	294	538	159	150

*DK = 7%

SOURCE: Commission on the Legislature Study

portion of the total sample that mentioned turning to
MPP's with complaints or suggestions—suggests that the
question must have received an accurate response. A further 26 per cent said that they occasionally contacted their
MPP's, but their contact must have been quite casual indeed. The vast majority of respondents (68 per cent) stated
that they had never contacted their MPP by letter or phone.

What is especially important to note is the degree of
difference that exists between respondents with different
levels of education. A study of Tables 3 and 4 makes it clear
that differences in access are directly associated with the
degree of education: the better the education (and, as we
have seen, along with that the higher the social status) the
more likely one is to complain, make suggestions, and
contact one's MPP. The lines from public to government are
on the face of it open to everyone; but because better
educated, higher status people are more inclined to use
them the message is only a partial one. The voice of the
people seems to speak from only one corner of its mouth!

Although relatively few people actually seem to make
contact with MPP's in the normal course of their lives, the
vast majority of the people in Ontario would like to see
opportunities improved for closer contact with MPP's
through the establishment of an office in the constituency
where people can go for information and assistance. When
this suggestion was put to them in a survey of opinion 71
per cent strongly agreed with the idea and opposition was
restricted to 7 per cent of the sample. The vast majority
also agreed with the statement, "My MPP should keep me
well informed of his activities in the provincial legislature";
in this case only 12 per cent disagreed with the proposition.
Presumably some interest exists, and if opportunities were
made more readily available—in a form which would
satisfy the needs of the less well-educated majority of
citizens in Ontario—perhaps the MPP would be more frequently looked to than he is now.

Some support for this notion comes from a further
analysis of the responses to the questions. Although there
were no great differences according to the respondent's
level of education (except that support for the idea of an
office in the constituency was highest from those with only
nine to ten years of education) there were differences
according to the respondents' sense of political efficacy. In

this case (and in contrast to the general pattern) those with a lower sense of political efficacy were a little more inclined than the most politically efficacious to say that they favoured both having the office and being kept informed by the MPP. The differences between the groups were not very great (in any case the vast majority of the sample agreed with both propositions) but the analysis suggests that those respondents who feel most impotent politically want these developments most.

The survey revealed that, of a number of methods suggested for dealing with the provincial government, going through the MPP at Queen's Park using letters and phone calls was the most popular. The idea of an information officer working for an MPP in his constituency was favoured by only a slim majority. The pattern of responses suggests that the Ontario public was not simply displaying an aversion to the more impersonal methods of communicating with government; rather, there is some evidence of a positive preference for working through MPP's, although it is possible that "support for the MPP" in this case was merely a preference for the known and an avoidance of the new.

This, then, is the general character of the linkages between individuals and the government of Ontario. What of the relationship between organized groups—interest groups, pressure groups, or, as they are often called, "lobbies"—and the political process? Although interest groups have been around for some time at the provincial level (the efforts of the Ontario Medical Association, for example, have been visible for many years) their character and numbers have been affected by two important postwar developments. The first is the considerably greater interventionist role played by the Ontario government, and the second is the concentration of political power in the hands of the executive and especially the bureaucratic sectors of the government.

A glance at the yellow pages of the Toronto telephone book under the entry for associations reveals scores of groups and associations, almost all of which exist in large part to attempt to influence the provincial government to favour their particular interest. There are, of course, some interest groups at work in the province which are not so well-organized or long-established that they have an office

286 / David Hoffman

or even a listed telephone number, and some of these may be quite vocal and visible for short periods of time, depending on the prominence of their particular concern. But these interest groups represent only a tiny fraction of the ongoing process of pressure group politics in the province. Even among the more formally organized groups there is a hierarchy—one which can be classified in terms of impact on the decision-making process. Closely correlated with the degree of impact is the extent to which the interest group has managed to establish regularized relations with government. For example, it may participate on advisory commissions of government, and, even more important, maintain close relations on a day-to-day, personal basis between its representatives and its opposite numbers at the senior levels of the Ontario civil service. Linkages between public and government when conducted by groups such as these— of which the Ontario Federation of Agriculture and the Ontario Chamber of Commerce are good examples—are very close indeed. But it must be remembered that proximity to political power such as this is reserv l for only a subset of the people—a specialized or privileged public who usually have something to give to government in the form of assistance with regulation of an industry or specialized information.

Some groups or associations are privileged in their relation with government because they are in fact the creatures of government. Far from being organized to attempt to influence some government policy, they have actually been created by the government to assist in the orderly regulation of a particular sector of the economy. In a thought-provoking essay, written for the Economic Council of Ontario, Donald Richmond called attention to a variety of interest groups of this type:

> Some are political institutions, in that they are established by legislation and empowered to regulate the affairs of their members in the public interest—professional associations for example. Others have been created to administer specific policies—farm marketing boards. The groups form a grey area; partially public, in the sense that they have been delegated specific powers by government; and partially private, in the sense that they represent the interests of their members and act as private bodies. Beyond the

semi-autonomous groups are those associations that exist solely to promote the common interest of their members, and although they may be incorporated by government, they act as independent agencies.[3]

Even independent bodies like Pollution Probe can be dependent upon the provincial government to some extent for financial support to keep them going.

The tactics of pressure groups vary depending upon their status in the system. Generally speaking, the groups which have close relations with the bureaucracy because their interests concern the establishment of and administration of regulations, fee schedules or prices do not resort either to the public campaign or even to "feeding" the opposition in the Legislature with the fundamentals of their case. They rely on quiet negotiations of an essentially bureaucratic nature with low political visibility. Only over the big issues, ones which require major decisions of policy at the political level do they move into the more public arena and then more often to oppose government initiatives through publicity campaigns than to fight for legislative innovation. The efforts of the OMA documented in the case of "How Medicare came to Ontario" on pages 34–45 illustrates this phase of a large and normally effective interest group's activity.

Nearly all the interest groups expend effort in trying to influence the politicians, either by sending briefs or communiqués to cabinet ministers and MPP's or through more formally organized presentations to cabinet. Only a relatively few are accorded the honour of annual presentations of briefs to a meeting with cabinet. Certain groups, such as the Ontario Federation of Labour, apparently value these formal arrangements because the occasion attracts more attention, especially in the press, than is normal for the cause of organized labour in the province. However, the government is considering replacing or supplementing the annual ceremony, perhaps with a series of presentations to cabinet committees. This is the practice with an increasing number of organized groups who are starting to follow the pattern introduced by the Ontario Chamber of Commerce: a number of "standing committees" of volunteer business-

3 D. R. Richmond, *Towards The Planning State*, Ontario Economic Council (Toronto: Queen's Printer, July 1973), p. 22.

men meet with each specific ministry of relevance to the interest of the organization and these contacts are supplemented by the OCC's secretariat on a daily basis. The OMA does not present an annual brief, either; instead, members of the OMA executive committee (usually four or five people including the president, vice-president and perhaps the past president) meet with the Minister of Health on a regular basis, usually every four or five weeks. The OMA does occasionally present briefs on specific issues, but these meetings with the minister are held simply to keep in touch and not necessarily to deal with specific topics.

Obviously the "specialized publics" which operate at this level of sophistication and familiarity in the system have resources far beyond those available to the ad hoc pressure group. The OMA, for example, has a permanent staff of forty-five; the Ontario Federation of Labour has a permanent staff of fourteen and the Ontario Federation of Agriculture has a Toronto-based staff of sixteen and a field staff of twenty. Many of the interest groups operate on a smaller scale, often sharing accommodation with other associations or the officers of the national association, as is the case with the Ontario Chamber of Commerce. The Ontario Forest Industries Association operates with a manager and two clerks, with the former relying on committee members for assistance when problems arise. Pollution Probe, which began with volunteer staffing, has gradually moved in the direction of permanent staffing in order to improve its effectiveness through greater continuity of research.

The experience of Pollution Probe, incidentally, illustrates one aspect of the question of the most effective strategy for groups who wish to make major changes in the system. It seems that there has been considerable controversy within the organization about what the strategy should be and the discussion has focused on whether efforts "within the system" are worthwhile at all. Some of the Pollution Probe staff feel that attempting to influence environmental policy through the accepted channels will only bring about short-term benefits, and that longer-term results require "confrontation" strategies—that is, challenges to the entire system of decision-making. Partly in response to this difference of opinion the staff has now been divided into four distinct "teams," each of which tends to have its own approach to influencing public policy. The energy team, for example, participates actively on various government boards and hearings, but an educational team that operates in Ward 3 of the City of Toronto, on the other hand, is deeply committed to the promotion of citizen participation.

The same kind of issue faces many interest groups when they conclude that quiet negotiation or the submission of the briefs to ministers have become futile and more dramatic activity is required. The backlash that followed upon the more vociferous tactics of the Working Committee of the Association of Catholic High School Boards, documented in the case study of the separate school issue on pages 17–32, illustrates the risks that are taken when an interest group becomes so visible in its efforts that counter groups are encouraged to organize. Specialized publics, with their more intimate relationship with decision-makers, do not normally have to face the frustrating effects of counter-interest-group activity.

It is difficult to assess how important is the linkage between an interest group and the Legislature. Those groups which fall outside the privileged (the small associations and the ad hoc groups fighting for attention to their problem) customarily make their case known to the members of Legislature, particularly to members of the opposition. One has only to thumb through the index of *Hansard* to see that references are made all the time in debates to the views of interest groups, particularly at question period or in debates on departmental estimates. But the significance of the activity is not clear. In many ways, the citation of an interest group's position in the Legislature is a kind of game; the opposition parties tend to trade publicity for the interest group's cause in the Legislature (and hopefully in the press) for pressure group-inspired information with which they hope to embarrass or harass the government. The government, on the other hand, when the conditions are right, is just as prone to use the positions of interest groups as support for the correctness of their policy. Often a tight corner is evaded by ministerial references to on-going consultation with the interest concerned.

It would be wrong to suggest that the only effective interest groups are the specialized or privileged; they may win more often than the rest but it is not the only route to influencing the Ontario government. Briefs from general interest pressure groups may go for months being quietly ignored, but a particular set of circumstances, usually attention in the Toronto press, has moved an issue to political prominence and resolution. Sometimes further ingredients are required. The Stop Spadina (Expressway) movement and the case study by Henry Jacek on how regional government came to Hamilton-Wentworth (pages 48–62), suggest that local pressure groups can be quite effective at the provincial level if the group can cut across party lines and in particular mobilize support from party workers from the Conservative party. In the former case, pressure of just this kind built up for three of the cabinet members holding inner-city ridings where the opposition was strongest and this fact must have played an important role in influencing the decision to stop further building of the expressway. Groups which appear as merely partisan, as CORRA apparently does (it is perceived as simply a tool of the NDP), tend to be ignored by the Conservative cabinet as unrepresentative of public opinion generally.

The government of Ontario is a complex business, as is the society which it is presumed to serve. Linkages between the public and the government exist in a variety of forms, but the effectiveness of the "transmission belts" varies enormously.

As far as relations between individuals and the government are concerned, certain limitations of the representative process were revealed. Overall, it seems that while MPP's are generally well regarded, many people do not actually know who their MPP is and even fewer have ever tried to use them to convey "inputs" to government. Only a relatively small proportion of the electorate is well informed about politics and active in the process, and in this respect, people of higher-than-average education, social status and income are the most inclined to participate in the political system and to take advantage of the representative institutions that exist. Differences in knowledge of the political process or feelings about involvement in it were shown to be related either to the size of the community in which the person lived or to the use of a language other than English in the home, but the pattern was not as consistent with regard to the entire set of variables as it was with the socio-economic.

The situation with organized groups is fundamentally similar. The better organized, with the inside track to the decision-makers through cabinet or bureaucracy connections, have a much easier time putting the "public's" case than those which are less advantaged.

Earlier it was suggested that confusion over which level of government is responsible for a particular policy may explain the low level of interaction between individuals and the provincial government (although the problem certainly does not apply for many interest groups which know only too well where to go!). However, the evidence suggests that the linkages between individuals and the other levels of government were no more developed; the vast majority of individuals do not connect with government at any level.

To some extent individuals may not need to interact with government because their interests are being well served by the activities of pressure groups. Interestingly enough, however, those whose interests are cared for by the organized groups are to a very great extent the same individuals who feel personally efficacious in the political system. It is the unorganized, the lower status, more poorly educated people who do not tend to have organizations speaking directly for their interests that are left out in the cold. Paradoxically, it may be the very success of the organized interests that cause the weak to feel that they can have no significant impact on the system. And who can say that they are wrong?

SELECTED BIBLIOGRAPHY

Citizen Involvement. Prepared for the Committee on Government Productivity, Toronto, 1972.

CORBETT, D. C. "The Pressure Groups and the Public Interest," in R. E. Hodgett and D. C. Corbett, eds., *Canadian Public Administration.* Toronto: Macmillan, 1960.

DRAPER, J. A., ed. *Citizen Participation in Canada.* Toronto: New Press, 1971.

PRESTHUS, ROBERT. *Elite Accommodation in Canadian Politics.* Toronto: Macmillan, 1973.

SZABLOWSKI, GEORGE J. *The Public Bureaucracy and the Possibility of Citizen Involvement in the Government of Ontario.* Prepared for the Committee on Government Productivity, Toronto, 1971.

TAYLOR, MALCOLM G. "The Role of the Medical Profession in the Formulation and Execution of Public Policy," *Canadian Public Administration* III (1960), 233–55.

VAN LOON, RICK. "Political Participation in Canada: The 1965 Election," *Canadian Journal of Political Science* III, no. 3 (September 1970), 376–399.

17
R.J. DRUMMOND

Voting Behaviour:
The Blueing of Ontario

I T HAS been customary in recent years for political
scientists to de-emphasize the importance of elections in
the political life of western democracies. However, none
of the important aspects of Ontario politics can be fully
comprehended without reference to the voting activity of
the province's citizens. Voting for members of the Legislative Assembly is the only directly political act that most
citizens will ever perform at the provincial level, and it is
the one opportunity most have to exert any influence on
their political leaders. In 1968 nearly 93 per cent of a
sample of Ontarians eligible to vote indicated that they
voted regularly or occasionally, while only 20 per cent said
they regularly or occasionally gave personal assistance to a
party or candidate; less than 15 per cent gave monetary
assistance, and only about 10 per cent attended political
protest meetings. Moreover, 70 per cent indicated that
voting was "the only way" that people like them could have
a say about "how the government runs things."[1]

Through general elections, the government of the day is
selected and the margin of its security in office is defined;
for the partisan make-up of the Assembly dictates the degree of the administration's support. Elections also serve to
delineate for the observer the major political figures of the
time and to spotlight the issues around which the political
interests of the province contend. By examining the conduct of elections and the behaviour of electors, we may
learn something about the variation of provincial opinion
on political matters, the strength and prospects of particular political movements, and the likelihood of stability
or change in the political life of the province.

ONTARIO'S ELECTION LAWS

What are the "rules of the game" for elections in Ontario,
and how have they developed? At the time of Confederation
in 1867, the Ontario electorate numbered slightly more than
200,000; the franchise was restricted to holders of property
over a certain value, and women had no vote. In the first
Ontario election 74 per cent of the eligible voters cast a
ballot. In the most recent Ontario election (1971) when 73

1 These figures are from a survey of political and social attitudes of
Ontario voters conducted by David Hoffman and Fred Schindeler
(with the assistance of the author) in 1968. Data are deposited in
the IBR Data Bank, York University, Downsview, Ontario.

per cent of those eligible cast a vote, over four and a half million men and women were on the voters' list and there were no property restrictions on the franchise.

Although property restrictions were effectively abolished in Ontario before the turn of the century, it was not until 1954 that inmates of charitable institutions (other than war veterans) and Indians living on reservations were permitted to vote in provincial elections. Women were first enfranchised for Ontario elections in 1917, but it was 1943 before the first woman was elected to the Legislative Assembly.

Under current Ontario law, a person is eligible to vote in provincial elections if he or she is eighteen years of age on or before polling day, is a Canadian citizen or other British subject, is not disqualified by the Election Act or otherwise prohibited from voting, has resided in Ontario for twelve months prior to polling day, and is ordinarily resident in the electoral district in which he or she intends to vote. Returning officers and election clerks are banned from voting, as are inmates of penal or reform institutions, mental hospitals, or homes for the mentally incompetent.

Candidates for election to the Legislature must be of voting age, be Canadian citizens or British subjects, have been resident in the province for twelve months, and not be disqualified by any other provincial statute (particularly the Legislative Assembly Act). Candidates must be nominated by one hundred duly qualified electors (a voter's signature may appear on the nomination papers of more than one candidate) but, in contrast to federal elections no monetary deposit is required.

The current Legislature is composed of 117 members elected by simple plurality in single-member districts (the last two-member districts in Ontario having been abolished in 1925). An independent commission appointed in 1962 drew the present constituency boundaries and they were approved by the Legislature in time for the election of 1967. This re-districting was the first in which the province employed an independent body, and the precedent has been followed in the redistribution being undertaken in 1974. The present constituencies vary in eligible voter population from around 20,000 to over 60,000, although the smallest in 1971 had 16,829 and the largest, 95,596. The new boundaries should reduce the size of the largest seats by creating new ones, but little can be done about some of the smaller seats since they involve large areas which are sparsely populated. Voting is by secret ballot of course, and great precautions are taken to ensure that no breach of the privacy of the polling booth takes place. Ballots bear only the names of the candidates in alphabetical order, unless two or more candidates have such similar names that confusion is likely, in which case all candidates are listed with their addresses.

There are few grounds allowed for questioning the validity of a particular election (for example, irregularities in the preparation or revision of the voters list are not grounds for invalidating the vote) but penalties are provided for the grosser forms of election fraud. Little else in the way of campaign conduct or election finance is really controlled; although there are requirements that campaign expenditures be reported and donations be listed, there is virtually no machinery of enforcement. Professor T. H. Qualter comments:

> None of the provinces (except Quebec) has any adequate enforcement provisions for the control or reporting of election expenses. The controls themselves exist and could be effective, but in no province is there any willingness on the part of election administrators, candidates, party officials, or members of the public to see that the law is observed and that penalties are imposed for its violation.[2]

ONTARIO'S ELECTORAL HISTORY

A history of electoral districts in the province of Ontario prepared by Roderick Lewis, the Chief Electoral Officer, in 1968 indicates that candidates have stood for election in Ontario under forty-three different party labels. However, the electoral history of the province can be described fairly completely by considering the fortunes of the four parties which have been either the government or the official opposition: the Conservative (later Progressive-Conservative) party, the Liberal party, the United Farmers of Ontario, and the Co-operative Commonwealth Federation (later the New Democratic Party). Indeed, 99.4 per cent of the votes cast in the 1971 election went to the Progressive-Conservative, Liberal, and New Democratic parties.

2 T. H. Qualter, *The Election Process in Canada* (Toronto: McGraw-Hill, 1970), p. 157.

When Ontario was formed at Confederation in 1867, there was already a history of two-party competition in the Assembly of the united Canadas. The Tory group (forerunner of the Conservative party) was led by the spiritual descendants of the Family Compact and the centralizing nation-builders of Sir John A. Macdonald. The Reform group (precursor of the Liberal party) was dominated by the "Clear Grits" from the southwestern part of the province. It is essential to recall however that party lines were rather weakly drawn in this early period, and it was possible to offer oneself for election as a supporter of the ministry—whichever party should form it. Thus when the provincial election of 1867 produced a deadlock in seats and a very narrow difference in popular vote, the Conservative leader, J. Sandfield Macdonald, was able to form a government with the aid of several nominal Liberals. The coalition lasted only until the election of 1871 when the controversion of several Conservatives' elections deprived Macdonald of his legislative majority. He was forced to resign on a vote of confidence and Edward Blake became the province's first Liberal premier.

Blake also held a seat in the federal House of Commons and, when legislation was passed forbidding a member to hold office in both the Commons and a provincial legislature, he was forced to give up one post. He chose to leave the provincial leadership for the federal cabinet and Oliver Mowat became premier. During the next four elections the Liberals consistently outpolled the Conservatives by only one percentage point of the popular vote. However, they never had less than a ten-seat majority in the Legislative Assembly because of their concentration in the over-represented rural areas.

Ontario remained a two-party province in terms of the popular vote from 1867 to 1919. The combined vote of the Liberal and Conservative parties fell below 90 per cent only once in the period, and only three times did it fall below 95 per cent. The election of 1894 foreshadowed the federal contest of two years later in which minor party votes were to play a significant role, as the Patrons of Industry (a farm organization) took seventeen seats in the ninety-four-seat Assembly with 15 per cent of the popular vote. A further 4 per cent of the vote went to candidates of the Protestant Protective Association; 41 per cent went to the

Liberals; 35 per cent to the Conservatives, and the usual 5 per cent to assorted independents and other candidates. The success of the Patrons was short-lived, however, and the two-party division was re-established in 1898.

Between 1867 and 1872, the Liberals had allied themselves with the mainly Methodist and Presbyterian farmers of the rural southwest, but in the 1872–96 period they had added the support of a large segment of the Catholic population—increasingly French—in eastern and northern Ontario. They had lost some Protestant support to the Conservatives (who were at first more closely identified with the Anglican and Roman Catholic establishments). However their greatest problem in years to come would stem from the fact that they had not attracted at the provincial level the support of the growing population of Ontario's towns. The province was an urbanizing one at the beginning of the twentieth century, and the Liberals remained wedded to the countryside.

When Mowat left to join Laurier's first cabinet in 1896, he was succeeded by A. S. Hardy, who was in turn replaced in 1899 by George Ross. The Liberals narrowly won the elections of 1898 and 1902, but they had slipped behind the Conservatives in the popular vote and they left office in 1905 on a wave of scandal surrounding electoral practices. Identification with the national Liberal party was costly in terms of urban, British Ontario's reactions to Prime Minister Laurier's nationalist (allegedly pro-French) and agrarian policies. The national party could not seem to be of much assistance either in providing organizational support. The Liberals in Ontario slipped from a total of 50 seats (out of 98) in 1902 to 19 (of 106) in 1908. After losing both federal and provincial elections in 1911, they moved provincially to 25 of 111 seats in 1914 with 38 per cent of the popular vote.

By the time of the 1919 provincial election, the Liberal party had been considerably weakened by the split in its ranks engendered by the conscription crisis of 1917 and the defection of some prominent members (notably the Ontario leader, Newton Rowell) to the ranks of Prime Minister Robert Borden's Union government. The once-dominant party of Reform could contest only 65 of the 111 seats (59 per cent) and could win only 28. The Conservatives contested all but 7 seats, but could win only 25. The electorate rejected both old parties, and the United Farmers of Ontario, with candidates in only 72 seats, won 45 of them on 24 per cent of the popular vote. As the largest group in the Legislature they sought to form a government, and with the 11 elected members of the Independent Labour Party, they were able to command a bare majority.

By 1923, however, intra-party disputes were beginning to weaken the UFO government. Although the Farmers received only two points less of the popular vote than they had garnered in 1919 (in about the same number of contests), the Conservative share of the vote increased dramatically from 33 per cent to 50 per cent in an election when the overall turnout declined from 74 to 56 per cent.

Turnout continued to be low in the elections of 1926 and 1929 and, as the UFO and ILP declined, the Conservative and Liberal votes increased. The Conservatives maintained a clear dominance in votes and seats; the Liberals could muster only 21 seats in 1926 and their total fell to 13 in 1929 —the lowest they had had since Confederation. Strangely the popular vote for the Liberals *increased* between 1926 and 1929 from 22 to 32 per cent.

The dominance of the Conservatives, first under the leadership of Howard Ferguson and later of George Henry, seemed secure. But the Liberals elected a leader in 1930 who was to lead them to an overwhelming victory four years later. How important the depression conditions were to the Conservative defeat is hard to judge, but there was an element of personal magnetism involved in the Liberal victory:

> To say that Mitchell Hepburn saved the Liberal party in Ontario is both an exaggeration and an understatement. In the furious election campaign of 1934 . . . Hepburn *was* the Liberal party.[3]

Because Hepburn's victory was so closely tied to his own personal style, the return to power did not rejuvenate the tired Liberal party organization. Nor, more importantly,

3 John Wilson and David Hoffman, "A Three-Party System in Transition," in M. Robin, ed., *Canadian Provincial Politics* (Scarborough, Ont.: Prentice-Hall, 1972), p. 214.

could Hepburn seem to mould the party into an engine of social reform which would create in modernizing, urban, industrial Ontario a province-building coalition such as had sustained the Liberals in office prior to 1905. As Mackenzie King was adapting the federal Liberals to meet the changes of the interwar and war years, Hepburn was carrying on a crusade against industrial unionism and a bitter personal feud with the Prime Minister. The Liberals remained the party of rural, southwestern Ontario in policy if not in support, and although he was able to lead them once again to victory in 1937, Hepburn failed to build a party which could continue to succeed after his departure from office. He retired in 1942 and was followed by Gordon Conant and Harry Nixon in quick succession. The election of 1943 reduced the Liberals to minor party status from which they have not clearly recovered even today.

From a high of 70 seats in 1934 (in a Legislature of 90 seats—the largest total ever for a Liberal government in Ontario) they plummeted to 16 seats. They managed to retain about a third of the popular vote—a figure which they have been able to maintain to the present—but they were replaced as official opposition by the Co-operative Commonwealth Federation.

Although the CCF had been formed in 1932, it had never made a strong showing in Ontario prior to 1943. The party had contested fewer than half the seats in 1934 and 1937 and had elected one candidate in the former year. In 1943 it contested all but 4 seats and won 34 (to the Conservatives' 38) with 32 per cent of the popular vote. The 1945 election saw a decline in CCF support and the beginning of thirty years of Conservative one-party dominance.

In a sense the 1943 election marks the beginning of the modern era of Ontario electoral history. The electorate has increased since 1943 from around two and a quarter million to over four and a half million, but the fluctuation in popular vote for the province's three principal parties has not been as dramatic as one might have expected in such circumstances. The Conservative party's popular support in the eight elections from 1943 to 1967 averaged 44.25 per cent; in 1971, they received 44.5 per cent of the vote. The Liberals averaged 32.5 per cent of the vote in the same eight elections, and although their 1971 total was only 27.5 per cent, that was the first time it had fallen below 30 per cent since 1926. The fluctuations for the CCF/NDP have been somewhat greater. Averaging 22 per cent across the eight elections, they scored 27.15 per cent of the vote in 1971, but their vote total has been as high as 32 per cent of the electorate in 1943 and as low as 16 per cent in 1963.

There is one other clear indication that 1943 marks the beginning of the current three-party system in Ontario. Between 1902 and 1937, the winning party had 50 per cent or more of the popular vote in every election except that of 1919; since 1943 no party has had a majority of the popular vote in any general election.

Large variations in seat totals caused by slight changes in popular vote are common in single-member, simple-plurality systems, but Ontario elections since 1943 provide some remarkably clear examples. Between 1948 and 1951, for instance, the Liberal party gained two percentage points in the popular vote and lost six seats. Between 1955 and 1959, the CCF proportion of the vote remained the same and the party gained two seats. In the same period, the Liberal party gained four points in the vote and increased its representation by eleven seats. Table I indicates the ratio of seat share to vote share in the elections since 1943. It is notable that the winning party (the Conservatives in each case) are consistently over-represented and the losing parties (with the exception of the CCF in 1943) are consistently under-represented.

TABLE I

Year	% of Votes			% of Seats			No. of Seats	% Seats ÷ % Votes		
	PC	LIB	NDP	PC	LIB	NDP		PC	LIB	NDP
1943	36	31	32	42	18	38	90	1.17	.57	1.18
1945	44	30	22	73	16	9	90	1.66	.52	.40
1948	41	30	27	59	16	23	90	1.44	.52	.86
1951	48	32	19	88	9	2	90	1.83	.28	.12
1955	49	33	17	86	11	3	98	1.75	.34	.18
1959	46	37	17	72	22	5	98	1.57	.63	.30
1963	48	35	16	71	22	6	108	1.49	.63	.41
1967	42	32	26	59	24	17	117	1.40	.75	.66
1971	45	28	27	66	17	16	117	1.48	.61	.60

Note: In addition to seats won by the three major parties, there were two Communist candidates elected in 1943, 1945, and 1948, and one in 1951.

302 / R. J. Drummond

(i) Issues

Accounting for the variations in support for Ontario's principal parties is not an easy task. In 1968 David Hoffman and Fred Schindeler conducted a sample survey of eligible voters in Ontario. Nearly sixteen hundred interviews were completed, and the responses should shed some light on partisan preferences. When respondents in the Hoffman-Schindeler study were asked what factors helped them make up their minds when voting, over 80 per cent said that party, party platform, and party leader were important considerations. They rejected the notion that the candidate's religion or country of origin were important and they would not agree that the views of their friends, neighbours, or relatives helped them decide. However, another survey conducted by John Wilson and David Hoffman in 1967 indicated that the party images were fairly vague among electors. Only around one third of the respondents in that survey could think of anything they liked or disliked about any of the parties. It is possible, of course, that the interview situation is an artificial environment in which to ask a voter to choose; during an election campaign, voters may be able to articulate more clearly the reasons for their party selection, and their reasons may indeed be linked to platforms and leadership.

Nevertheless, if one looks for relationships between some likely issues (on which the parties divided) and party support, the results are not comforting. During the 1971 election campaign, the Liberal and New Democratic parties both supported the extension of the separate school system into the high school years through the provision of government aid to Roman Catholic high schools; thus the public-private system at the secondary level would be replaced by a dual-public system like that which prevails at the elementary level. The Conservative government opposed this plan. Although the issue was perhaps not as salient in 1968 as in 1971, one might have expected that there would be variation in support for the parties based on the views of the electors regarding the separate school system. The Ontario study conducted by Hoffman and Schindeler found little variation, however: 60 per cent of Conservative supporters in that study, and 62 per cent of NDP supporters declared themselves opposed to separate schools (presumably at any level); 50 per cent of Liberal supporters were also opposed. Even this slight difference between Liberals and the others virtually disappears when one considers Protestants and Roman Catholics separately.

Respondents in that study were also asked to declare whether "the government ought to be doing" a variety of things (no difference was indicated between the federal and provincial governments). Table II indicates the proportions of party supporters agreeing the government ought to do the things in question.

TABLE II

Percentage of each party's supporters (i.e., voted for the party in 1967 election) saying the government ought to be . . .

	Liberal	Progressive Conservative	New Democratic
Trying to even out differences in wealth	47	41	55
Relaxing divorce laws	52	57	62
Forcing industry to bear the costs of stopping air and water pollution	83	83	87
Increasing taxes on business	40	35	49
Providing free university education for all who have good marks	71	63	79
Providing public housing for low income earners	78	79	81
Increasing social welfare payments and programs	50	37	50

SOURCE: Hoffman-Schindeler Ontario Study, IBR, 1968.

Clearly there are some differences among party supporters, but they are not very large even in the most striking instances, and for some "issues" they are non-existent.

(ii) Leadership

What about party leadership? Both the mass media and the candidates in the 1971 election stressed the importance of choosing "the next Premier of Ontario" and the advertising campaigns of the PC's and New Democrats particularly featured the party leaders. Was the issue of less importance in 1967?

In 1967, the leaders of the three parties most prominent in Ontario electoral politics were John Robarts (Premier and leader of the Progressive-Conservatives), Robert Nixon (leader of the official opposition, the Liberals), and Donald C. MacDonald (leader of the New Democrats). If party leader were an important determinant of the vote, then one might expect a high level of knowledge in the electorate respecting these figures. The results are disappointing.

The Ontario study respondents were asked to indicate only the level (federal or provincial) and party for each of the three federal and provincial leaders. Robert Nixon fared best among the provincial leaders, with 39 per cent getting both his party and level correct. A further 34 per cent knew he was in provincial politics, but did not know to which party he belonged. Only 3 per cent knew he was a Liberal but were wrong about his level of government. The rest (24 per cent) did not know either his party or his level.

Premier Robarts was readily recognized by only 32 per cent of the sample, while 35 per cent knew he was a Conservative but did not know at which level he served. Six per cent knew only that he was in provincial politics, and the remainder (26 per cent) did not recognize at all the names of the province's first minister.

Donald C. MacDonald suffered from two handicaps in seeking recognition from the Ontario public. First, he was the leader of only the third strongest party in the province. Second, his name was very similar to those of a federal cabinet member (Donald S. Macdonald), and the then President of the Canadian Labour Congress (Donald Mac-Donald). In any event, he was correctly identified by only 27 per cent of the sample; 16 per cent correctly named his level, but not his party; 11 per cent knew his party, but not his level. The remaining 46 per cent did not recognize his name.

In fairness to the hypothesis that leadership is of importance, one must note that the greatest degree of non-recognition was among non-voters, but Table III indicates that all three leaders were better recognized by supporters of a party other than their own. Perhaps party leaders have only a negative effect on the vote?

It is possible, of course, that the issues we have been able to explore were not those which best discriminated among party supporters. We had no questions on medicare, for

TABLE III

Leadership Recognition and Provincial Vote
1967 Vote

| | D. C. MacDonald | | | |
	LIB	PC	NDP	Other and no vote
Both right	30	39	36	15
Level only	20	19	14	11
Party only	12	9	16	11
Both wrong	38	33	34	63
Total	100%	100%	100%	100%
N	371	432	164	631

| | John Robarts | | | |
	LIB	PC	NDP	Other and no vote
Both right	36	40	43	22
Level only	6	5	9	7
Party only	38	47	27	28
Both wrong	20	9	22	42
Total	100%	101%	101%	99%
N	371	432	164	631

| | Robert Nixon | | | |
	LIB	PC	NDP	Other and no vote
Both right	46	55	44	24
Level only	33	33	31	36
Party only	4	3	6	2
Both wrong	17	9	19	38
Total	100%	100%	100%	100%
N	371	432	164	631

SOURCE: Hoffman-Schindeler Ontario Study, IBR, 1968.

example, or on Ontario's labour laws; nothing was asked
about the Workmen's Compensation Board, regional government, or the right of teachers to strike. While all of
these have been campaign issues in the last few years, they
are relatively transitory when expressed in so specific a
form.[4] It is as representatives of enduring issue-clusters,
or as the bases for delineating long-term socio-political

4 For evidence of the transitory nature of campaign issues at the
federal level, see J. A. Laponce, *People vs. Politics* (Toronto:
University of Toronto Press, 1969), especially pp. 77–104.

cleavages, that such issues can be of use to the scholar who wants his explanations of electoral behaviour to be good for more than one election.

With this fact in mind it is possible to discover, on most of the issues examined, a degree of greater support for the "left" position (greater government activity in the provision of social well-being) among NDP supporters and a degree of greater support for the "right" position (reduction of government intervention in the life of society) among Conservative supporters. On some issues the Liberals seem closer to the NDP; on others, to the Conservatives. That these differences exist is not surprising. That they are so small is astonishing.

(iii) Party Images

The NDP is often perceived as more hostile to the status quo than either of the older parties. Indeed, the party often appears proud of this fact. Nonetheless, the differences between NDP supporters on the one hand, and supporters of the Liberals and Conservative parties on the other, are not very wide when responsibility to question government policies is considered. While 92 per cent of the NDP supporters in the sample agreed citizens had such a responsibility, 89 per cent of Liberal supporters also agreed, as did 95 per cent of the Conservatives. When it came to joining demonstrations to support the things one believes in, New Democrats were again only slightly different from the others. Twenty per cent of the NDP voters said people had an "essential" responsibility to join such demonstrations, as against 13 per cent and 15 per cent for Conservatives and Liberals respectively. There were virtually no differences among the three support groups regarding a citizen's responsibility to join a political party, assist a candidate for office financially, or convince others to vote in accordance with one's wishes.

Perhaps the single most salient difference between Liberal and Conservative voters is in their apparent orientation to the federal and provincial levels of government. Liberals tend to be much more federally oriented with respect to party identification. Fully 35 per cent of those who identified with the Liberal party indicated that they had not voted in the 1967 provincial election, compared to 25 per cent of Conservative, and 32 per cent of NDP identifiers. More notable than this slight difference is the fact that, of those who did vote, over 90 per cent of Conservative and NDP identifiers supported their party, while only 75 per cent of Liberal identifiers supported theirs. Indeed, when Professor John Meisel asked party identifiers in 1968 whether their identification applied to both federal and provincial elections, 94 per cent of New Democrats and 97 per cent of Conservatives stated that their support extended to their party at both levels, while only 81 per cent of the Liberals made that statement.[5] Fully 11 per cent of those who identified themselves as Liberals with respect to federal politics, said they were Conservatives in provincial contests.

One aspect of the location of the parties with respect to one another in the minds of the electorate can be gauged from an exploration of the alternative vote which supporters would exercise if there were not a candidate available from their own party. About 60 per cent of 1967 Liberal voters, 67 per cent of Conservatives, and 72 per cent of New Democrats could imagine voting for one of the other parties in such circumstances. However, while one and a half times as many NDP voters would support a Liberal candidate as would support a Conservative, two and a half times as many Liberals would support a Conservative as would support a New Democrat, and three times as many Conservatives would vote Liberal as would vote NDP.

(iv) Socio-economic Cleavages

When knowledge of party leaders is inadequate to provide a basis for intelligent differentiation among the parties, and when the long-term values and beliefs assumed to underlie transitory campaign issues are only imperfectly measured, the researcher may be forced to look at the distribution of votes across categories of socio-economic cleavage in the hopes of finding some explanation for party choice. Such cleavages presumably reflect enduring conflicts, and these conflicts will be related to party electoral support, insofar as they give rise to contemporary issues on which parties can appeal for votes. Table IV summarizes a number of these distributions, and again the similarity of party support across social groups is the most striking result.

5 Calculated from the 1968 National Election Study, John Meisel, principal investigator, using only the Ontario respondents.

308 / R. J. Drummond

TABLE IVa
Socio-economic Characteristics and Vote in 1967
Provincial Election

Variable	Category	LIB	PC	NDP	Other and no vote	Total	N
Region[1]	North	26	21	17	37	101	150
	Southwest	26	29	12	33	100	296
	"Mississauga conurbation"	26	29	8	38	101	241
	Central	19	29	8	44	100	209
	East	17	29	2	52	100	98
	Ottawa Valley	22	36	4	38	100	190
	Toronto and Yorks	23	22	14	42	101	414
Community Size	Rural	26	32	6	37	101	203
	Small towns[2]	22	33	7	38	100	395
	Small cities[3]	26	24	15	35	100	304
	Windsor	15	17	20	49	101	41
	London	18	33	3	48	102	40
	Ottawa	19	34	4	43	100	134
	Hamilton	28	14	9	48	99	64
	Metro Toronto	23	22	14	42	101	414[4]
Income Group (Annual Family)	Under $5,000	27	26	11	36	100	371
	$5,000–$7,999	24	24	12	40	100	464
	$8,000+	23	33	11	32	99	516
	DK/NA, Refused	15	21	5	60	101	247
Occupation Groups	Managerial	21	47	3	30	101	105
	Prof-technical	26	31	11	32	100	157
	Clerical	20	30	11	39	100	167
	Sales	27	37	7	29	100	73
	Service	26	21	9	44	100	121
	Transport–Communications	18	15	15	52	100	33
	Primary[5]	31	28	12	28	99	67
	Industrial	24	18	15	43	100	372
Trade Union Membership	Respondent	26	13	20	41	100	218
	Someone else in household	21	21	16	42	100	248
	No-one else in household	23	31	7	39	100	1132
Subjective Social Class	Working class	25	18	13	45	101	272
	Middle class	22	37	6	35	100	264
	Ambivalent[6]	20	26	7	48	101	219
	Confused[7]	24	28	12	36	100	782
	Reject class	21	16	8	54	99	61

1 The regions are combinations of electoral districts. Details obtainable from the author.
2 Incorporated municipalities with from 1,000 to 14,999 population in 1961 census.

TABLE IVb

Socio-economic Characteristics and Vote in the 1967 Provincial Election

Variable	Category	LIB	PC	NDP	Other and no vote	Total	N
					1967 Vote (as reported in 1968)		
Education Level	Elementary or less	26	20	10	43	99	503
	Secondary or technical	22	29	12	38	101	873
	University	23	39	6	32	100	178
	Other and NA	11	18	7	64	100	44
Age Groups	21–39	17	22	11	51	101	662
	40–59	27	30	11	32	100	598
	60+	30	33	7	29	99	309
	DK/NA, Refused	21	24	10	45	100	29
Sex	Male	24	27	12	37	100	763
	Female	22	27	9	42	100	835
Religious Preference	Roman Catholic	35	16	10	39	100	417
	United Church	20	38	8	35	101	368
	Anglican	19	34	7	41	101	286
	Presbyterian	22	36	12	30	100	133
	Baptist	17	32	18	33	100	66
	Other Protestant	15	26	14	45	100	133
	Jewish	37	15	11	37	100	27
	Other	13	15	7	65	100	69
	None	20	14	16	50	100	99
Ethnic Origin	British	21	33	9	37	100	907
	French	28	16	11	45	100	115
	German	18	33	21	29	101	73
	Italian	36	12	10	42	100	69
	Other European	24	20	15	41	100	226
	Other	34	17	9	40	100	77
	NA and "Canadian"	24	19	3	53	99	131
Party Identification	Liberal	49	14	2	35	100	638
	Prog.-Conservative	3	68	3	25	99	362
	NDP	1	6	61	32	100	170
	Independent	15	35	10	40	100	113
	Other, DK/NA	10	15	7	68	100	315

3 Cities with from 15,000 to 75,000 population in 1961 census + Sudbury.

4 Total N does not add to 1598 because of three coding errors.

5 Mainly farmers.

6 Respondents who said that both "working class" and "middle class" described them fairly well.

7 Respondents who said either that both "working class" and "middle class" described them very well, or that one term described them very well and the other fairly well.

SOURCE: Hoffman-Schindeler Ontario Study, Institute for Behavioural Research, York University, 1968. Row totals vary from 100% because of rounding.

Perhaps the easiest variable to isolate (and the most difficult to explain fully) is intra-provincial region. What is the distribution of support across definable areas of the province? The Conservative party does not appear to be weak in any part of Ontario, but there are areas of greater and lesser PC strength, and the Liberals and New Democrats are fairly localized in their support. Of the 22 seats the Liberals currently hold in the Legislature, 13 are located in the southwest or west central parts of the province and 5 more are in Metro Toronto. Of the 19 seats held by the NDP, 7 are in Metro and 6 in northern Ontario. The distribution of seats accentuates and exaggerates the distribution of votes. In the eastern and central regions, the Liberals and Conservatives contend without much serious threat from the NDP. (Although the NDP doubled its vote in some eastern ridings in 1971, it continued to finish a distant third in most of them.) In the northern region, the Liberals and the NDP are relatively strong, but the Conservatives are not without substantial support in this, their weakest area. The Metro Toronto and southwestern regions display the clearest three-party competition, as do some parts of the Mississauga conurbation (the Golden Horseshoe from Niagara to Oshawa, omitting Toronto) to a lesser extent.

An examination of the vote distribution across categories of community size provides a further elaboration of the regional breakdown. In the north and southwest, the rural areas are predominantly Liberal, whereas in the east, central, and Mississauga region, the rural areas are predominantly Conservative. The NDP fares best in the small cities of the north and the southwest, and in Windsor, Hamilton and Metro Toronto. The Conservatives do well in the small towns of all regions (except Metro Toronto of course and the Ottawa Valley region in which 71 per cent of the respondents are resident in Ottawa). Conservative support is strong in the cities of London and Ottawa.

Moving from the geographic to the socio-economic variables, what patterns of support emerge? As far as income groupings are concerned, there is hardly any variation in party support which appears to be linked to this variable. There is only a very slight increase in Conservative support in the $8,000+ annual family income group and very little change in support for the other parties. Occupation groups provide a somewhat greater degree of variation, with the Conservatives doing best among managerial, clerical and sales workers; the New Democrats attract the bulk of their support from among industrial workers, and employees in the transportation and communication industries. The Liberals also do well in these groups and in the service and primary industry occupations.

Education level is a variable related both to information-processing capacity and to economic status; one might expect it to have some impact on party choice, but again the relationship is quite weak. The NDP vote declines somewhat in the university-educated group, and there is a general increase in Conservative support as education level rises. The Liberals obtain around one quarter of each group's support.

More direct indicators of socio-economic status may be found in trade union membership, and self-perception in class terms. There appears to be a negative relationship between membership in a trade union and support for the Conservative party. The relationship between union membership and NDP support is positive; between union membership and Liberal support, weakly positive. Given the formal links between the Canadian Labour Congress and the NDP, one might have expected a greater degree of support for the party among rank-and-file unionists, but we have measured only membership in unions, not commitment to their political goals.

As regards subjective class evaluation, the picture in Ontario is somewhat confused. Nearly 25 per cent of the sample in the Hoffman-Schindeler study said that the terms "working class" and "middle class" both described them very well! A further 14 per cent said both terms fit them "fairly well," and 4 per cent rejected both terms entirely. Nonetheless, when the respondents with a clear class self-description are isolated the pattern is somewhat sharper. New Democrats do twice as well among working-class identifiers as among middle-class identifiers; Conservatives do twice as well among the middle class; the Liberals do equally well in both groups.

What is the distribution of the vote across age and sex categories? The only variation by gender appears to be a slightly greater tendency for men than women to support the NDP. Age appears negatively related to NDP support and positively related to Conservative and Liberal support, but as usual the relationships are weak.

Perhaps the strongest link between Ontario voting behaviour and membership in a social category remains that between religious affiliation and vote. To a lesser extent, ethnic origin is also a factor. However both these variables are still only weakly related to party choice. The Liberals do best among Roman Catholics and Jews (and thus not surprisingly, among persons of French, Italian, and "other European" origin). Conservatives do best among the major Protestant denominations (and among British and German-origin respondents). The NDP is most successful among the minor Protestant denominations and among those with no religious preference.

It would appear from these figures that, despite the enduring importance of ethno-religious issues related to education and cultural policy, and despite the contemporary relevance of regional and economic groupings to social welfare, taxation and industrial development policies, there are very few clear relationships between party electoral choice and membership in the social categories related to these issues. Is it that Ontario's cleavages overlap, so that a desire to support party A in one issue-area is tempered by a desire to support party B in another? Is it that the components of party images which are truly relevant to the voter's choice have not yet been adequately explored? Or is it that most Ontarians don't perceive their society to have any politically relevant cleavages at all?

There is probably a little truth in all these suggestions. It is not that there are no relationships, but that they are weak. It is not that there are no social cleavages, but that they are of only limited salience. It is not that there are no issues, but that they are changeable and hard to measure. Given this lack of clear definition in our picture of Ontario voting behaviour, what can be said with confidence about the future of electoral politics in the province?

CONCLUSION

The single most pervasive fact about Ontario electoral history since 1943 is the dominance of the Conservative party. As long as the province remains the most prosperous in Canada, is there any likelihood that such a long-term dominance can be altered? The sheer length of time in office can become a detriment in itself, for as governments grow complacent, the electorate becomes easier to convince that "it's time for a change." However, the Conservative party has shown a great ability to select a new leader, and undergo a substantial replacement of personnel, just before those elections when it appeared they were in danger of losing critical electoral support. The importance of leadership image was again evident in the 1971 election, but some observers felt that the major factor in that particular Conservative success was simply an abundance of money lavishly spent on advertising. Controls on election spending may have some effect on such largesse, but controls in other jurisdictions have seldom been so strict as to reduce severely the level of expenditure; and in any case, it is difficult to attribute over thirty years of dominance to spending in one or two elections. Indeed, the fact that such money is readily available may be testimony of the certainty of contributors that their party will continue to be successful.

Opposition weakness may be a factor in Conservative dominance, for if there is to be change in Ontario, it will probably have to come from one of the existing opposition parties. The question arises whether either one of them is capable of achieving power without the destruction of the other.

The Liberals were heartened in 1973 by two by-election victories—one rural, one urban—while the NDP took consolation from the fact that they had managed in the 1971 election virtually to match the Liberals in both votes and seats. The concentration of attention by Ontario Liberals on the federal level has meant that personnel have been harder to come by at the provincial level. The relatively greater success of the Liberals in federal politics, combined with the centrality of Ontario in determining the strength and security of Liberal administrations, has meant that rewards for the Liberal party faithful, in terms both of jobs and of policy-making influence, have been disproportionately at the federal level. Thus the party opted to remain with its current leader, Robert Nixon, despite changes in the other parties' leaders since 1967, partly because prominent federal Liberals were unwilling to accept the task of rejuvenating the Ontario party when Nixon considered stepping down.

The Liberal party is not likely to disappear, however, while it continues to have such substantial federal strength in the province. At any rate, it seems likely from considerations of alternative vote, that the principal beneficiary of a Liberal demise would be the Conservatives. The NDP continues to draw fairly consistent support from the working class in Ontario's cities and towns, however, and unless some major event intervenes it would appear that Ontario is destined to be a three-party system "in transition" for some time to come.

SELECTED BIBLIOGRAPHY

ALFORD, ROBERT R. *Party and Society: The Anglo-American Democracies.* Chicago: Rand McNally and Company, 1963.

ANDERSON, GRACE M. "Voting Behaviour and the Ethnic-Religious Variable." *Canadian Journal of Economics and Political Science,* XXXII, 1966.

GAGNE, WALLACE and S. PETER REGENSTREIF. "Some Aspects of NDP Urban Support in 1965." *Canadian Journal of Economics and Political Science,* XXXIII, 1967.

GROSSMAN, L.A. "Safe Seats: The Rural Urban Pattern in Ontario." *Canadian Journal of Economics and Political Science,* XXIX, 1963.

HOFFMAN, DAVID. "Intra-Party Democracy: A Case Study." *Canadian Journal of Economics and Political Science,* XXVII, 1961.

JACEK, HENRY et al. "The Congruence of Federal-Provincial Campaign Activity in Party Organizations." *Canadian Journal of Political Science,* V, 1972.

JEWETT, PAULINE. "Voting in the 1960 Federal By-elections at Peterborough and Niagara Falls." *Canadian Journal of Economics and Political Science,* XXVIII, 1962.

LAPONCE, JEAN A. "Non-Voting and Non-Voters: A Typology." *Canadian Journal of Economics and Political Science,* XXXIII, 1967.

———. *People vs. Politics.* Toronto: University of Toronto Press, 1969.

LEWIS, RODERICK. *Centennial Edition of a History of the Electoral Districts, Legislatures and Ministries of the Province of Ontario 1867–1968.* Toronto: Queen's Printer, 1968.

MCDONALD, LYNN. "Religion and Voting: A Study of the 1968 Canadian Election in Ontario." *Canadian Review of Sociology and Anthropology,* VI, 1969.

MEISEL, JOHN, ed. *Papers on the 1962 Election.* Toronto: University of Toronto Press, 1964.

———. "Religious Affiliation and Electoral Behaviour." *Canadian Journal of Economics and Political Science,* XXII, 1956.

———. *Working Papers on Canadian Politics* (enlarged edition). Montreal: McGill-Queen's Press, 1973.

MORTON, DESMOND. "The Effectiveness of Political Campaigning: The NDP in the 1967 Ontario Election." *Journal of Canadian Studies,* IV, 1969.

PERLIN, GEORGE and PATTI PEPPIN. "Variations in Party Support in Federal and Provincial Elections: Some Hypotheses." *Canadian Journal of Political Science,* IV, 1971.

QUALTER, T. H. *The Election Process in Canada.* Toronto: McGraw-Hill, 1970.

REGENSTREIF, S. PETER. *The Diefenbaker Interlude: Parties and Voting in Canada.* Toronto: Longmans, 1965.

———. "Some Aspects of National Party Support in Canada." *Canadian Journal of Economics and Political Science,* XXIX, 1963.

SCARROW, HOWARD. *Canada Votes: A Handbook of Federal and Provincial Election Data.* New Orleans: The Hauser Press, 1962.

———. "Federal-Provincial Voting Patterns in Canada." *Canadian Journal of Economics and Political Science,* XXVI, 1960.

WILSON, JOHN. "Politics and Social Class in Canada: The Case of Waterloo South." *Canadian Journal of Political Science,* I, 1968.

——— and DAVID HOFFMAN. "The Liberal Party in Contemporary Ontario Politics." *Canadian Journal of Political Science,* III, 1970.

—— and DAVID HOFFMAN. "Ontario: A Three-party System in Transition," in Martin Robin, ed., *Canadian Provincial Politics*. Scarborough, Ont.: Prentice-Hall, 1972.

WRONG, DENNIS. "Ontario Provincial Elections 1934–55: A Preliminary Survey of Voting." *Canadian Journal of Economics and Political Science*, XXIII, 1957.

Ontario Political Parties: Fish or Fowl?

WHAT is the nature of political parties in Ontario? Some would tell us that they are ephemeral bodies that have substance only during election campaigns. Others see the Progressive Conservative party as a massive, well-oiled, precision-built Big Blue Machine that levels everything in its path; the Liberal party as a decrepit tool of its federal Big Brother; and the New Democratic Party the captive of union bosses or wide-eyed socialists. Still another analysis finds that the NDP is a democratic mass-membership party, while each of the others is no more than a parliamentary caucus linked to a self-chosen clique of wealthy Bay Street businessmen. The latter is perhaps closest to the academic perception of the parties and follows the now classic taxonomy of Maurice Duverger.[1] Examining parties throughout the world (though with very brief references to Canadian parties), Duverger found two basic types: the cadre, elite or legislative party, and the mass-membership party. The former had its origins in the legislature where cohesion was provided by the glue of patronage. In general its parliamentarians dominate the party, but centralization is frowned upon and the party operates more as a federation of locally based elites, including legislators. Party structures are vague and seasonal and the central institutions that do exist are rendered impotent by the presence of ex-officio positions. Party membership is an ill-defined concept to which the party attaches little significance.

The mass-membership party had its origins outside the legislature in a popular movement, the members of which were primarily concerned with policy issues and ideological questions. The organizational base of the party consists of branches which actively and without discrimination recruit members who, in turn, have clear rights and obligations, one of which is the financing of party activities through their membership dues. The base, in turn, is integrated into a disciplined, centralized, complex, yet precisely defined organization which does not allow itself to be dominated by those whom it elects to parliament. Historically, the elite type of structure has been typical of conservative, middle-class parties, while the

1 M. Duverger, *Political Parties* 2nd ed. (London: Methuen and Co., 1959), Introduction and Book I.

mass-membership model was the hallmark of socialist parties.

Duverger admits that the theoretical distinctions are not always clear in practice and Canadian parties are certainly a case in point. In fact, Canadian (and Ontarian) parties are composites. They are alliances—sometimes close and harmonious, sometimes distant and strained—of elites who owe their positions to more or less democratic procedures, and a membership base of rather modest proportions. There are many ways in which this could be illustrated, but the present article will attempt to do so by looking at party origins, the provincial office, membership, leadership, annual meetings, and the provincial party's relationship with its constituency associations.

EARLY PARTY HISTORY

If one looks first at their origins, the Conservatives would seem to be a clear case of a legislative or elitist party, the Liberals a mass-membership party, and the CCF/NDP somewhere in between. The Ontario Conservative party had its beginnings with the Family Compact Tories in the Executive Council and Legislative Assembly of Upper Canada in the first decades of the nineteenth century. The Liberal party, on the other hand, is descended from Reform and Clear Grit movements outside the Legislature beginning in the 1820s. The CCF was born following a series of meetings by farm, labour and intellectual groups in the West in the early 1930s. However, unlike the typical socialist party, it began as a decentralized federation and already had a small parliamentary contingent, the Ginger Group, one of whom became the leader of the party. The origins of the Ontario CCF party also showed a divergence from the mass-membership model. Agnes Macphail, a former Progressive who represented an Ontario riding in the federal House, brought the new party to Ontario and induced remnants of the UFO party to affiliate with it. More typically, labour groups and socialist clubs helped to provide some kind of popular base and the party began without any representation in the Ontario Legislature.

The subsequent history of all three parties shows how the elitist and mass-membership components have waxed and waned. Throughout the nineteenth century, various attempts were made to give Upper Canadian Reform (later

Ontario Liberalism) a permanent province-wide organization. The branch, based on a small geographical area, is the
foundation of the mass-membership party and, as early as
1818, the first attempt to organize Reformers systematically
throughout the province involved meetings in every township to support a petition of grievances. From then until
fairly recent times this small geographical unit provided
the organizational base for the Liberal party. By the 1820s
this model was used when Reform candidates were nominated for Assembly elections and, by mid-century, most
constituencies at the very least had nominating conventions
following more or less the same procedures as those used
today. But the attempt to create a permanent, province-
wide organization was frustrating. Typically, some enter-
prising person would have the idea that a convention of
representatives from the constituencies throughout the
province would help to unify the party, would galvanize
the rank-and-file into activity at the constituency level and
would give the party a program that all agreed on. The
convention would be enthusiastically attended and it would
create a hierarchy of committees similar to those of earlier
Reform organizations: an executive committee in Toronto
supported by county and township committees throughout
the province. But a year or two later, there would be complaints that nothing had happened and that the provincial
association had collapsed again. As one writer has said,
"the history of the organization of the Liberal party in
Ontario is one of continual rebirth and disintegration."[2]
Although it had begun as a membership party, the legislative caucus later became clearly dominant.

The Conservatives were prompted to follow the Liberal
example and adopted the same form for nominations. But
they had less need of a permanent, provincial organization.
John A. Macdonald kept such a close watch on party matters throughout what was later Ontario that he constituted
a kind of one-man organization. He also had assistance in
elections from two organizations with which he had carefully constructed alliances: the Orange Order and the
Roman Catholic Church. Newspapers, which were partisan
in a way that is most unusual now, also did much of the
organizational work of the two parties.

2 E. V. Jackson, "The Organization of the Canadian Liberal Party,
1867–1896," MA Thesis, University of Toronto, 1962, p. 73.

THE PROVINCIAL OFFICE

Towards the end of the nineteenth century it was the legislative party that succeeded in giving the extra-parliamentary Liberal party a degree of permanence. In the mid-1870s, a salaried organizer or secretary was appointed who gave a continuity and motive force which had hitherto been lacking. G. R. Pattullo, a journalist, was followed in 1883 by W. T. R. Preston, another journalist and in 1893 by Alexander Smith, a lawyer. They prodded local riding associations out of their dormancy and into electoral activity, advised them and took stock of political conditions throughout the province. About the same time the Conservatives also appointed a paid secretary, H. H. Smith and later Robert Birmingham, and both parties have maintained such a position and a party office in Toronto more or less continuously up to the present.

The existence of a party bureaucracy is an important feature of the mass-membership party and it is now a prominent part of all three parties' operations. Although activity accelerates in the lead-up to an election, the office is busy throughout the year and has primary responsibility for organizing provincial and district party meetings, for producing a party newsletter, for conducting research that will aid the party in planning election strategy and for ensuring that riding associations are active and effective. To do this, the office of the Liberal Party in Ontario (LPO), at its unfashionable Duncan Street address, has a staff of sixteen or seventeen and about four organizers on short-term appointments working in the field at the riding level. The NDP office at the foot of Church Street employs a staff of similar size and five field organizers, two of whom are paid by the United Steelworkers of America. The Ontario Progressive Conservative office is in the plushest building, above Hy's Restaurant in the heart of the Bay Street district, but employs the smallest staff: six plus two field organizers.

Any discussion of the provincial party bureaucracy should mention the sometimes competing staff in the Premier's and the opposition leader's offices. The Premier's office, which costs the Provincial Treasury $1.1 million a year to run, employs top-level advisers, whose responsibilities inevitably intermingle governmental and party business. The opposition leader's office is geared, even more than the Premier's office, to party activities such as the search for prospective candidates. Unlike the Conservative party headquarters which is concerned almost exclusively with provincial politics, the LPO office attempts to serve the provincial and federal levels of the party; though the office has been used more by the latter than the former. Sometimes in the past, the LPO has not been particularly impressed with the way the Queen's Park people have planned their election campaigns and there has been a certain coolness (not to say disdain) in the relationship between the two. Furthermore, the caucus of Liberal MPP's has included a number of individualists not much interested in party matters; in contrast the members of the Ontario federal caucus have tended to be party men, actively concerned with party affairs.

The Conservatives will not reveal anything about how much it costs to operate their provincial office or where the money comes from. The Liberals publish a full financial statement. Excluding the atypical item of the 1973 leadership convention, the cost of running the party office in that year was $191,843, the major items being salaries, printing equipment and annual meeting expenses. The NDP pays out more in salaries; their total expenses in the same year were $213,153.

MEMBERSHIP

The mass-membership party is theoretically financed through the sale of party memberships and all three of Ontario's political parties have a membership base, but does that make them mass-membership parties? Duverger found that many elitist parties have attempted to imitate mass-membership parties; but, though members exist, there is no systematic registration or dues collection. The true mass-membership party has a more formal procedure for enrolling members. They have to pledge themselves to uphold party principles and are subject to regularly collected fees which provide the party with its principal funds for financing party operations and election campaigns. According to these criteria, the NDP comes closer than Ontario's other two parties to being a mass-membership party: prospective members undertake to abide by the principles of the party and they have to have their applications forwarded to the provincial secretary for approval. Individual membership fees are $10 and must be renewed by 31 March of each year. (There are lower fees for additional members of a family, students and senior citizens; affiliated membership is open to trade unions, farm organizations, cooperatives and other similar organizations who pay an annual fee of $1.20 per member.)

The NDP constitution is rigorous in denying membership to members of other political parties (in practice, excluding Communists and Trotskyites) and the party took a very tough line against its most recent ginger group, the Waffle. In 1970 the party welcomed "the constant stimulus provided by groups like the Waffle"; but in 1972 the provincial council forbade groups within the party to hold any public activities and forced the breakup of the Waffle and the resignation of a considerable number of prominent Wafflers. The incident could be interpreted as the characteristic action of a left-wing mass-membership party anxious to maintain its ideological purity or, more plausibly, as a decision taken by a pragmatic, somewhat elitist party that was worried about how the electorate viewed the Waffle's socialist rhetoric and the divisions within the party.

Membership in the older parties is a more casual undertaking. For a long time their constitutions did not say anything about rank-and-file members and the relationship between the provincial party and the individual member of a riding association remained vague. Then in 1964 the constitution of the Liberal party was changed to define an individual member of the party, how he became a member and the rights he acquired. The present Conservative constitution likewise defines the "duties of active members." They are expected "to uphold Progressive Conservative principles," to assist PC candidates, to attend association meetings and to participate in their discussions. Neither party's new members are subject to any screening process, but new Liberals are not allowed to vote at party meetings unless they have joined at least 72 hours beforehand.

Of the three parties, the NDP is by far the most successful in financing its operations through the sale of memberships. The provincial party gets 50 per cent of the proceeds, which amounted to $90,483 in 1973. Affiliation fees, largely from unions, provided another $53,561 and other income amounted to $17,789. The party, nevertheless, had an excess of expenditures over income of $51,320. Other operations of the party which are financed separately are the *New Democrat* (the party newspaper), the biennial convention, provincial and federal elections. In 1971, provincial election expenses were largely paid for by $100,000 in union contributions and $95,000 in quota payments which were levied on the riding associations. Membership fees in the past have gone into the provincial election campaign fund only indirectly as a transfer from the provincial party's operating account; that was about $20,000 in 1971. Even the most successful mass-membership parties elsewhere have had to rely on sources other than membership dues and in 1973, the Ontario NDP launched a "Wipe out the Debt Fund" that was more typical of the fund drives of middle-class American parties than of European working-class parties. Instead of attempting to collect innumerable small contributions, the party sought sizable donations of $100 each from just one thousand individuals. Within eighteen months, it had collected $74,000.

Liberal membership fees are used solely to finance riding activities. The LPO is financed by a combination of traditional elitist and middle-class American techniques. In 1973 $60,000 and $15,000 were turned over to the provincial office from federal and provincial fund-raisers who collected donations from corporations and wealthy individuals in the manner that is characteristic of the elitist party; on the other hand, the annual $100-a-plate Prime Minister's dinner in Toronto brought the provincial party $59,000 and the Red Carnation Fund another $22,123. The fund—in the manner of the NDP "Wipe out the Debt Fund"—asks for contributions of up to $500, which are specifically used, not for elections, but for financing the party's year-round operations. The party does not publish a statement of income and expenses for its provincial election campaigns, but it is probably safe to assume that funds are raised in the traditional elitist manner.

In terms of membership numbers, no Ontario party can really be described as a membership party with a mass base. Neither the Conservatives nor the Liberals keep a central registration of members, although the Liberals estimate that the constituencies across the province have about 40,000 members. The NDP have about 22,000–24,000 individual members and approximately 200,000 affiliated members. Compared with mass-membership parties elsewhere, these figures are modest. Liberal membership represents one half of 1 per cent of the province's population; NDP individual membership is one quarter of 1 per cent and, even with affiliated members, is just over 3 per cent. In Britain, almost 2 per cent of the population have individual memberships in the Labour party and, including affiliated members, the figure is 11 per cent. Austria and Sweden, with populations comparable to Ontario's, have socialist parties with memberships of 700,000 and 900,000 respectively. In Saskatchewan, where political participation is also high, NDP membership is 3½ per cent of the population and the Liberal party has almost as many members. Even in Ontario, CCF party membership was over 18,000 in the 1940s, when the population was half what it is now. Compared, also, with other Ontario associations, the political parties are small. Both the Anglican and United Churches claim an "active" or "participating" membership of over half a million and the largest trade unions have about 100,000 dues-paying members.

When affiliated members are included, the NDP looks more like a mass-membership party and the party considers affiliated members to be an integral part of the' membership along with individual members. There are good reasons, however, for suggesting that the actual membership of the NDP is a good deal less than the figure of a quarter of a million that includes affiliated members. First of all, surveys show that only one quarter of trade unionists vote NDP. Less than a third of trade unionists in Ontario are affiliated to the NDP, but they are undoubtedly not the only unionists who vote NDP. In other words, it must be that many affiliated NDP members do not vote for the party. They can hardly be considered members, except in the most nominal sense. Secondly, members of affiliated unions have to take the initiative of opting out if they do not want a portion of their union dues to be paid in affiliation fees to the NDP. In Britain, trade unionists had, for a time, to opt in if they wanted affiliated membership in the Labour party and affiliated membership then dropped to about half of what it had been previously. In Ontario, a union usually affiliates about 80 per cent of its membership as a way of meeting the objections of those who do not want affiliated membership in the NDP; but the British experience suggests that affiliated membership would be much lower if the individual trade unionist had to exercise his initiative —as he must to join either of the other parties. Thirdly, the party itself implicitly recognizes the phantasmal quality of its affiliated membership: the rules for representation at provincial conventions are such that a constituency association with, say, two hundred individual members is entitled to the same number of delegates as a union with nineteen hundred affiliated members; furthermore, every delegate to the provincial convention and the provincial council must be an individual member of the party. The main reason, of course, for having affiliated memberships is to provide a large, dependable source of funds and paid organizers which partly compensate for the corporate donations that largely go to the other two parties. As one writer has said, "The trade union movement in terms of affiliation, fees, donations at election time and full time organizers, is the only thing (or almost the only thing) which stands between the poor house and a vibrant, active party organization."[3]

Finally, the new federal legislation on party finance and the recommendations of the Camp Commission, examined in the next chapter by Jo Surich, are likely to have a profound influence on party membership and membership dues. The Conservative and Liberal parties will probably, as a result, put more emphasis on having a wider and more regularized membership base and all three parties will certainly have more funds.

LEADERSHIP SELECTION

The leadership convention is perhaps the most compelling piece of evidence for claiming that all three parties give the ultimate power to their membership, although this has not always been the case. From 1867 until after the First World War, Conservative and Liberal party leaders were chosen in a manner typical of legislative parties. (Before 1867, the party membership's recognition of a man as Liberal or Reform leader was, with one exception, crucial to his actually heading the party in the Legislature, even though there was no formal procedure for election by a convention.) When the party was out of office, the legislative

3 J. Surich, *The New Democrat* (Sept./Oct. 1973), p. 9.

caucus chose the leader; when in power, the party's leader was chosen by the Lieutenant-Governor, by the retiring premier or, in one instance, by the cabinet who were aided by a carefully phrased letter from the recently deceased premier.

In 1918, when Newton Rowell quit the leadership of the provincial Liberal party to join Borden's Union government, the party decided to call a convention which would give the party new policies as well as a new leader for the upcoming elections. Other provinces had held conventions at which new leaders had been chosen but this democratizing process was somewhat diluted by there being only one candidate. The Ontario Liberals had the distinction of holding probably the first contested leadership convention in the country. The federal leadership convention followed a couple of months later and one writer has noted with what surprising readiness this form was accepted.[4]

The convention innovation was most attractive to an opposition party which had only a small caucus and recognized the need to capture the public's attention. So, with the UFO (United Farmers of Ontario) in power after 1919, the Conservatives followed suit and elected Howard Ferguson at their first leadership convention the next year. The convention proved to be a successful device for getting publicity and reinvigorating the party rank-and-file. The first federal Liberal and provincial Conservative leadership conventions were followed by victories at the polls and the convention became an established device by which a party could rebuild its popularity with the electorate. The most recent example of that was the 1971 Conservative convention, discussed by David Surplis in Chapter 5. While the leadership convention sometimes looked like becoming an overworked talisman, experience also suggested that a party ignored at its peril the democratic selection of the leader.

When Howard Ferguson resigned as premier to become High Commissioner in London, he advised the Lieutenant-Governor to call on George Henry, who was unanimously confirmed as party leader six months later at a so-called "Special Meeting" of the Conservative Association. Henry

4 J. C. Courtney, *The Selection of National Party Leaders in Canada*, p. 65.

328 / Joseph Wearing

was reported to have had more cabinet support than his rival, William Price, the Attorney General; but Charles McCrea, the Mines Minister, would have been the favourite to carry a convention, according to one account.[5] Four years later the Conservatives were decisively defeated in the general elections; since then, every Conservative leader has been chosen at a keenly contested convention—in 1966 six ministers and the Speaker fought it out for six ballots—and all but one (Earl Rowe, elected in 1936) led their party to victory at the next election.

The Liberals' experience with the leadership convention has been less heartening and, at times, the party has shied away from it. The wisdom of the latter course has not, however, been borne out by the results. Neither of the party's first two leaders chosen in convention stayed at the helm for very long and in 1923 the third leader in four years (William Sinclair) was chosen by the caucus to be their "temporary leader"; but he led the party for seven years through two electoral defeats. The party's return from the political wilderness followed an electrifying convention which chose Mitch Hepburn to lead the party. When Hepburn was named leader for the second time, shortly before the 1945 election, it was by a meeting midway in size between a party caucus and a full-blown convention; the election dealt the party its worst defeat in over a decade.

After Hepburn withdrew from public life, the party held off calling a convention for two years, hoping to entice some attractive federal ministers into the contest. None entered and the eventual convention chose the House leader, Farquhar Oliver, to lead the party. Another convention, three and a half years later, called forth more numerous and more attractive candidates and the party's popular vote went up, though its representation in the Legislature fell to a catastrophic level. Once again the party made Oliver acting leader. Two years passed without a convention; then Oliver won the leadership again in the face of minimal opposition. He improved the party's position slightly in an election and then resigned for the second time. There followed one of the most hotly contested

5 Q. Thompson, "In the Absence of Mr. Ferguson," *Maclean's* magazine, August 15, 1931, p. 19.

leadership contests in the party's history. The new leader, John Wintermeyer, brought a dramatic improvement in the party's fortunes in the 1959 election.

Leadership contests have not by any means solved the party's problems. In 1961 the Tories had their own keenly contested leadership race which was won by John Robarts. In the election two years later, he strengthened his party's hold on the electorate, while the Liberals more or less held steady and their leader lost his own seat. Another hotly fought convention put Andrew Thompson into the leadership in 1964, but a combination of bad health and bad luck forced him to resign before he could prove himself in electoral battle. When the party held its seventh leadership convention in twenty years, there was only one candidate, Robert Nixon. Under him, the party's electoral strength has fallen off and in 1972, Nixon decided to resign as leader; but two dramatic by-election victories made him reconsider and the following year he defeated three other challengers to retain the post.

The ccf/ndp has had only three leaders and all have been chosen by convention. The party was slow to choose its first provincial leader because in its early years ccf'ers focused more attention on Ottawa than on Queen's Park and the federal leader, J. S. Woodsworth, led the party in the 1937 provincial election. Finally in 1942 a party convention elected E. B. Jolliffe, who led the party in its most impressive election to date. From nowhere, the party won thirty-four seats, just four less than the leading Conservative party. In the next ten years Jolliffe and the party were severely buffeted by the electoral breezes. Both he and most other members of his caucus lost their seats in 1945. They regained lost ground in 1948, only to suffer an even worse defeat in the 1951 election. Without a seat in the Legislature and faced with rumblings against his leadership, Jolliffe retired in 1953 to devote himself to his law practice. His successor, Donald C. MacDonald, defeated two rivals at a leadership convention later that year and under MacDonald's leadership the party steadily improved its position in the next four elections until it stood just below its high point achieved in 1943. Unlike the other two parties, the ndp constitution provides for the leader to be elected at every biennial provincial meeting. Usually the incumbent leader is re-elected without opposition, but in

1968 MacDonald's leadership was challenged. He won handily, but Stephen Lewis made moves to contest the leadership at the next biennial convention and MacDonald retired to "avoid a messy internal struggle." Lewis won the leadership but failed to improve the party's showing at the subsequent general election.

All three parties use the same balloting procedures for leadership conventions as they do for constituency nomination meetings; that is, the lowest-placed candidate is dropped from successive ballots until one candidate receives an overall majority of votes cast. American party conventions have the same overall majority requirement (although there is no rule that the lowest placed candidate must be dropped), but in recent years, pre-convention campaigning in the United States has wrapped up delegate votes to such an extent that even a second ballot is rarely needed. In Ontario, there has been a trend in the opposite direction and conventions have gone on to third, fourth, or sixth ballots. Furthermore, whereas Canadian national leadership conventions have always been won by the candidate who led on the first ballot, in Ontario the overall majority requirement has not been superfluous. In three instances the man who eventually won had placed second on the first ballot, although admittedly very close to the man who placed first. In 1958 Walter Harris, long a minister in St. Laurent's government, led John Wintermeyer at first; but there was resentment against Harris as the supposed nominee of the Liberal brass and the "federal gang" and anti-Harris votes shifted strongly to Wintermeyer on the second ballot, although he needed another ballot to win. At the 1953 CCF convention Fred Young had a first-ballot lead over Donald C. MacDonald and Andrew Brewin, who had been tipped as the favourite by the *Globe and Mail*. When Brewin was dropped, the greater part of his support went to MacDonald. In 1961 four Conservative candidates were tightly packed together on the first ballot, with John Robarts seven votes behind Kelso Roberts. Robarts had two advantages: the party establishment supported him and, as the only non-Toronto candidate on the fifth and sixth ballots, he got the votes of the small-town Tories who mistrust Torontonians.

Those who have led the two older parties over the last century share a number of characteristics. All have been male and almost all have been Protestants (United Church, Anglican or Presbyterian) of British descent. All but three were born in Ontario and twenty-five of the thirty were either lawyers or farmers.

The most striking difference between Conservative and Liberal leaders is that the Liberals have had such difficulty finding leaders to stay with the job, even when the party has been in power. The typical Liberal has led his party for just over three years, while the typical Conservative has led his for eight and a half. In the early years, the counter-attractions of Ottawa accounted for the loss of several Liberal leaders, one after just nine months as premier. In more recent years, four have given up the leadership after losing in their own constituencies. (Such a fate has befallen only two Conservatives.) In three other cases quite vocal dissatisfaction in party ranks has convinced a leader to retire after just one election defeat. When the Conservatives were in opposition they were more patient and allowed W. R. Meredith to lead the party to defeat in five elections before he retired gracefully to a chief justiceship. Unlike the federal party, the provincial Conservatives have harried out only one leader, George Henry, and in recent years the party has demonstrated a most orderly succession of leaders, each of whom has held the top post for a decade and retired in his own time. More recently the Liberals appear to be following the earlier Conservative example: Robert Nixon will be the first Liberal to take his party into another election after having led it in two defeats.

Because the CCF/NDP has had only three leaders, few generalizations can be made. All came to the position in their thirties and the first two leaders stayed even longer than most Conservatives. The backgrounds of the three men are more varied than those of the more numerous leaders of the other two parties (in this respect the NDP is more like a mass-membership party than the other two): an Anglican lawyer born in China, a Unitarian journalist born in British Columbia, and a Jewish teacher from Toronto.

Until recently, neither of the older parties' constitutions said anything about renewing a leader's mandate or re-placing him. On the other hand, neither had really had much trouble in getting rid of unwanted leaders. At their 1952 annual meeting there was a strong feeling amongst

332 / Joseph Wearing

Liberals that Walter Thomson should resign (partly because he had ignored the party's policies that had been passed by the mass party in convention), and he is reported to have come to the meeting with two speeches—a fighting speech and a swan song. He delivered the latter and a blood-bath was avoided. Nevertheless, the trauma of Diefenbaker's exit from the federal Conservative leadership made both parties realize the wisdom of having leadership review clauses in their constitutions. The NDP's biennial election of a leader provided an obvious model, but a convention might occur prematurely before the party was really ready to elect a new leader. Under the NDP arrangement the incumbent, once re-elected, is there for a two-year term. Consequently, the two constitutions were amended to give the Liberal Executive Board and the Conservative Executive Council the authority to call a leadership convention at any time. The Liberals added the requirement that one must be called within the two years following a provincial election.

Probably no other political parties in the world have gone as far to make their leaders directly responsible to the party membership. The only possible fly in the democratic ointment lies in the selection of delegates who attend these conventions. All three party constitutions allow for the possibilities of flies: Conservative delegates-at-large, Liberal standing-committee delegates, and NDP union delegates. Delegates elected in the constituencies (and by campus clubs) are the rank-and-file representatives of the membership of the three parties. But at the most recent leadership conventions of the Conservatives and Liberals, constituency delegates accounted for two-thirds of the total number of delegates and about half at the last NDP convention which elected a new leader. All three parties gave automatic or ex-officio status to their governing bodies: the twenty-two people on the Conservative executive plus about two hundred officers of women's, youth, and district associations; the forty-member Liberal executive board; and the 158 members of the NDP provincial council. Ontario MP's and MPP's were also there ex-officio, as were Conservative and Liberal constituency presidents, former Liberal MP's and MPP's and Liberal defeated candidates and Ontario senators. Finally, the Conservative president and executive appointed fifty-eight delegates-at-large; people who were appointed to Liberal standing committees became ex-officio delegates; affiliated trade unions named 830 delegates to the NDP convention.

All (except the senators) owed their delegate status to some sort of party election; but, because they were not elected to their positions for the purpose of attending a leadership convention, their presence somewhat diluted the voting strength of the constituency delegates who were elected by constituency members in order to represent them at the convention. There are even good arguments for appointing some ex-officio delegates, such as esteemed party veterans who are no longer active enough in a constituency to be elected as riding delegates. The Conservatives have limited the possibility of abuse by restricting the number of delegates-at-large to no more than half the number of provincial constituencies. Liberal standing committees, which have numbered between eight and ten, have up to thirty-two members each. Half of these may be elected district representatives, but can be appointed in the case of districts which have not held annual meetings. What is worse, a committee may be more or less inactive until a leadership convention is called. Then the committee chairman, who may not have called a meeting all year, can stick his friends on his committee and they get to be ex-officio delegates. At the party's 1974 annual meeting, the constitution committee proposed making only the committee chairmen ex-officio delegates, but that seemed too drastic a reduction and the proposal was tabled for further discussion. In any case, the actual number of ex-officio standing committee delegates at the party's last leadership convention was just 175 out of 1,738.

The union contingent at NDP conventions raises a similar sort of problem. We have already examined the peculiar position of the affiliated trade union membership in the NDP and, even though the constituencies get more delegates per member than the unions, the latter can still wield a lot of votes. In fact, the unions tend not to send nearly as many delegates as they are entitled to and, at the 1974 convention, riding delegates outnumbered union delegates by more than two to one. However, in 1970, when a new leader was to be elected, a great effort was made to get the union delegation to the convention in support of Stephen Lewis, who, as the party's labour critic in the Legislature, had

been in a good position to win union support. According to
UAW leader Dennis MacDermott, Lewis got 99 per cent of
the UAW's large block of 265 delegates; he perhaps got 80
per cent of the rest. The contest between Lewis and Walter
Pitman for constituency delegate votes was very much
closer and it was difficult to tell whether Lewis's overwhelming union support provided the necessary margin of
victory or not. In any case, the convention did raise questions about the impact of large, monolithic union delega-
tions at NDP conventions.

It is perhaps deceptively easy to imagine that the constituency delegates alone are the democratic embodiment
of the Conservative, Liberal and New Democratic parties.
The ideal does not necessarily match the reality. For one
thing, none of the parties has a membership base that is so
large or diverse that it can claim to be a reflection of the
province as a whole. Secondly, there are occasionally
charges that constituency meetings have been packed by
one of the leadership contenders. As would befit a centralized, disciplined party of the mass-membership type, all
three parties have attempted to tighten these constituency
elections in order to prevent abuses. The Conservative
constitution provides that delegates must be elected at
general meetings for which fifteen days' notice has been
given to all riding members; the NDP require applications
for party membership to be forwarded to the provincial
secretary for approval; the Liberal constitution requires
that seven days' notice of meetings should be given, that
new members must have joined at least three days before
such a meeting, and that the provincial president may,
at his discretion, name someone to conduct the riding
election.

How democratic are these conventions in reality? For
one thing, the voting is done by secret ballot, so no matter
what pledges are given or what pressures applied, no one
knows what the delegate will do when he gets to the voting
booth. For another thing, there have been enough upsets
or near upsets to cast doubt upon claims that conventions
can be controlled. The winner at each of the last two Conservative conventions was apparently the preferred heir of
the retiring leader; but in one case, it took six ballots to
elect him and in the other, he won on the fourth ballot by
just forty-four votes. Rebellions by Liberal delegates have
been legion. In 1919 the temporary leader, William Proud-

foot, placed a poor third; in 1947, Ontario federal ministers, led by C. D. Howe, campaigned vigorously for Colin Campbell, but he was beaten in one ballot; in 1950, the "Feds'" man, John Brown, placed third; in 1958 there were rumours of splits and revolts if the convention was carried by the nominee of the party brass, Walter Harris, a former federal cabinet minister. One of the candidates was even quoted as saying, "We're being run by a group of men in Toronto who couldn't win an election for pound-keeper. . . . The only people who are for Walter Harris are the professional politicians who are clinging to their jobs." As the convention opened, Harris was considered to have the best chance of winning on the first ballot, but he lost to Wintermeyer on the third. As for the NDP, the favourite of the 1953 convention was eliminated on the first ballot. At the very least, the parties' conventions are unpredictable; they can make a good claim to being pretty free and democratic as well.

ANNUAL MEETINGS, CONVENTIONS AND POLICY RALLIES

It might be somewhat arbitrary to say which of the pre-Confederation Reform rallies in Toronto was the first to bring delegates together from all across what is now Ontario. Certainly, by the late 1870s, both the Liberals and the Conservatives were holding regular provincial conventions and the practice has continued, with only an occasional break, up to the present. The most notable lapse came after Mitch Hepburn became premier in 1934. He dispensed with annual meetings of the Liberal party and was able to get away with such high-handed behaviour, because T. B. McQuesten, who had been elected to the presidency at the party's annual meeting in 1932, was in his cabinet. When Hepburn's government collapsed, the executive of the extra-parliamentary party, the management committee, were able to head off attempts by McQuesten and the parliamentary wing to gain control of the membership organization. In 1943 it drastically revised the party's constitution, barring ministers, parliamentarians and civil servants from the party presidency. (This clause was later dropped from the party's constitution and the presidency has recently been held by both an MPP and an MP. The NDP constitution has retained a similar disqualification clause.)

The annual meeting, like the leadership convention, is a delegated meeting of the rank-and-file membership of the extra-parliamentary party and the two forums constitute the highest decision-making authority in the membership party. (NDP biennial conventions, besides electing or re-electing leaders, transact business similar to that which occupies the annual meetings of the other two parties. The Liberals occasionally hold meetings which deal almost solely with policy and these are called policy rallies.) Between annual meetings or conventions, authority to act for their respective parties is given to the conservative executive, the Liberal executive board and the NDP provincial council. (The Conservative executive council, which includes the executive, is a large body that carries out "such duties as are entrusted to it from time to time.") With 158 members, the NDP provincial council is about three times the size of the Conservative executive council and the Liberal executive board. It is the only one of the three that includes a representative from each riding executive and has been described as a "mini-parliament of the party."

The annual meeting receives reports, discusses policy, amends the party's constitution and elects the party's executive: president, secretary, treasurer and a number of vice-presidents and executive or board members. Attended by up to one thousand delegates, it is part business session, part social get-together, with the Conservatives giving more emphasis to the latter and the NDP more to the former. In one recent Conservative meeting, for example, eleven hours were given over to dances and receptions and two hours to resolutions. A recent Liberal meeting devoted five hours each to receptions, policy, dinner speeches and three hours to party business. The 1974 NDP convention scheduled a three-and-a-half-hour reception, twelve hours of resolutions, three and a half hours of speeches and five and a half hours of party business. NDP conventions are not for the faint-hearted or the social butterfly!

Occasionally the executive elections are an occasion for the extra-parliamentary party to make a display of independence. The election of W. J. Henderson to the Liberal presidency was a victory for the reformers who started to rebuild the party after its shattering defeat in the federal election of 1958.

The election of a new Conservative party president in 1968 provided a similar show of independence by the Conservative annual meeting. For years the president of the

Ontario party had been the leader's right-hand man. A. D.
Mackenzie, president from 1944 to 1960, was Leslie Frost's
political *alter ego*. It was his job to keep his finger on the
political pulse of the province and he reported to the
Premier regularly over breakfast. When Mackenzie died,
Frost retired. On Robarts' becoming leader, Mackenzie's
position was filled by two men: Ernie Jackson and Elmer
Bell, the party president. Jackson held no official position,
but he took on the full-time job of keeping the Premier in
touch with grass-roots opinion across the province. The
team worked well and Robarts led his party to two impressive election victories. Robarts, however, was not really
interested in party affairs and the party began to feel
lethargic and fretful. In 1968, Alan Eagleson charged that
the party had become moribund and was heading for
electoral defeat. He ran for the party presidency on that
issue and won. The rank and file of the party had registered
their disenchantment and two years later the message was
reinforced with Allan Lawrence's campaign for the leadership. As a result the parliamentary leadership has tended
to take the extra-parliamentary or membership party more
seriously. There followed a revitalization of the party
executive and party committees, an almost complete
change in the personnel of the party office and the Premier's
office, an enhanced role for the post of executive director
and the party office, and a much more professional approach to party organization.

Similarly, at the 1974 NDP convention, Jo Surich had been
the favourite to win the presidency against Pat Chefurka.
But a proposal by Surich's finance committee to raise extra
membership funds through a $100 J. S. Woodsworth mem-
bership got the delegates' backs up. The rank and file disliked the idea of naming a deluxe membership after the
saintly ascetic, who had been the first CCF federal leader,
and denied the party presidency to the proponent of the
scheme.

The making of party policy by the rank and file is theoretically one of the main preoccupations of the mass-membership party. The NDP constitution states unequivocally that
"the provincial convention . . . shall have final authority in
all matters of principles, policies, constitution and program." The constitution of the Liberal party in Ontario is
both more explicit and, at least by implication, more

guarded. Policy rallies are to "develop and determine policy" and the constitution adds a so-called accountability clause requiring a representative of the leader to report to the rally on decisions made by the leader and caucus on resolutions passed at the previous policy rally. The implication is clear that, although the leadership must answer to the delegates for diverging from policies voted on, such divergence is possible if the meeting does not specifically negate the leadership's own policy position. The Ontario PC Association constitution simply states that the association provides "a forum for the membership of the Party to participate in political discussion and to advise with respect to Party policy" and does not even include policy discussion as a regular item of business at annual meetings.

All three parties make some attempt to have their party membership involved in policy-making, but the practical problems are enormous. How can one thousand delegates debate and vote intelligently on three or four hundred policy resolutions over a period of two or three days? Traditionally, policy groups met in the various constituencies several weeks before the convention and sent in resolutions on a variety of subjects. These were channelled to the floor by a watchful resolutions committee who ensured that matters did not get out of hand nor that the convention passed policies which would embarrass the leadership. A resolutions committee is still a prominent part of NDP conventions and its presence is sometimes a source of frustration for the rank and file. No resolution can be directly amended from the floor, but must be referred back to the resolutions committee with instructions to amend it. Delegates may be warned that shortage of time could militate against a resolution re-emerging from the resolutions committee; it may be better to accept half a loaf than none at all. On rare occasions a determined resolutions committee can even ignore the instructions that accompany a motion referred back to them and return it to the floor in a form that suits them. Consequently, procedural arguments can get intense, as they did in 1972. At the party's 1974 convention, debate went much more smoothly and several resolutions were successfully amended in the interests of reaching a broad party consensus. But, although the 1974 convention actually voted on more resolutions than is customary, there were many more that had to be referred to the provincial council for final determination.

In recent years, the other two parties have experimented with various sorts of policy meetings held apart from regular party meetings. The Conservatives, in particular, have had policy sessions that could be unconventional and free-wheeling only because they did not pretend to be setting policy for the party. Before the 1971 election the Liberals developed policy over a two-year period beginning with a "thinkers' conference" in Guelph in August 1969 and culminating in a policy rally in Ottawa seventeen months later. Before the rally, resolutions were drafted in consultation with the leader, caucus and other party members. Delegates to the rally were divided into various policy forums to discuss and amend the resolutions or to replace them with new ones. A plenary session debated the revised resolutions and, finally, delegates voted on them all by means of a ballot. A high proportion of these policy ideas eventually appeared in the party's election manifesto, "Blueprint for Government"; though, in retrospect, some of the party elite concluded that the Liberal campaign had given too much emphasis to this mass of detailed policy proposals. Since 1971 participation by the Liberal membership in policy-making has fallen off noticeably. Nevertheless, in preparation for an election in 1975, the party held a small conference to toss over new policy proposals at McMaster University in August 1974, to be followed by a full policy rally in February 1975.

There is always a question as to how seriously the parliamentary party will treat the three-day deliberations of one thousand delegates representing the membership party. The classic dilemma is posed when a convention endorses a policy to which the leadership is resolutely opposed. The most spectacular case occurred when a British Labour party conference passed a resolution on unilateral nuclear disarmament which was disavowed by the leader, Hugh Gaitskell. In Canada such bitter confrontations have been avoided. The fact that 72 per cent of the 1971 Liberal election manifesto came from the party's policy rally was enough to cause pleasant surprise.[6] On the other hand, Con-

6 S. Clarkson, "Policy and the Media: Communicating the Liberal Party Platform in the 1971 Ontario Election Campaign." Paper given at the Canadian Political Science Association meeting, June 1974, p. 12.

servative and Liberal leaders have occasionally repudiated convention resolutions with relative impunity (though we have already referred to the recent moves by the Liberal party to make leaders more accountable to the membership party). The NDP, for its part, indulges in a bit of "guided democracy," by means of its resolutions committee and often some pretty firm chairmanship, to ensure that the leadership gets policies it can live with. But the delegates will not always be guided. The 1974 convention balked at passing a resolution on natural resources that did not include a long-term commitment to public ownership. Stephen Lewis made it known that he would be very unhappy with an amendment along these lines and it was clear that his view coincided with the position taken by his primary base within the party, the conservative trade union leadership. As the convention progressed, however, one of its most notable features was the extent to which Lewis made a personal declaration of independence from many trade union views and that included a compromise which essentially embodied the position taken by the centre-left within the party on eventual public ownership of natural resources. In any case, an NDP leader always has open to him a device which NDP premiers in Saskatchewan and British Columbia have fallen back on occasionally. He can agree that a certain unwanted resolution *is* party policy —adding that it is, however, near the bottom of the list of the leader's and the caucus's own priorities. Still, there is no denying that such disagreements are regarded more seriously in the NDP than in the Conservative party, with the Liberals falling somewhere in between.

THE PROVINCIAL PARTY AND THE CONSTITUENCIES

Finally we look at the relationship between the provincial party and the lower levels of the organization: regional and district associations, the constituencies and the members, recalling that, for Duverger, the structure's complexity, as well as its degree of centralization, indicate whether it is a mass-membership party or not.

The Conservatives have district associations, the NDP have area councils, and the Liberals have both regions and district associations. (These intermediate bodies have representation on their parties' governing bodies, but not enough to frustrate intra-party democracy. There is no parallel with the indirect election of higher committees which is used to disguise autocracy in parties elsewhere.) The Liberal constitution describes in considerable detail the operation of the party's three regions and lower-level district associations, but in practice these and similar bodies in the other two parties are largely inactive. There are notable, though rare, exceptions. The Conservative Western Ontario Association is the most active district in the party and provided an important base for John Robarts in his bid for the leadership. After the federal election defeat of 1958, the Liberal Toronto and District Association sparked the whole rebuilding of the party and the attempt to democratize the party structures in the 1960s. The party tried to use the "T & D" model in other parts of the province and the country but nowhere else did it work as well.

Traditionally, the riding associations of the two older parties have jealously guarded their independence and have resented interference or attempts to centralize the party structures. No doubt the transitory nature of central party institutions during the early years of both parties accustomed the ridings to being self-governing entities. In particular, the absolute right of riding conventions to nominate candidates for general elections without any outside dictation has always been fiercely defended. The leader and the provincial office have, of course, always taken a close interest in the search for candidates, because in Canada a good candidate still can pull up to 10 per cent of the total vote.[7] The problem, however, is usually more one of finding good potential candidates than of finding ridings for them. In any case, the constituencies have to be handled very diplomatically and even gentle attempts to guide the ridings in matters of candidate selection have backfired as often as they have been successful.

The ridings have, however, been willing to submit to more centralization and discipline with respect to procedures, laid down by both the Liberal and NDP constitutions, that ensure democratic and open nomination meetings. Fourteen days' notice of NDP nominations normally must be given to all members. New members joining within that

7 R. Cunningham, "The Impact of the Local Candidate in Canadian Federal Elections," *Canadian Journal of Political Science* (1971), pp. 287–290.

fourteen-day period are ineligible to vote. The provincial council can refuse to endorse the person selected by a nominating convention and, if a riding fails to call a convention, the provincial council may do so.

The Liberals amended their constitution after a particularly embarrassing incident in the 1963 federal election. The constituency executive of the Ottawa East Liberal Club decided not to hold a nomination meeting under the pretext that the nomination meeting held before the 1962 election made another one superfluous. The decision did not sit well with one particular member of the executive, Yves Parisien, who had lost that nomination by just seventeen votes. He and two others resigned in protest from the executive. Thereupon a rival Ottawa East Liberal Association was formed and announced that an open nomination meeting would be held on 7 March. Then, three days before the meeting, the original executive, under pressure from the provincial office, relented and announced that it would hold a nomination meeting after all, on the same evening as the breakaway group. Parisien ran for the new Ottawa East Liberal Association nomination, while the sitting MP, Jean Richard, faced opposition from an Ottawa professor, Bill Boss, at the meeting of the Ottawa East Liberal Club. The club's executive did not facilitate matters for Boss. At first he understood that he could be nominated from the floor, but he was subsequently informed that nomination papers, signed by ten members of the club, had to be filed the day before the nomination. Three hours before the deadline, he was allowed access to the membership list, but allowed to copy only fifteen names. Boss had time to collect only seven signatures and, at the meeting, his nomination was ruled unacceptable. The meeting was a delegated one, as opposed to a meeting that any riding member could vote at. Delegates had been chosen by "party workers under the supervision of five ward chairmen," who had in turn been picked by Richard. In the election, Richard and Parisien faced each other as rival Liberal candidates (placing first and second respectively), but the provincial association moved quickly to prevent that sort of thing occurring again.

Gordon Blair, vice-president of the Ontario Liberal Association, who had sat through the antics of the club nomination meeting, wrote to Robert Nixon, then the president of the provincial association, and suggested that the provincial executive had to insist on a complete re-organization in Ottawa East. A general meeting open to all Liberals in the riding would have to elect a new Executive. He went on to say, "This episode raises even larger issues for the Ontario Liberal Association. The Association consists of all the provincial constituency organizations but, as far as I am aware, we have no control over how these associations operate and have not even, as a matter of policy, established basic procedures which must be followed as a condition of membership in the Ontario Liberal Association. . . . I would suggest that the Ontario Liberal Association insist on receiving copies of the constitution of all constituency associations. Two basic provisions in these constitutions should be insisted upon at least, namely, open membership for all Liberals and the nomination of candidates by properly organized nominating conventions."[8]

The following year, the party's constitution was amended to require that riding associations adhere to a number of guidelines. As it now stands, the constitution insists that every riding association have a written constitution; that the provincial executive board be enabled to call a nominating convention if the riding executive fails to do so and to call an annual meeting if the riding executive fails to call one within a year of the previous one; that riding members receive seven days' notice of nominating conventions and other meetings; that new members must have joined the party at least three days before a meeting in order to vote. For a time delegated meetings, like that held by the Ottawa East Liberal Club, were prohibited; but in 1974 the party's constitution was amended to permit huge, sparsely populated northern ridings to hold delegated meetings. These would be closely scrutinized to ensure that undemocratic practices did not creep back in.

There is good reason to suspect that not all Liberal ridings in the province have incorporated these minimum requirements into their own constitutions, as they are required to do.[9] Nevertheless, there is little doubt that nomination meetings and delegate election meetings are

8 National Liberal Federation Papers, Vol. 694, File: Election 1963, K. Davey; Blair to Nixon, 27 March, 1963.
9 R. F. Freeman, "Ontario Party Organization: The Myth and the Reality of the Classification of Parties," MA thesis, University of Waterloo, 1969, pp. 38, 42–44.

much more tightly supervised than they were in the past. In all three parties the degree of local autonomy that operates in the actual choosing of candidates makes them look like decentralized elitist parties, while the limits that Liberal and NDP constitutions put on that freedom make them look like centralized mass-membership parties. Once again, they are neither Duverger's fish nor his fowl.

Even in their election campaigning at the riding level, the parties look remarkably similar. The NDP is supposed to have invented the intensive house-to-house canvass which the press "discovered" when the party successfully exploited the technique in the 1964 Riverdale by-election.[10] In fact, the other two parties have issued detailed booklets on canvassing techniques that date back to 1887[11] and canvassing was certainly employed even before that. The NDP's contribution to the science of getting out the vote is the triple canvass[12] as opposed to the more usual double canvass. In fact, anyone who has worked for a party in an election knows that each party has a great deal of difficulty getting all of its polls expertly canvassed and covered on election day. It is furthermore difficult to say just how much effect the local organization has on the electoral outcome now that all three parties are relying more and more on province-wide advertising, public opinion studies and the building of favourable leadership images.

CONCLUSION

While each of Ontario's political parties has its own traditional approach to organization, the degree of similarity among them should occasion no surprise. All three have grown out of the same political culture and the innovations of one have been taken over by the others. While there may be some truth to the statement that the Ontario Conserva-

10 D. Morton, *NDP: The Dream of Power*, pp. 53–54.
11 Public Archives of Ontario, "To the Liberal-Conservative Party of Ontario," pamphlet. See also in the Public Archives of Canada, Progressive Conservative Headquarters Papers, Reel 1140, E. Owen, "Plan of Electoral Organization," pamphlet, n.d. (probably c. 1940); C. J. Bowie-Reed, "The Structure of a Political Party," pamphlet, three editions, 1949–1951; Hon. A. W. Roebuck, "Campaign Management and How to Win Elections," pamphlet, n.d. (probably c. 1955).
12 D. Morton, *Campaign Guide: The New Democratic Party*, 4th ed., pp. 30–31.

tive party is merely an appendage of the cabinet; that the LPO is so obsessed with federal politics that it barely operates as a provincial party; and that the NDP is a democratic, grass-roots party—there *is* another side to the story.

APPENDIX

Ontario Party Leaders
with date of accession to the leadership

Conservative

- Sir M. C. Cameron, 1871
- Sir W. R. Meredith, 1878
- George F. Marter, 1894
- *Sir James Whitney, 1896
- *Sir William Hearst, 1914
- *Howard Ferguson, 1920
- *George Henry, 1930
- Earl Rowe, 1936
- *George Drew, 1938
- *(T. L. Kennedy, interim—1948)
- *Leslie Frost, 1949
- *John Robarts, 1961
- *William Davis, 1971

CCF/NDP

- E. B. Jolliffe, 1942
- Donald C. MacDonald, 1953
- Stephen Lewis, 1970

Liberal

- Archibald McKellar, 1867
- *Edward Blake, 1869
- *Sir Oliver Mowat, 1872
- *A. S. Hardy, 1896
- *Sir George Ross, 1899
- G. P. Graham, 1907
- Alexander MacKay, 1907
- N. W. Rowell, 1911
- (William Proudfoot, temporary —1918)
- Hartley Dewart, 1919
- F. Wellington Hay, 1922
- William Sinclair, 1923
- *Mitch Hepburn, 1930, 1945
- *Harry Nixon, 1943
- Farquhar Oliver, acting leader— 1945, 1952, 1963; leader—1947, 1954
- Walter C. Thomson, 1950
- John Wintermeyer, 1958
- Andrew Thompson, 1964
- Robert Nixon, 1967

*also premier; three other premiers were not leaders of any of the three major parties: John Sandfield Macdonald headed a coalition ministry from 1867 to 1871; E. C. Drury was premier, 1919–23, of the United Farmers of Ontario ministry; Gordon Conant was premier for seven months following Hepburn's resignation in October 1942, but he did not become leader of the party.

SELECTED BIBLIOGRAPHY

CAMERON, DAVID MURRAY. "The NDP and The Ontario Election of 1963." MA thesis, University of Toronto, 1964.

Canadian Annual Review of Public Affairs, 1901–1937/38. Toronto: Canadian Annual Review Company.

Canadian Annual Review, 1960–1970. Toronto: University of Toronto Press.

Canadian Annual Review of Politics and Public Affairs, 1971–72. Toronto: University of Toronto Press.

CAPLAN, GERALD L. *The Dilemma of Canadian Socialism: The* CCF *in Ontario.* Toronto: McClelland and Stewart, 1973.

CLARK, LOVELL C. "The Conservative Party in the 1890's." Canadian Historical Association, *Annual Report* 1961, pp. 58–74.

Communiqué. Monthly newsletter published by the Liberal party in Ontario.

CLARKSON, S. "Policy and the Media: Communicating the Liberal Party Platform in the 1971 Ontario Election Campaign." Paper given at the Canadian Political Science Association annual meeting, June 1974.

COURTNEY, JOHN C. *The Selection of National Party Leaders in Canada.* Toronto: Macmillan of Canada, 1973.

DRURY, E. C. *Farmer Premier.* Toronto: McClelland and Stewart, 1966.

HOFFMAN, D. "Intra-Party Democracy. A Case Study." *Canadian Journal of Economics and Political Science,* XXVII, 1961, 223–235.

HUMPHRIES, CHARLES W. "The Sources of Ontario 'Progressive Conservatism' 1900–1914." Canadian Historical Association, *Reports,* 1967, pp. 118–129.

"Constitution of the Liberal Party in Ontario," mimeo, 1973.

MANTHORPE, JONATHAN. *The Power and the Tories.* Toronto: Macmillan of Canada, 1974.

MCKENTY, N. *Mitch Hepburn.* Toronto: McClelland and Stewart, 1967.

Momentum. Monthly newsletter published by the Ontario Progressive Conservative Association.

MORTON, D. "The Effectiveness of Political Campaigning. The NDP in the 1967 Ontario Election." *Journal of Canadian Studies* IV, August 1969, 21–33.

———. *NDP: The Dream of Power.* Toronto: Hakkert, 1974.

New Democrat. Bimonthly newsletter published by the New Democratic Party of Ontario.

"Constitution of the New Democratic Party of Ontario," pamphlet, 1972.

OLIVER, PETER N. "Sir William Hearst and the Collapse of the Ontario Conservative Party." *Canadian Historical Review*, LIII, 1972, 21–50.

――――. "Howard Ferguson, the Timber Scandal and the Leadership of the Ontario Conservative Party." *Ontario History*, LXII, 1970, 163–178.

PRANG, MARGARET. "The Evolution of a Victorian Liberal. N. W. Rowell." *Profiles of a Province*. Toronto: Ontario Historical Society, 1967.

PRESTON, W. T. R. *My Generation of Politics and Politicians*. Toronto: Rose, 1927.

"Constitution of the Ontario Progressive Conservative Association," mimeo, 1973.

STEWART, M. and D. FRENCH. *Ask No Quarter. A Biography of Agnes MacPhail*. Toronto: Longman's, 1959.

TENNYSON, BRIAN D. "The Succession of William H. Hearst to the Ontario Premiership, September 1914." *Ontario History*, LVI, 1964, 185–189.

――――. "Sir Adam Beck and the Ontario General Election of 1919." *Ontario History*, LVIII, 1966, 157–162.

THOMPSON, Q. "In the Absence of Mr. Ferguson." *Macleans*, August 15, 1931, p. 19.

WEARING, JOSEPH. "Pressure Group Politics in Canada West before Confederation." Canadian Historical Association *Annual Report* (1967), pp. 75–94.

WILSON, JOHN and DAVID HOFFMAN. "The Liberal Party in Contemporary Ontario Politics." *Canadian Journal of Political Science*, III, 1970, 177–205.

――――. "Ontario, A Three-Party System in Transition," in Martin Robin, ed., *Canadian Provincial Politics*. Scarborough: Prentice-Hall, 1972.

WRONG, D. H. "Ontario Provincial Elections, 1934–55. A Preliminary Survey of Voting." *Canadian Journal of Economics and Political Science*, XXIII, 1957, 395–403.

19
JO SURICH

Keeping Them Honest: Election Reform in Ontario

PARLIAMENTARY democracy demands that the system by which leaders and governments are chosen be beyond criticism. Ever since representative government was invented and since competing political parties fought for office politically knowledgeable people have worried about the effect of the electoral system on the process of elections. The representative principle demands that each vote shall have approximately the same weight within the political system, but two aspects of the electoral process have consistently interfered with this principle: methods of fund-raising used by the political parties for electoral and other purposes have raised question of propriety and occasionally of dishonesty; and the distribution of constituencies has often meant that some sectors of a population are unequally represented.

Fund-raising techniques come to public attention only infrequently. One such event in recent Ontario history was the discovery by the Toronto *Globe and Mail* that $50,000 had been paid to the Ontario Progressive Conservative Party by the Fidinam Corporation, a Swiss-based development firm, only one month after the Ontario cabinet had approved a contract for a new Workmen's Compensation Board building with the company.[1] Almost at the same time, suspected improprieties in the letting of a lease-back contract for a new Ontario Hydro building to a company controlled by a close personal friend of the Premier, William Davis, were being investigated by a select committee of the Legislature. This investigation came to be known as the "Hydrogate" affair.[2]

As is typical in such cases, tremendous pressure was exerted on the government by the opposition parties and the media to launch an investigation of the Fidinam affair also. After a great furor in the Legislature, the Attorney General, Mr. Dalton Bales, finally agreed to an investigation of the Fidinam allegations on December 1, 1972 and the Premier announced a few days later on December 13 that the Camp Commission on the Legislature would be charged

1 See Toronto *Globe and Mail*, various issues, November 1972.
2 The investigations were underway while the Watergate investigation was gaining much public attention in the United States. The select committee eventually produced a report which exonerated the Premier but raised doubts about the propriety of some aspects of the affair.

with the task of analysing the whole process of political fund-raising in Ontario with a view to establishing formal rules which would call for the full disclosure of all donations to political parties.

Almost at the same time the federal Parliament was considering substantial amendments to the federal Election Act partly as a result of recommendations arising out of the Barbeau Commission Report on election finances. These discussions led to the passage of Bill C-203 through the Canadian Parliament and the introduction of new federal finance rules on August 1, 1974. The most notable of the provisions of the federal scheme include some measure of public financing of election campaigns both through a system of rebates to candidates and a system of tax credits for donations to parties and candidates, some limitations on total allowable expenditures by parties and candidates, and provisions for the disclosure of political donations in excess of $100.

Quite clearly, the new federal legislation was going to have a fundamental effect on the ways in which parties carried out their fund-raising, and it became quite clear to the Camp Commission that any new provincial legislation would have to dovetail with it. As will be seen, federal activity in this sensitive field was to lead to an apparent limitation of the options open to the Ontario Commission.

The other critical area of election reform which gained prominence shortly after the start of the investigation of financing was the question of redistribution. The distribution of constituencies can have a profound effect on the chances of parties within the system, a fact which has not escaped politicians in most jurisdictions. In the latter part of the nineteenth century, Ontario's Liberals under Sir Oliver Mowat were able to retain their hold on the province partly because of their ability to redistribute constituencies with "partisan ingenuity."[3] The rural areas of the province, which in those days consistently supported the Liberal

3 For a brief discussion of this point see John Wilson and David Hoffman, "The Liberal Party in Contemporary Ontario Politics," *Canadian Journal of Political Science*, iii, (June 1970), 177–204. Also, John Wilson and David Hoffman, "Ontario: A Three-Party System in Transition," in Martin Robin, *Canadian Provincial Politics* (Scarborough: Prentice Hall, 1972), pp. 198–239.

party, received grossly excessive representation in the Legislature. A period of rapid urban growth and industrialization and of rural stability and even decline made it possible to concentrate a large number of Conservative voters in a relatively small number of urban ridings. Through the 1960s most of the growth in Ontario occurred in urban areas, and more specifically in the suburbs of the major metropolitan regions. Indeed, where the average Metropolitan Toronto constituency in 1971 had 44,260 electors, with a range from 20,947 to 95,596, the average rural riding in eastern Ontario had 26,845 voters with a range from 18,019 to 32,608.[4] The effect of an outdated distribution of constituencies, last undertaken on the basis of the 1961 census, was to leave some voters with a theoretically greater representation than others, often even within the same region. It required approximately half as many voters to elect a rural member in Ontario as it did to elect an urban one. If the principles of democratic government demand that each vote should have equal weight, the Ontario constituencies had to be redistributed.

In recognition of the inequities, an Electoral Boundaries Commission was struck on December 5, 1973 to redistribute the provincial electoral district boundaries in light of the 1971 census. The membership of the commission consisted of Roderick Lewis, the Ontario Chief Election Officer and Clerk of the Legislature, Mr. Justice Campbell Grant as chairman, and Professor T. Robert Sansom of the Political Science department at the University of Western Ontario.

The Electoral Boundaries Commission was instructed to take into account such factors as community or diversity of interests, means of communication, topographical features and existing municipal and ward boundaries and so on. Wherever possible the commissioners were to follow a 25 per cent rule which would allow constituencies to fluctuate no more or less than 25 per cent around an average. Special consideration with regard to this rule was to be given to areas in which large, sparsely populated territories were involved. In addition, the commission was given the power to add up to eight additional seats to the

4 Ontario, Legislative Assembly, *Ontario Elections: Return from the Records* (Toronto: Queen's Printer, 1972), for results of the 1971 election.

Legislature and was prevented from reducing the number of seats then in northern Ontario.

The background of electoral reform in Ontario in the mid-1970s consists, then, of the Camp Commission studying the problem of election and party finance, and the Electoral Boundaries Commission working to bring the distribution of constituencies in Ontario more in line with existing realities. The results of their efforts will prove to be fundamentally different in content and focus.

FINANCIAL REFORMS

In searching for a new formula of election financing, the Camp Commission set out to establish a system

> to which the parties themselves will adhere, which will not invite violation or circumvention, a system that is equitable and comprehensible, and one that can and must be regularly monitored and vigorously enforced. . . . If such is to be achieved, it can only be done by a mixture of method and means, including tax credits to encourage individual donors, a tax check-off to encourage mass participation in party financing, statutory limits upon the size of all contributions, corporate or otherwise, and, given certain qualifying requirements, a degree of public funding of the election expenses of candidates.

Over the years, attempts in other democracies to reform the system of political funding have resorted to a fairly large range of options—disclosure of contributions, spending limitations, methods of encouragement of small donors, limited public financing, and so on.[5] The Camp Commission in its report resorted to all these measures to some extent. It produced an amalgam of approaches which it felt best served the interests of political parties in the province. And in some ways it broadened the principles embodied in the new federal election expenses act, and occasionally improved them. Furthermore, the Camp Commission, which was made up of three experienced politicians representing all of the parties active in the Ontario political system, steered away from any attempt to influence through legis-

5 See K. Z. Paltiel, *Political Party Financing in Canada* (Toronto: McGraw-Hill, 1970), pp. 3–10.

lation the methods which parties employed to run election campaigns.

The Camp Commission was particularly concerned with the provisions in the new federal act which touched on direct contributions to the political parties. While limits are placed on the total amounts that parties can spend during elections, no limits are set on the size of contributions. Indeed, it is possible for an individual, corporation or other organization to donate $100 to each candidate of a party without having the identity of the donor revealed.

The federal legislation, despite its disclosure provisions, continues to allow the political parties to depend heavily on large donations from a few sources, and it is precisely this type of dependence which the Camp Commission was trying to eliminate. The Fidinam allegations were dangerous because they served as an example of the level of dependence on special interests which the political parties face. Given the scope of governmental activity in the modern age, it becomes nearly impossible to deal with firms which will not also be involved in donations to political parties and candidates. Under these conditions it is argued that disclosure at least assures the public that nothing clandestine has been done. The limitations of donations to relatively small amounts would remove even further doubt.

The Camp Commission also recognized that the major difficulty with all previous legislation, including that which governed the mere reporting of campaign income and expenses by candidates, was that it tended to be virtually impossible to enforce at least in part because candidates very often failed to understand the nature of the legislation and its intent. The commission therefore strove to provide proposals which would be simple to administer and which would do the least violence to the methods by which parties in Ontario had traditionally operated.

Indirectly, any new legislation concerning the financing of political parties and their election campaigns will have a profound impact on the ways in which the parties operate. Spending ceilings, for example, may determine that parties will not use the most expensive campaign tools such as the electronic media. The Camp Commission argued that it is not the job of election legislation to "restrict" the parties in their activities. Instead, the objective is to provide a means of assuring the public that politics is carried on in as open a fashion as possible. Instead of recommending that media expenditures be limited, therefore, the commission suggests that there are "natural" limits which will be imposed on the total expenditures of the parties because of suggested changes in fund-raising procedures.

The Camp Commission's recommendations will greatly influence two levels of party activity: candidates and election campaigns, and the day-to-day operations of the parties. Let us first investigate the effect on the normal year-round activities. As their most basic recommendation, the commissioners suggest that a Commission on Election Expenses (CEE) be established on a permanent and independent basis. While the new federal election expenses legislation had assigned supervisory powers to the Chief Election Officer, the Camp Commission envisages a body which will not only enforce the new legislation but which will also work actively to assist the parties and candidates in complying with it. The membership of the CEE will consist of two members nominated by the leaders of each of the political parties with at least four seats in the Legislature and a bencher on the Ontario Law Society. The Provincial Auditor and the Chief Election Officer are to be ex-officio members, and a chairman is to be appointed by the Lieutenant-Governor-in-Council for a maximum period of ten years.

The CEE is to be given sweeping powers to make decisions over activities to which the new rules will apply. One of its initial functions will be the registration of political parties, their constituency organizations and candidates. Without registration the solicitation of funds will be illegal. Registration of political parties is to be incumbent on four conditions: parties must hold a minimum of four seats in the Legislature; or they must have contested at least half the constituencies in the previous election; alternatively, they may have nominated candidates in at least half of the Ontario ridings after the issuance of the writ for an election; and finally they may be registered if they provide the names of five thousand persons of voting age who are eligible Ontario voters and who attest to the registration of the political party concerned. It was argued by the Camp Commission that the last two provisions would allow new groupings or parties to form.

One of the more interesting aspects of the registration proposals will be the increased legal recognition for the existence of political parties, and the increased legal power which will be given party leaders to discipline their riding associations. The CEE will register riding associations only on the advice of a party leader, thereby giving the leaders the formal power to decide which grouping in a constituency shall constitute the official party organization. This is a power which leaders previously held only informally. A constituency organization which is not registered will, of course, not be able to solicit funds under the proposed rules. One of the likely outcomes of the Camp proposals will be the much greater legal recognition given to parties, converting them from organizations which have never before been formally recognized. In much the same way federal election reforms which provided for the placing of a party label on the ballot formally gave national party leaders the power to determine who the official candidate for the party would be in each constituency.

In the Canadian setting, the most novel suggestions of the Camp Commission revolve around the methods of fundraising which are to be open to the political parties. The commissioners recommend that the substantial dependence of our political parties upon the large contributions of a few be terminated. They propose a system which relies on the support of many, at all levels of society, and in which, in the end result, no particular group or segment can be deemed to wield more influence, or bear more of the cost of political financing than another.*

They recommend that with few exceptions only two kinds of political donations be allowed. Only individuals, corporations and trade unions are to be allowed to make direct contributions to political parties and furthermore the amounts which they are to be allowed to give would be severely limited. It is suggested that the maximum contribution to a registered political party in any one year will be $2,000 plus an additional aggregated total of $500 to the constituency organization of a registered party. Tax credits of the kind which are now operable under the new federal

*For the Davis government's proposed legislation based on the Camp Commission's report, see page 363.

legislation would be available to individuals,[6] and corporations would be able to claim up to $4,000 as an income tax deduction. For election years the allowable contributions would be doubled.

Combined with the recommendations for limits on total campaign donations are proposed rules for the disclosure of political donations. The proposals demand that records of all contributions in excess of $10 be kept and that the names of all contributors of $100 or more be disclosed. Furthermore, the Camp Commission specifically excludes the acceptance of cash donations by the parties except for membership fees.

One of the major difficulties in enforcing both limitations and disclosure rules arises because of the possibility that individuals and corporations might "launder" their contributions through front organizations of various kinds. A large number of contributions could theoretically be made to a series of non-profit corporations which could then make donations to political parties. To avoid this problem, the Camp Commission recommended that donations from such organizations be allowed only where the contribution is made up of individual donations, all of which must be disclosed and itemized as to source and amount, and all of which, in conjunction with any other contributions the individual may have made, must be within the limitations set down in the Act. In other words, the individual or corporate sources of all funds given by such organizations must be disclosed completely.

The restrictions on the size of political contributions are likely to have important effects on the operations of all of the political parties in Ontario. Parties will have to forego large contributions from a few donors, and will have to seek to collect the same amounts from a vast number of smaller contributors. It will be more difficult and time-consuming to collect the fairly substantial sums which the parties need in order to sustain their year-round operations, to say nothing of election campaigns.

6 Federal tax credits for donations to registered political parties and their agents provide for a tax credit of 75 per cent for the first $100 of a contribution, 50 per cent of the next $450 and one-third of the remainder up to a maximum tax credit of $500. The Camp Commission recommended that no maximum be set on the allowable tax credit.

One of the major failures of past election acts has been the lack of enforcement of financial provisions, and the commission proposes very tough penalties for non-compliance with the provisions. Fines ranging from $1,000 for individuals and constituency organizations to $10,000 for political parties are to be levied for transgressions. It is hoped by the commissioners, of course, that the Act will be sufficiently logical that parties will be able easily to adhere to it.

Finally, the Camp Commission proposes a novel way of helping the provincial parties to meet their day-to-day expenses. While the tax credit provisions are expected to make it somewhat easier for individuals to give larger amounts of money to their parties, a direct system of tax check-off is proposed. Individuals who are taxpayers in the province of Ontario are to be allowed to assign two dollars to the registered party of their choice without any direct cost to them personally. In other words, the registered parties would be listed on the Ontario part of tax returns and the individual will be allowed to assign the money to his party. The commission felt that this method would encourage the participation of larger numbers of individuals in the funding process since it would require people to act in order to have public funds given to a political party. The commissioners felt it important, in any system of tax check-off, that it encourage the individual's voluntary participation in specific party financing. No realistic estimate of the total return to the political parties of this system is, of course, possible. However, it must be noted that it further legitimizes and formalizes the existence of political parties.

Registration would also be required for candidates and their financial committees. Such candidates may either be registered as the candidate of a registered party or its constituency organization, or as individuals. While this provision makes it theoretically possible for independent candidates to register as easily as those running for a registered party, this may, in fact, not be the case. Since candidates cannot register until they have been officially nominated after the issuance of a writ for an election, they will not be able to legally solicit funds until after the call of an election and after their official nomination. Candidates for registered political parties, on the other hand, would be able to ask their constituency organizations to solicit funds on their behalf. Two possible effects may result from the proposal that registration will only be possible after an official nomination: either independent candidates will ignore the rules, or alternatively they will be discouraged from running. If the latter effect were to result, electoral competition would be further restricted to the existing political parties.

The limitations on the size of contributions which are discussed above with respect to the ordinary operations of the parties also apply during election campaigns, so that the effective contribution during a provincial election year would be double that allowed in a normal year. Furthermore, the Camp Commission proposed that specific limits be set on the amounts national parties might give to their provincial wings during an election. The total contributions are to be limited to a maximum of $100 times the number of provincial electoral districts. The Camp Commission suggested this rule on two grounds. One, it was concerned about the possibility of circumvention of the provisions of the proposed Act if federal parties were to be allowed to contribute unlimited amounts, and second, it appeared to be committed to the notion that the Ontario parties are independent organizations.

An element of public funding is also introduced during elections with specific reference to candidates. A system of rebates is to be introduced which would return to candidates some part of their election expenses. Unlike the federal legislation, however, which pays rebates according to the number of electors in a constituency, the Camp Commission proposed that rebates be paid to candidates who received more than 15 per cent of the vote in their constituency on the basis of the difference between the candidate's audited expenses and income. The maximum reimbursement is to be $7,500 and is never to exceed the difference between income and expenses.

The problem faced by any commission which attempts to reform the system of party financing, and which sets out to do as little violence to existing party structures and practices as possible, lies in the fact that structures and practices vary widely. Particularly the difference between a major emphasis on fund-raising through membership donations such as that engaged in by the New Democratic

Party and alternatively a major emphasis on direct donations of larger amounts which the Liberal and Progressive
Conservative parties focus on is likely to cause major
difficulties. In fact, the rules proposed by the Camp Commission do violence to all three political parties and the
methods they employ.

For example, the limitations on the total contributions
to be allowed by individuals and corporations would probably mean that both the Liberals and the Conservatives will
have to engage in a somewhat different method of fund-
raising from much larger numbers of smaller donors. The
NDP benefits from these provisions since it has always
depended to a large extent on much smaller donations and
since the tax credit provisions will make donations from
small donors less burdensome. No accurate data are currently available on the sources of Conservative and Liberal
funding either during elections or during off years. However, it would probably be safe to assume that the major
sources of funding for those two parties would be partly
dried up by the proposed rules.

THE PROPOSED REDISTRIBUTION

Where the Camp Commission had made a serious attempt
at facing the problems of party and election-financing
squarely, the Electoral Boundaries Commission was ac-
cused in some quarters of having worked essentially to
ensure the survival of the current Ontario government. In
fact, the commission appears to have proceeded on the
same basis as the commission which redrew boundaries in
time for the 1967 general election.[7] From a position of
apparent independence it presented a set of new boundary
proposals on June 8, 1974. It had increased the number of
seats in the Legislature from 117 to 125 but had failed to
eliminate many of the inequities that had previously existed. Since it can be argued that even the 25 per cent rule
allows too much latitude serious questions must be asked
about the fact that the commission returned proposals
which included new ridings which fell outside the rule. On
the basis of the 1971 census, seven of the new ridings in
southern Ontario fell more than 25 per cent below the
average population of ridings in tht part of Ontario. In the

7 Terence H. Qualter, *The Election Process in Canada* (Toronto:
   McGraw-Hill, 1970), pp. 107–109.

north, four had populations more than 25 per cent below the northern average while three were to have populations greater than the rule might have allowed for. All of the former were rural seats, while all of the latter were urban. The Electoral Boundaries Commission's work proposed a distribution in Ontario which was more uneven than even the 25 per cent rule allowed, and furthermore it tended to ignore population trends in Ontario. It is quite clear that even by the time of the provincial election expected in 1975 when the new boundaries are to be used for the first time, growth in the suburbs will have been sufficient to allow many of the suburban ridings to exceed the 25 per cent limit. A strong bias, therefore, continues to exist in favour of the rural areas of the province. Some of the apparent over-representation of rural areas can, of course, be explained in terms of problems of accessibility and the difficulties MPP's face in servicing vast areas of the province, particularly in the north. Even given such a consideration, a great deal of violence appears to be done to the principle of one man, one vote. An even distribution of constituencies within certain physical restraints provides the backbone of a democratic representative parliamentary system. The Ontario proposals appeared to ignore that principle.

Some other concerns can be expressed with the work of the commission. Even though its instructions had suggested as much adherence as possible to existing political boundaries, the commission, in fact, ignored the boundaries of the new regional governments in its first report. Since any reasonable principle of representation might also include concerns about the closeness of a community to its elected representatives, it might have been useful for the commission to consider the need of these new units of local government to develop a sense of community. A more faithful adherence to regional government boundaries was evident in the revisions which were made in response to public criticism. Similarly, ward boundaries in Toronto, which might be said to represent communities of interest were ignored in favour of "strip" ridings which include a broad cross-section of people in Toronto.

As a corollary to the uneven distribution which the commission proposed, a pattern emerges which appears to largely favour the government party. This in itself is not unusual since that has been the traditional way in which redistributions in most jurisdictions were carried out, but it appears to be odd in light of the government's apparent willingness to allow for a dramatic overhaul of the system of party financing. An effort at fairness and openness on the one hand appears to be contradicted by an effort to ensure the government's survival by a "political" redistribution on the other hand. A clear bias exists in the proposals of the commission in favour of some rural seats, and more specifically in favour of rural seats in strongly Conservative areas.

What then were the partisan effects of the proposed new boundaries? It must first of all be recognized that any attempt to eliminate some of the small rural seats in southwestern Ontario was likely to hurt the Liberal party most, while such an attempt in eastern Ontario would hurt the Conservative party. However, when the results of the 1971 Ontario election are cast into the new boundaries, the Conservative party emerges as the winner with 86 seats, the New Democratic Party second with 22 and the Liberals third with 17.[8] The evidence of systematic bias in favour of the government party appears to be overwhelming. A good part of the bias appears to be introduced by a selective application of the 25 per cent rule. All seven of the seats in southern Ontario which fall below the rule are to be found in eastern Ontario, and all are held and would be held by the Conservative party. While the Liberals held a number of seats in the southwest which were small also, none fall outside the rule as a result of the proposed redistribution. Indeed, some estimates can be made of the effect of selective ignoring of the rule.

Since 1971 data are most readily available in terms of the numbers of electors while those for the new areas are census data, some estimate has to be made of the number of voters a given population represents. It appears that a rule of thumb which suggests that 60 to 65 per cent of the population are electors makes sense. On the basis of such an estimate, where the average Liberal rural riding in southwestern Ontario had 24,857 voters in the 1971 election, the average Liberal riding in this area under the new distribution would have approximately 34,000 voters, an increase of more than 40 per cent. In the process, the

8 These data do not include the effect of by-elections held in 1973 in Huron and St. George and in 1974 in Stormont and Carleton East.

Liberals lose one seat in the Essex County area, and another becomes a very close and difficult proposition at best.

In eastern Ontario, on the other hand, populations are increased from an average of 26,845 in Conservative rural seats to about 29,500, an increase of only 9 per cent. Where it might be argued that the Liberals were over-represented in the southwest, the same argument can be applied with equal validity to the eastern sections of the province. The bias against urban areas is likely to have the greatest effect on NDP representation, but this is somewhat more difficult to document.

The evidence is, of course, quite clear. The Electoral Boundaries Commission acted as an agent of government objectives rather than as a truly independent body. Reform of the redistribution process according to what might be democratic principles demands an independent commission of the kind which now undertakes federal redistributions, free from political pressures either from government or opposition.

One other aspect of the work of the Ontario Electoral Boundaries Commission can be viewed with interest. While federal independent commissions open their proposals to extensive public debate and questioning, the Ontario commission decided to ask for public participation only in the form of written responses which could not be debated in meeting with the commission. In other words, public participation in the process of redistribution was severely limited. Direct questions were particularly asked by the NDP caucus at the Legislature which asked for a meeting with the commissioners. In a press conference which followed the refusal of the commission to meet with representatives of the caucus, a group of NDP MPP's suggested that "the Commission was independent in name, but with rare exceptions, its proposals bolster or perpetuate the government party's strength."[9]

In short, the commission proposed a new set of electoral district boundaries which can at best be called political, at worst a gerrymander.

9 New Democratic Party Caucus, *Brief Submitted to the Ontario Electoral Boundaries Commission*, September 10, 1974.

APPENDIX

Bill 200, Tabled in the Ontario Legislature,
February 13, 1975

As this book was going to press, Bill 200 was introduced into the Legislature to implement the Camp Commission proposals. Certain alterations to the commission's recommendations were made, as follows: (1) Whereas Commissioners Camp and Fisher, with Commissioner Oliver dissenting, recommended that there be no ceilings on campaign media expenditures because of the extreme difficulty in policing them (see pages 353–54 of this essay), the bill permits a registered party in a general election to spend 25 cents for each name on the registered voters' list of the electoral district where they have a candidate, and a registered constituency association or independent candidate 25 cents for each name on the revised voters' list of the electoral district. (2) Whereas the Camp Commission recommended tax credits parallelling those in the federal legislation (pages 356, 357), no such provincial tax credits were included in the first draft of the bill, because of unresolved difficulties with the federal income tax authorities. (3) Whereas the Camp Commission proposed disclosure of the names of all contributors of $100 or more (page 356), the bill requires disclosure for contributors of amounts in excess of $100 only. (4) Whereas the Camp Commission proposed a check-off of $2 for each person filing an income tax to be given to the party of his choice from the public treasury (page 357), the first draft of the bill made no such provision, again because of unresolved difficulties with the federal income tax authorities. (5) Whereas the Camp Commission recommended a maximum reimbursement of $7,500 for each candidate's local budget, the bill opted for an alternative formula: namely, the aggregate of 16 cents for each of the first 25,000 voters and 14 cents for each voter in excess of 25,000 in the electoral district.

Premiers and Leaders
of the Opposition,
1867-1975

LEGISLATIVE ASSEMBLY OF ONTARIO: PREMIERS AND LEADERS OF THE OPPOSITION, 1867–1975

Legislative Session	Premier	Leader of the Opposition
1st. (Dec. 1867–Feb. 1871)	John Sandfield Macdonald (CONS)	Edward Blake (LIB) Dec. 1869–Dec. 1871
2nd. (Dec. 1871–Dec. 1874)	Edward Blake (LIB) Sir Oliver Mowat (LIB) *appointed Oct. 1872*	Matthew C. Cameron (CONS) Dec. 1871–1878
3rd. (Nov. 1875–Mar. 1879)	Sir Oliver Mowat	Matthew C. Cameron
4th. (Jan. 1880–Feb. 1883)	Sir Oliver Mowat	William R. Meredith (CONS) Oct. 1878–Oct. 1894
5th. (Jan. 1884–Mar. 1886)	Sir Oliver Mowat	William R. Meredith
6th. (Feb. 1887–Apr. 1890)	Sir Oliver Mowat	William R. Meredith
7th. (Feb. 1891–May 1894)	Sir Oliver Mowat	William R. Meredith
8th. (Feb. 1895–Jan. 1898)	Sir Oliver Mowat Arthur S. Hardy (LIB) *appointed July 1896*	G. F. Marter (CONS) Oct. 1894–Apr. 1896 James P. Whitney (CONS) Apr. 1896–Jan. 1905
9th. (Aug. 1898–Mar. 1902)	Arthur S. Hardy George W. Ross (LIB) *appointed Oct. 1899*	James P. Whitney
10th. (Mar. 1903–Apr. 1904)	George W. Ross	James P. Whitney

Legislative Session	Premier	Leader of the Opposition
11th. (Mar. 1905–Apr. 1908)	James P. Whitney (CONS)	George W. Ross (LIB) Feb. 1905–Jan. 1907 George P. Graham (LIB) Jan.–Aug. 1907 Alexander G. Mackay (LIB) Aug. 1907–1911
12th. (Feb. 1909–Mar. 1911)	James P. Whitney	Alexander G. Mackay
13th. (Feb. 1912–May 1914)	James P. Whitney	Newton W. Rowell (LIB) Dec. 1911–1917
14th. (Feb. 1915–Apr. 1919)	James P. Whitney William H. Hearst (CONS) *appointed Oct. 1914*	Newton W. Rowell William Proudfoot (LIB) Feb. 1918–Oct. 1919
15th. (Mar. 1920–May 1923)	E. C. Drury (UFO)	H. H. Dewart (LIB) 1919–Oct. 1921 F. W. Hay (LIB) Mar. 1922–June 1923
16th. (Feb. 1924–Apr. 1926)	George H. Ferguson (CONS)	W. E. N. Sinclair (LIB) Aug. 1923–June 1934
17th. (Feb. 1927–Mar. 1929)	George H. Ferguson	W. E. N. Sinclair
18th. (Feb. 1930–Apr. 1934)	George H. Ferguson George S. Henry (CONS) *appointed Dec. 1930*	W. E. N. Sinclair
19th. (Feb. 1935–Mar. 1937)	Mitchell F. Hepburn (LIB)	George S. Henry (CONS) July 1935–Dec. 1938
20th. (Dec. 1937–Apr. 1943)	Mitchell F. Hepburn Gordon D. Conant (LIB) *appointed Oct. 1942* Harry C. Nixon (LIB) *appointed May 1943*	George S. Henry

		Premier	Leader of Opposition
21st.	(Feb. 1944–Mar. 1945)	George A. Drew (CONS)	E. B. Jolliffe (CCF) Aug. 1943–June 1945
22nd.	(Mar. 1946–Apr. 1948)	George A. Drew	Farquhar R. Oliver (LIB) July 1945–June 1948
23rd.	(Feb. 1949–Apr. 1951)	Thomas L. Kennedy (CONS) Leslie M. Frost (CONS) *appointed May 1949*	E. B. Jolliffe (CCF) July 1948–Nov. 1951
24th.	(Feb. 1952–Mar. 1955)	Leslie M. Frost	Farquhar R. Oliver (LIB) 1951–Apr. 1958
25th.	(Jan. 1956–Mar. 1959)	Leslie M. Frost	Farquhar R. Oliver J. J. Wintermeyer (LIB) Apr. 1958–Aug. 1963
26th.	(Jan. 1960–Apr. 1963)	Leslie M. Frost John P. Robarts (CONS) *appointed Nov. 1961*	J. J. Wintermeyer
27th.	(Oct. 1963–June 1967)	John P. Robarts	Farquhar R. Oliver (LIB) Oct. 1963–Sept. 1964 Andrew E. Thompson (LIB) Sept. 1964–Nov. 1966
28th.	(Feb. 1968–July 1971)	John P. Robarts William Davis (CONS) *appointed Feb. 1971*	Robert F. Nixon (LIB) Feb. 1967–
29th.	(Feb. 1972–)	William Davis	

Contributors

KENNETH BRYDEN. Formerly MPP for Toronto Woodbine; Department of Political Economy, University of Toronto.

R. J. DRUMMOND. Institute of Behavioural Research, Department of Political Science, York University, Toronto.

FREDERICK J. FLETCHER. Formerly with the Vancouver *Province*; Department of Political Science, York University, Toronto.

DAVID HOFFMAN. Institute of Behavioural Research, Department of Political Science, York University, Toronto; on leave of absence (1974–1975) with Ministry of State for Urban Affairs; co-author of "A Three-Party System in Transition," in Martin Robin, ed., *Canadian Provincial Politics*.

HENRY J. JACEK. Department of Political Sience, McMaster University, Hamilton, Ontario.

DONALD C. MAC DONALD. MPP for York South, former leader of the New Democratic Party of Ontario; lecturer in the Government and Politics of Ontario at Atkinson College, York University, Toronto.

A. K. MC DOUGALL. Department of Political Science, University of Western Ontario, London, Ontario; author of forthcoming biography of John P. Robarts in the Ontario Historical Studies series.

JONATHAN MANTHORPE. Formerly Queen's Park reporter for the *Globe and Mail*, now with that newspaper's Ottawa bureau; author of *The Power and the Tories* (1974).

DESMOND MORTON. Department of History, Erindale College, University of Toronto; author of *Mayor Howland: The Citizens' Candidate* (1973).

ALLAN O'BRIEN. Formerly mayor of Halifax; Department of Political Science, University of Western Ontario, London, Ontario.

NORMAN PEARSON. Town planning consultant; Department of Political Science, University of Western Ontario, London, Ontario.

WALTER G. PITMAN. Formerly MPP for Peterborough; Dean of Arts and Science, Trent University, Peterborough, Ontario; President of Ryerson Polytechnical Institute, Toronto (1975).

DON SCOTT. Formerly lecturer at Laurentian University, Sudbury, Ontario; lecturer on business at Cambrian College, Sudbury.

PETER SILCOX. Department of Political Economy, University of Toronto.

JO SURICH. Department of Political Science, University of Waterloo, Waterloo, Ontario.

DAVID SURPLIS. Department of Political Science, University of Guelph, Guelph, Ontario.

GEORGE J. SZABLOWSKI. Department of Political Science, York University, Toronto.

JOSEPH WEARING. Department of Political Science, Trent University, Peterborough, Ontario.

M. W. WESTMACOTT. Department of Political Science, University of Western Ontario, London, Ontario.

JOHN WILSON. Chairman, Department of Political Science, University of Waterloo, Waterloo, Ontario; co-author of "A Three-Party System in Transition," in Martin Robin, ed., *Canadian Provincial Politics.*